Hungarian Dances and Musical Life
in Eighteenth-Century Vienna

Hungarian Dances and Musical Life in Eighteenth-Century Vienna

CATHERINE MAYES

OXFORD
UNIVERSITY PRESS

Oxford University Press is a department of the University of Oxford.
It furthers the University's objective of excellence in research, scholarship,
and education by publishing worldwide. Oxford is a registered trade mark of
Oxford University Press in the UK and certain other countries.

Published in the United States of America by Oxford University Press
198 Madison Avenue, New York, NY 10016, United States of America.

© Oxford University Press 2025

All rights reserved. No part of this publication may be reproduced, stored in a retrieval system, transmitted, used for text and data mining, or used for training artificial intelligence, in any form or by any means, without the prior permission in writing of Oxford University Press, or as expressly permitted by law, by license or under terms agreed with the appropriate reprographics rights organization. Inquiries concerning reproduction outside the scope of the above should be sent to the Rights Department, Oxford University Press, at the address above.

You must not circulate this work in any other form
and you must impose this same condition on any acquirer.

Library of Congress Cataloging-in-Publication Data
Names: Mayes, Catherine, 1979– author.
Title: Hungarian dances and musical life in eighteenth-century Vienna/ Catherine Mayes.
Description: [1.] | New York, NY : Oxford University Press, 2025. |
Includes bibliographical references and index.
Identifiers: LCCN 2025016057 (print) | LCCN 2025016058 (ebook) |
ISBN 9780197805763 (hardback) | ISBN 9780197805794 |
ISBN 9780197805770 (epub)
Subjects: LCSH: Music—Austria—Vienna—18th century—History and criticism. |
Music—Social aspects—Austria—Vienna—History—18th century. |
Dance—Austria—Vienna—History—18th century. |
Dance—Hungary—History—18th century. |
Music—Austria—Vienna—Hungarian influences—History—18th century.
Classification: LCC ML246.8.V6 M27 2025 (print) | LCC ML246.8.V6 (ebook) |
DDC 780.9436/1309033—dc23
LC record available at https://lccn.loc.gov/2025016057
LC ebook record available at https://lccn.loc.gov/2025016058

DOI: 10.1093/oso/9780197805763.001.0001

Printed by Marquis Book Printing, Canada

The manufacturer's authorized representative in the EU for product safety is
Oxford University Press España S.A., Parque Empresarial San Fernando de Henares,
Avenida de Castilla, 2 - 28830 Madrid (www.oup.es/en).

Contents

List of Illustrations vii
Acknowledgments ix
List of Abbreviations xi
Note on Sources xiii

Introduction: Cross-Cultural Encounters in Music and Dance   1

1. Staging Hungary at the Habsburg Court   25
2. Experiencing Vernacular Music   65
3. Playing Hungarian Dances at the Keyboard   102
4. Dancing the *Ungarischer*   132

   Epilogue   161

Appendix: Descriptions of Hungarian Dances Issued in Connection with Dances for Keyboard   165
Bibliography   171
Index   185

Illustrations

Figures

1.1. Jean-Baptiste Haussard, "Hongrois" (1714) — 35
1.2. Jean-Baptiste Haussard, "Hongroise" (1714) — 36
1.3. Martin van Meytens, *Joseph II. als Kronprinz mit sechs Geschwistern* (ca. 1750) — 41
1.4. Joseph Starzer, *Ballets de Nations, Tome premier*, title page of the first violin part (1760) — 56
2.1. *Im Café Seidl* (1794) — 75
2.2. *Gaststube des Wirtshauses "Zur Schnecke" im Prater* (1772) — 76
2.3. Georg Emanuel Opitz, *Altwiener Kellerwirtshaus* (1803) — 77
2.4. Johann Hieronymus Löschenkohl, *Am Spittelberg im Extrazimmer* (1783) — 81
2.5. Joseph Richter, *Taschenbuch für Grabennymphen auf das Jahr 1787*, engraving 9 (1787) — 84
4.1. *Contredanses Hongraises pour le Clavecin*, title page (1788) — 133
4.2. Carl Joseph von Feldtenstein, *Erweiterung der Kunst nach der Chorographie zu tanzen*, table 2 (1772) — 151

Music Examples

1.1. Joseph Starzer, *L'Hongrois*, no. 1, "Mad: Bodin," mm. 1–8 (1754/1755) — 58
1.2. Joseph Starzer, *L'Hongrois*, no. 4, "Sig:^re Angiolini," mm. 1–4 (1754/1755) — 60
1.3. Joseph Starzer, *L'Hongrois*, no. 6, complete (1754/1755) — 60
1.4. Joseph Starzer, *L'Hongrois*, no. 10, mm. 1–8 (1754/1755) — 61
3.1. Joseph Bengraf, *XII. Magyar Tántzok Klávicembalomra Valók/XII. Danses Hongroises pour le Clavecin ou Piano-Forte*, no. 3 (1790) — 112
3.2. *22 Originelle Ungarische Nationaltänze für das Clavier*, vol. 1, no. 1 (1806/1807) — 113

3.3. Johann Nepomuk Hummel, *Balli ongaresi*, op. 23, no. 1, "Ballo patetico" (1806)   126
3.4. Execution of trills in Hummel's *Balli ongaresi*, op. 23, no. 1 (1807)   127
4.1. *Contredanses Hongraises pour le Clavecin*, no. 5 (1788)   134

Tables

1.1. Descriptions of three representative mid-century Viennese pantomime ballets   53
1.2. Joseph Starzer and Franz Hilverding, *L'Hongrois* (1754/1755)   57

Acknowledgments

I am very grateful to the individuals and institutions who helped me take this book from idea to reality. At the University of Utah, a Virgil C. Aldrich Fellowship from the Tanner Humanities Center, a Faculty Release for Scholarly Pursuits from the University Research Committee, and a sabbatical leave gave me much-needed time away from teaching and service responsibilities. Smaller grants from the University Research Committee and the College of Fine Arts also underwrote portions of my work. I thank the directors of the School of Music, Miguel Chuaqui and Kim Councill, for supporting me in pursuing these opportunities. The American Musicological Society contributed to the publication of this book through a subvention from the Margarita M. Hanson Fund, supported in part by the National Endowment for the Humanities and the Andrew W. Mellon Foundation.

Lisa Chaufty, director of the McKay Music Library at the University of Utah, was unrelenting in helping me locate and obtain scans of archival materials; without her assistance, this book may not have come to fruition, as the global COVID-19 pandemic precluded travel for much longer than any of us expected in early 2020. Staff at the Gesellschaft der Musikfreunde and the Austrian National Library in Vienna, the State Regional Archives in Třeboň, and the National University Library in Turin kindly and promptly responded to requests for materials and allowed me to reproduce excerpts from them in this book. Personnel at the Wienbibliothek im Rathaus; the Wien Museum; and the HUN-REN Research Centre for the Humanities, Institute for Musicology in Budapest also kindly facilitated use of their materials.

I thank friends and colleagues near and far who generously shared time, expertise, and unpublished writing with me: Bruce Alan Brown, Elizabeth T. Craft, Stephanie Doktor, Glenda Goodman, David R. M. Irving, Estelle Joubert, Mira and Andrew Larson, Ralph P. Locke, Marie Sumner Lott, Melanie Lowe, Sarah McKibben, Stephanie Vial, and Steven Zohn. Participants and audience members at talks, conferences, and colloquia in Salt Lake City, Las Vegas, New York City, and on Zoom asked questions that helped me refine my ideas and their presentation. Peer reviews solicited by Oxford University Press were critical to shaping the manuscript in its final form and strengthened it tremendously. Finally, it is my very good fortune to count three exceptional scholars among my dearest friends; they gave selflessly of their time, believed in this project from beginning to end, and are always ready to laugh and commiserate with me about our favorite topics: parenting and academia. Mark Ferraguto read and commented on the entire manuscript more than once; Elizabeth T. Craft and Emily H. Green gave me feedback on critical portions of my work at various stages of development; and all three answered endless questions large and small. Any remaining errors and infelicities are mine alone.

I am indebted to Curtis Bryant for painstakingly transcribing countless handwritten eighteenth-century ballet parts into usable scores with patience and precision; to Mat Campbell for quickly and skillfully engraving the music examples in their final form; and to Erin K. Maher for creating a thorough index and assisting in proofreading under a very tight schedule. At Oxford University Press, Norm Hirschy expertly guided me through the publication process, and I thank him and Anna-Lise Santella for their interest in this book from our first conversations about it. I am grateful to Timothy DeWerff for his careful copyediting and to Zara Cannon-Mohammed and Narayanan Srinivasan for patiently overseeing production.

As I worked on this book in the shadow of the pandemic, I felt a certain kinship with the eighteenth-century women about whom I was writing; their long hours and days at home were a sign of their socioeconomic privilege, as they were of mine. Nonetheless, as the weeks turned into months of juggling what felt like impossible personal and professional demands, I was keenly reminded that time is the most valuable currency and family the most precious gift. In particular, I thank my parents, Greg and Louise Mayes, for their moral support from the other side of a closed border and especially for bestowing on me the unconditional love and education that have made all my accomplishments possible. I was fortunate to share the isolation of the pandemic—as well as many happier times—with my husband, Matt Cecil, and our young sons. Oliver and Julian, your unrelenting efforts to teach me about all creatures great and small, living and extinct, animal, vegetable, and mineral—and your deep dismay at my persistent lack of progress in these areas—serve as my daily reminders to keep my priorities in order. For that, I can never thank you enough.

Abbreviations

A-Wgm	Vienna, Gesellschaft der Musikfreunde
A-Wst	Vienna, Wienbibliothek im Rathaus
A-Wn	Vienna, Österreichische Nationalbibliothek
CZ-K	Český Krumlov, Státní oblastní archiv v Třeboni
D-Dl	Dresden, Sächsische Landesbibliothek—Staats- und Universitätsbibliothek
D-HR	Harburg, Öttingen-Wallersteinsche Bibliothek
H-KE	Keszthely, Helikon Kastélymúzeum Könyvtára
I-Tn	Turin, Biblioteca nazionale universitaria
US-CAt	Cambridge, MA, Harvard Theatre Collection
WZ	*Wiener Zeitung*

Note on Sources

This study relies on eighteenth-century sources in several languages: German, Hungarian, French, English. Where I have quoted from these sources in my own translation in the main text, I have provided the original passage in a footnote, retaining original orthography, capitalization, and punctuation and using "*sic*" only where most essential. Attentive readers will therefore notice many inconsistencies—and in some cases, errors—in the original passages, as well as in some of the music examples. In these also I have kept editorial alterations and corrections to a minimum, and they are signaled by square brackets.

Introduction: Cross-Cultural Encounters in Music and Dance

According to Friedrich Nicolai, the "primary purpose" of his travels through the German-speaking lands in 1781 was "to observe people."[1] Perhaps no stop on the German writer, editor, and book dealer's seven-month journey was better suited to this purpose than Vienna, for as he remarked, "there is no city, except possibly Amsterdam, where one sees so many nations all together as in Vienna. [...] There is certainly no city in Germany where foreigners are to be found in such large numbers as in Vienna."[2] The population of the imperial capital and its suburbs increased dramatically in the eighteenth century, by one conservative estimate growing by over 42,000 inhabitants, or about one quarter, between the years 1754 and 1785 alone.[3] Numerous descriptions of the city documented or satirized its growth and change, and as Germanist Kai Kauffmann has argued, they increasingly characterized Vienna as a unique metropolis, markedly different from other large European cities such as Paris and London.[4] While writers' assessments of Viennese attractiveness, education, and manners varied, virtually all commentators underscored that one of the city's most distinctive attributes was its ethnic and cultural diversity. Writing to her sister from Vienna as early as 16 January 1717, Lady Mary Wortley Montagu, wife of the newly

---

[1] Friedrich Nicolai, *Beschreibung einer Reise durch Deutschland und die Schweiz, im Jahre 1781. Nebst Bemerkungen über Gelehrsamkeit, Industrie, Religion und Sitten*, vol. 1 (Berlin and Stettin: n.p., 1783), "Aufenthalt in Koburg," 87: "Mein Hauptzweck war: Menschen zu beobachten."

[2] Nicolai, *Beschreibung einer Reise*, vol. 3 (Berlin and Stettin: n.p., 1784), "Ueber die Einwohner in Wien und ihre Anzahl," 170 and 182: "Es wird keine Stadt seyn, außer allenfalls Amsterdam, wo man so vielerley Nationen zusammensiehet, als in Wien [....] In Deutschland ist gewiß keine Stadt, wo Fremde in so großer Anzahl vorhanden sind, als in Wien."

[3] Ignaz de Luca, *Wiens gegenwärtiger Zustand unter Josephs Regierung* (Vienna: Wucherer, 1787), "Volksmenge," 392–95. De Luca's tabulation excludes military personnel and foreigners ("die Fremden"), by which he means visitors who were not permanent residents of the city, a category in which he included day workers. Johann Pezzl disputed de Luca's numbers, believing them to be too low; see Johann Pezzl, *Skizze von Wien* (1786–1790), as translated in H. C. Robbins Landon, *Mozart and Vienna* (New York: Schirmer, 1991), 64–65.

[4] Kai Kauffmann, *"Es ist nur ein Wien!" Stadtbeschreibungen von Wien 1700 bis 1873* (Vienna: Böhlau, 1994), 17.

Hungarian Dances and Musical Life in Eighteenth-Century Vienna. Catherine Mayes, Oxford University Press.
© Oxford University Press 2025. DOI: 10.1093/oso/9780197805763.003.0001

appointed English ambassador to the Porte, opined that "the Austrians are not commonly the most polite people in the world nor the most agreeable, but Vienna is inhabited by all nations, and I ha[ve] formed to myself a little society of such as [a]re perfectly to my own taste."[5] Almost seventy years later, the Viennese writer and civil servant Johann Pezzl, one of the eighteenth-century city's most avid chroniclers, captured its essence succinctly when he characterized it as "a conglomeration of all European nations."[6]

Pezzl penned a particularly colorful account of Josephinian Vienna's inhabitants, which reveals the pleasure he took in their diversity while also heightening their differences through exoticizing and unfortunately stereotypical language. The value of his description lies in the portrait it paints of the omnipresence of difference in daily Viennese life; the two conditions, of mundanity and distinctiveness, clearly coexisted in the Habsburg capital:

> A pleasant feast for the eyes here is the variety of national costumes from different countries. The city is not limited to the usual German costumes, all alike, as in most European cities. Here you can often meet the Hungarian, striding stiffly, with his fur-lined dolman, his close-fitting trousers reaching almost to his ankles, and his long pigtail; or the round-headed Pole with his monkish haircut and flowing sleeves: both nations die in their boots. — Armenians, Wallachians and Moldavians, with their half-Oriental costumes, are not uncommon. — The Serbians with their twisted moustaches occupy a whole street. — The Greeks in their wide heavy dress can be seen in hordes, smoking their long-stemmed pipes in the coffee-houses on the Leopoldstädter Bridge. — And bearded Muslims in yellow mules, with their broad, murderous knives in their belts, lurch heavily through the muddy streets. — The Polish Jews, all swathed in black, their faces bearded and their hair all twisted in knots, resemble scarecrows: a living satire of the Chosen Race. — Bohemian peasants with their long boots; Hungarian and Transylvanian waggoners with sheepskin greatcoats; Croats with black tubs balanced on their heads—they all provide entertaining accents in the general throng.[7]

---

[5] Lady Mary Wortley Montagu, *Turkish Embassy Letters*, introduction by Anita Desai, text edited and annotated by Malcolm Jack (Athens: University of Georgia Press, 1993), "Letter XXI, Vienna, 16 January 1717," 42.
[6] Pezzl as translated in Landon, *Mozart and Vienna*, 60.
[7] Pezzl as translated in Landon, *Mozart and Vienna*, 65–66.

INTRODUCTION   3

In descriptions such as Pezzl's, the salience of Vienna's diversity is met largely by silence about its effects on the city's musical life. Whereas many eighteenth-century writers chronicled how Vienna's mix of peoples shaped the dress, gastronomy, and economy of the city, they said curiously little about how it must also have defined its soundscape. Unlike the "chocolate made in Milan[,] pheasant raised in Bohemia[,] oysters fished in Istria[,] wine from the cellars of Tokay [the Tokaj region of the Kingdom of Hungary], [...] sable hunted in Siberia, silk woven in Lyons, [...] works of art and music from Italy, France's fashions, Germany's books" that are conjured for today's reader as for Pezzl's wealthy fellow Viennese "as if by rubbing Aladdin's lamp," eighteenth-century aural experiences of the capital are not so easily summoned.[8] Indeed, they are mostly limited to comments about language. A Viennese dialect of German was the most widely spoken one, and numerous eighteenth-century observers drew attention to French as the language of choice among socioeconomically privileged individuals. Still, Nicolai declared that "surely there is no [city] where one hears so many languages spoken," and Pezzl agreed that the "very mixture of many nationalities here produces an endless babel of tongues which distinguishes Vienna from all other European capitals."[9]

To this day, despite Vienna's historic and enduring diversity, most scholarship about Viennese music in the eighteenth century focuses on Haydn, Mozart, and Beethoven. To be sure, their contemporaries also strongly associated these composers with the city. In May 1808, for instance, in the "overview of the current state of music in Vienna" offered in the first month of publication of the Viennese newspaper *Vaterländische Blätter für den österreichischen Kaiserstaat*, descriptions of the accomplishments of the

---

[8] Pezzl as translated in Landon, *Mozart and Vienna*, 62. Montagu, *Turkish Embassy Letters*, "Letter XX, Vienna, 1 January 1717," 40–41, commented similarly: "The plenty and excellence of all sorts of provisions are greater here than in any place I ever was before, and 'tis not very expensive to keep a splendid table. 'Tis really a pleasure to pass through the markets, and see the abundance of what we should think rarities, of fowls and venison, that are daily brought in from Hungary and Bohemia. They [the Viennese] want nothing but shell-fish, and are so fond of oysters, that they have them sent from Venice, and eat them very greedily, stink or not stink." Indeed, according to historian David Do Paço's recent research, foreign merchants and diplomats, especially from the vast Ottoman Empire that bordered the Habsburgs' lands, were integral to Viennese economic and cultural life. See David Do Paço, *L'Orient à Vienne au dix-huitième siècle*, Oxford University Studies in the Enlightenment (Oxford: Voltaire Foundation, 2015); and David Do Paço, "Viennese Delights: Remarks on the History of Food and Sociability in Eighteenth-Century Central Europe," EUI Working Paper MWP 2014/23, https://cadmus.eui.eu/bitstream/handle/1814/33473/MWP_2014_23.pdf?sequence=1&isAllowed=y (accessed 20 January 2023).

[9] Nicolai, *Beschreibung einer Reise*, vol. 3, 170: "gewiß ist keine [Stadt], wo man so vielerley Sprachen reden hört[.]"; Pezzl as translated in Landon, *Mozart and Vienna*, 66.

deceased Mozart, "this rare genius," Haydn, "Vienna's pride," and Beethoven, "an unfettered and anomalous genius [...] an inestimable acquisition for Vienna," overshadow those of other contemporary composers in the city.[10] More forcefully, nearly 200 years later, musicologist and pianist Charles Rosen declared that "Haydn, Mozart, and Beethoven [...] and no others defined Viennese classical style," as he proclaimed also in the title of his highly influential and much celebrated monograph *The Classical Style: Haydn, Mozart, Beethoven*.[11] Countless articles and books with titles announcing a focus on some aspect of musical life in "Haydn's Vienna," "Mozart's Vienna," or "Beethoven's Vienna" seem to share this perspective. While this longstanding emphasis has illuminated the achievements of this justly famous trio as well as their importance in their own time and beyond, it has resulted in a disproportionately Austro-German picture of eighteenth-century Vienna's musical life.

How did Vienna's musical diversity shape everyday experiences, individual and collective identities, and boundaries of belonging in the eighteenth century? How did cross-cultural musical encounters vary by gender and class in a city in which these variables and their intersection decisively determined the rhythms and practices of daily life? In this book, I use Hungarian dance music as a lens through which to begin to answer these basic questions. By shifting my focus away from the Austro-German composers long synonymous with eighteenth-century Vienna, and to a large extent away from the circles of predominantly aristocratic men who supported them, emphasizing instead the city's multicultural nature and the experiences of women, I offer a fresh look at a music-historical time and place that have defined a canon of Western art. I investigate the ways in which gender and class mediated cross-cultural encounters in the Habsburg capital—at court-sponsored entertainments (chapter 1), in public sites of sociability (chapter 2), at the keyboard in domestic settings (chapter 3), and in social dancing (chapter 4)—and I explore how these encounters at times contested and at others reinforced sociocultural norms, perceptions, and

---

[10] "Uebersicht des gegenwärtigen Zustandes der Tonkunst in Wien," *Vaterländische Blätter für den österreichischen Kaiserstaat*, 27 May 1808, 42: "dieses seltene Genie"; "Wiens Stolz"; "ein Genie, ungebunden und regellos [...] eine sehr achtungswerthe Acquisition für Wien." David Wyn Jones has suggested that this article was likely penned by Ignaz von Mosel; see David Wyn Jones, *Music in Vienna 1700, 1800, 1900* (Woodbridge: Boydell Press, 2016), 117. The translation of the description of Beethoven is Jones's (p. 118).

[11] Charles Rosen, *The Classical Style: Haydn, Mozart, Beethoven* (New York: W. W. Norton, 1997), xvi. The original edition of Rosen's monograph was published by Viking in 1971.

hierarchies. In so doing, I demonstrate how historiographically marginalized music and dance were in fact integral to Enlightenment Vienna's cultural life as the capital of a multinational monarchy, and I resituate cultural traces and artifacts not as exotic marginalia but as critical evidence of pervasive social practices in a vibrantly multiethnic community.

Hungarian dances and their music constitute only a single strand within the large multicultural web of Viennese musical life, but their particularity makes them an especially productive and interesting thread to pick out. Nicolai himself noted that in Vienna, "one particularly sees many Hungarians and Transylvanians."[12] Indeed, eighteenth-century accounts of the city attest that Hungarians were relatively numerous there, outnumbered, according to the Austrian statistician Ignaz de Luca, only by the two broad categories of "Germans" and "Slavs."[13] As I explore in chapter 1, furthermore, the Kingdom of Hungary, and particularly elite Hungarians, claimed a privileged position within the Habsburg Monarchy. Hungarian dances and their music thus offer unique insights into the important roles that these art forms could play in imperial politics, establishing and at times shifting boundaries of cultural and political power and inclusion. At the same time, a variety of extant evidence—from newspaper articles and advertisements to ballet rehearsal and performance parts to copious quantities of sheet music for amateur enjoyment—reveals that Hungarian dances and their music were widespread and popular across venues and social strata in the Habsburg capital. Their broad appeal lay at least in part in a fascination with the Romani musicians who were their primary original performers. This fascination, however, coexisted with ongoing profound stigmatization of the Roma as a people.[14] Alongside Jews, they were Europe's internal racial Other, and descriptions of their musical performances were integral to their Orientalization. The appropriation and adaptation of their music for enjoyment in domestic contexts thus opens an interpretive window unique among the many national dance types performed in eighteenth-century Vienna.

---

[12] Nicolai, *Beschreibung einer Reise*, vol. 3, 171: "Besonders bemerkt man viele Ungarn und Siebenbürger [...]." Transylvania was part of the Kingdom of Hungary in the eighteenth century.

[13] Ignaz de Luca, *Topographie von Wien*, vol. 1 (Vienna: In Kommission bey Thad. Edlen v. Schmidbauer und Komp. am Graben zur blauen Krone, 1794), "Von den Einwohnern, ihrer ehmaligen Vermehrung, jetzigen Anzahl, Eintheilung derselben, Sitten, Sterblichkeit u.," 12: "Jetzt findet man hier von allen Nationen Menschen, darunter die Teutschen die größte Zahl machen, diesen folgen die Slaven, Ungern, Siebenbürger, Illyrier, Franzosen, Italiener, und Juden."

[14] I use "Roma" (the plural of "Rom") as a noun and "Romani" as the corresponding adjective throughout this book.

Music, Dance, and the Enlightenment

The central role of dance in shaping the music and culture of Habsburg Vienna has been well established, but scholarship has largely been restricted to Western European dances such as the minuet, contredanse, and waltz.[15] The ubiquity and functions of Hungarian dances—like others from Eastern Europe—in eighteenth-century Viennese life have yet to be examined in detail. Historian Mark Philp has argued, furthermore, for the centrality of embodiment to the Enlightenment, and specifically for the critical role that dance, along with music and song, played in identity formation because of its physicality. Dance, in particular, he has suggested, as a "heightened emotional, physical and mental experience of self-discipline, bodily coordination and social and sensual regulation and excitement was unlikely to have been entirely fleeting."[16] It had lasting effects on memory, self-perception, and identification with others in wider social and political contexts; its practice was thus much more than a merely agreeable and widespread pastime. Dance's intimate connection to music, furthermore, suggests its importance with respect to other aspects of culture—visual art or fashion, for instance—in the Enlightenment's construction of knowledge, to which, as Nicolai asserted, the observation of people was central. Travel was at the heart of this anthropological project, and as historian Vanessa Agnew has brilliantly explored, music was elevated in eighteenth-century aesthetic hierarchies hand in hand with its new valorization as an object of inquiry in apodemic literature.[17] Music's relationship to travel, Agnew argues, was both ontological and epistemological: "music facilitated travel, structured the cross-cultural encounter, and shaped its interpretation."[18] The English musician, composer, and music historian Charles Burney is a central figure for Agnew, for "by foregrounding music and producing a specialized travel account, [he] had done something new."[19]

---

[15] See, for instance, Wye Jamison Allanbrook, *Rhythmic Gesture in Mozart: Le Nozze di Figaro and Don Giovanni* (Chicago: University of Chicago Press, 1983); Eric McKee, "Ballroom Dances of the Late Eighteenth Century," in *The Oxford Handbook of Topic Theory*, ed. Danuta Mirka (Oxford: Oxford University Press, 2014), 164–93; Walter Salmen, ed., *Mozart in der Tanzkultur seiner Zeit* (Innsbruck: Helbling, 1990); Peter van der Merwe, *Roots of the Classical: The Popular Origins of Western Music* (Oxford: Oxford University Press, 2004); and Erica Buurman, *The Viennese Ballroom in the Age of Beethoven* (Cambridge: Cambridge University Press, 2022).

[16] Mark Philp, *Radical Conduct: Politics, Sociability and Equality in London 1795–1815* (Cambridge: Cambridge University Press, 2020), 218.

[17] Vanessa Agnew, *Enlightenment Orpheus: The Power of Music in Other Worlds* (Oxford: Oxford University Press, 2008).

[18] Agnew, *Enlightenment Orpheus*, 14.

[19] Agnew, *Enlightenment Orpheus*, 62.

If Burney's approach to the travelogue was novel for its focus on music, as a traveler, he was entirely typical of his day, embodying the qualities that his contemporaries identified as those of the model voyager: he was erudite and curious, and he possessed a refined sensibility.[20] These characteristics tacitly presuppose socioeconomic privilege, but their elaboration—physical and mental stamina, single-minded devotion to the object of study, firsthand experience of it and dissemination of resulting observations in lucid prose— also strongly imply that the eighteenth-century's ideal traveler was male. As I explore in chapter 2, women's ability to travel and to write about their travels was restricted by numerous factors—legal, financial, educational, social—in the eighteenth century. In cosmopolitan Vienna, furthermore, gender intersected with socioeconomic privilege to circumscribe women's access to the public sites of sociability in which they could have experienced a wide range of vernacular musics. This in turn contributed to women's disenfranchisement, for as Agnew has underscored, the high status of travel and related anthropological experiences and the literary undertakings that they enabled "conferred symbolic capital" and, in the case of many middle-class men, facilitated upward social mobility.[21]

By attending to typical areas of engagement and accomplishment of relatively privileged eighteenth-century women—reading, playing keyboard instruments, social dancing—I argue that we may understand how music made cross-cultural encounters possible for them too. Indeed, the very accounts of foreign musics that could raise a middling man's social capital and standing, as well as versions of these musics for amateur enjoyment at the keyboard and in social dancing, allowed women to travel imaginatively. Eighteenth-century descriptive literature about Hungarian music and music-making, moreover, intersected unusually directly with an especially large Viennese repertoire of accessible keyboard dances ostensibly adapted from the performances of Romani musicians. As I argue in chapter 3, this repertoire is thus particularly suggestive of the ways in which cross-cultural musical experiences—even, or perhaps especially, private ones—were critical to women's vicarious exploration of new identities, some of which pushed against sociocultural boundaries, without risk to their position or reputation. On the dance floor, in turn, the repertoire of Hungarian dances for keyboard lent itself to accompanying contredanses in social dance settings.

---

[20] Agnew, *Enlightenment Orpheus*, 62, 66.
[21] Agnew, *Enlightenment Orpheus*, 25.

As I explore in chapter 4, contredanse practices reinforced class hierarchies in the Habsburg capital, but they could also invite imaginative community across the border separating Vienna from the Kingdom of Hungary.

Beyond the "*Style Hongrois*"

As a social history, this book departs significantly from substantial existing scholarship on Viennese—and more broadly Western European—engagement with Hungarian music in the late eighteenth and nineteenth centuries. Authors of numerous studies have treated Hungarian music as a topic or style in Western European works—with Haydn's "Rondo, in the Gipsies' Style" from the Piano Trio in G Major, Hob. XV:25, and his "Rondo all'ungarese" from the Keyboard Concerto in D Major, Hob. XVIII:11, being perhaps the most discussed works from the eighteenth century—compiling inventories of Hungaricisms and often attempting to attribute influences or to trace borrowings to specific sources.[22] As I have argued in some of my own work, the strong association of the Hungarian style with dance music carried specific generic and syntactical implications when this topic was evoked in Western European compositions.[23] Many musicologists, furthermore, have sought to elucidate why composers such as Haydn, Beethoven, Schubert, Schumann, Brahms, and Liszt evoked in their own works the

---

[22] See, for instance, Ervin Major, "Miszellen: Ungarische Tanzmelodien in Haydns Bearbeitung," *Zeitschrift für Musikwissenschaft* 11 (1928–29): 601–4; Dénes Bartha, "Mozart et le folklore musical de l'Europe centrale," in *Les Influences étrangères dans l'oeuvre de W. A. Mozart, Paris, 10–13 octobre 1956*, ed. André Verchaly (Paris: Centre national de la recherche scientifique, 1958), 157–81; Bence Szabolcsi, "Joseph Haydn und die ungarische Musik," *Beiträge zur Musikwissenschaft* 2 (1959): 62–73; Ferenc Bónis, "Beethoven und die ungarische Musik," in *Bericht über den internationalen musikwissenschaftlichen Kongress Bonn 1970*, ed. Carl Dahlhaus et al. (Kassel: Bärenreiter, 1970), 121–27; Tibor Istvánffy, "All'Ongarese: Studien zur Rezeption ungarischer Musik bei Haydn, Mozart und Beethoven" (PhD diss., Ruprecht-Karls-Universität Heidelberg, 1982); Bálint Sárosi, "Parallelen aus der ungarischen Volksmusik zum 'Rondo all'Ongarese'-Satz in Haydns D-dur Klavierkonzert Hob. XVIII:11," in *Bericht über den internationalen Joseph Haydn Kongress Wien 1982*, ed. Eva Badura-Skoda (Munich: G. Henle, 1986), 222–26; Jonathan Bellman, "Toward a Lexicon for the Style Hongrois," *Journal of Musicology* 9, no. 2 (Spring 1991): 214–37; and Gerhard J. Winkler, "Der 'Style Hongrois' in der europäischen Kunstmusik des 18. und 19. Jahrhunderts: Ein geschichtlicher Abriss," in *Musik der Roma in Burgenland: Referate des internationalen Workshop-Symposions Eisenstadt, 5.–6. Oktober 2001*, ed. Gerhard J. Winkler (Eisenstadt: Burgenländisches Landesmuseum, 2003), 63–81.

[23] Catherine Mayes, "Turkish and Hungarian-Gypsy Styles," in *The Oxford Handbook of Topic Theory*, ed. Danuta Mirka (Oxford: Oxford University Press, 2014), 214–37.

music that Hungarian Romani musicians performed.[24] Conclusions have often been biographical: composers' personal identification with the Roma, a people living outside sociocultural boundaries and norms, not only led them to reference specific elements and practices of Hungarian Romani music-making, but, more broadly, provided a frame within which to push or even to defy the boundaries of stylistic, harmonic, and formal conventions. Existing scholarship, as musicologist Jonathan Bellman has summarized in his own seminal work on what he has termed the *"style hongrois,"* has thus both "examine[d] the musical speech itself" and "illuminate[d] the need for it, [...] identify[ing] those things the conventional musical language of the time was unable to express."[25] With respect to Schubert, for instance, Bellman has hypothesized that the composer was "identifying on a deeper level with the [...] Hungarian Gypsies, whose mistreatment, ostracism, defiance, and reputed reliance upon music as the expression of their sorrows had resonances in his own life."[26] Likewise, musicologist John Daverio has noted that "Brahms, Schumann, and the gypsy: each, in his own way was indeed an outsider."[27]

Such conclusions are in long-standing historiographical company. In his 1859 book *Des Bohémiens et de leur musique en Hongrie*, Franz Liszt declared:

> More than one kind of personal sympathy has long since drawn us closer to the Gypsies. [...] The memory of the Gypsies is linked to those of our own childhood and to some of its most vivid impressions. Later we became a wandering virtuoso, as [the Gypsies] are in our homeland. They drove

---

[24] See, most significantly, Jonathan Bellman, *The* Style Hongrois *in the Music of Western Europe* (Boston: Northeastern University Press, 1993); Ferenc Bónis, "Heldentum und Sehnsucht nach Freiheit. Zur Frage: Beethoven und die ungarische Musik," in *Fidelio/Leonore: Annäherungen an ein zentrales Werk des Musiktheaters—Vorträge und Materialien des Salzburger Symposions 1996*, ed. Peter Csobádi et al. (Salzburg: Verlag Müller-Speiser, 1998), 347–57; Csilla Pethő, "*Style Hongrois*: Hungarian Elements in the Works of Haydn, Beethoven, Weber and Schubert," *Studia Musicologica* 41, nos. 1–3 (2000): 199–284; John Daverio, "Brahms, the Schumann Circle, and the *Style Hongrois*: Contexts for the 'Double' Concerto, Op. 102," chap. 7 of his *Crossing Paths: Schubert, Schumann, and Brahms* (Oxford: Oxford University Press, 2002), 191–242; Matthew Head, "Haydn's Exoticisms: 'Difference' and the Enlightenment," in *The Cambridge Companion to Haydn*, ed. Caryl Clark (Cambridge: Cambridge University Press, 2005), 77–92; Julie Hedges Brown, "Schumann and the *Style Hongrois*," in *Rethinking Schumann*, ed. Roe-Min Kok and Laura Tunbridge (Oxford: Oxford University Press, 2011), 265–99; and Shay Loya, *Liszt's Transcultural Modernism and the Hungarian-Gypsy Tradition*, Eastman Studies in Music 87 (Rochester, NY: University of Rochester Press, 2011).
[25] Bellman, *The* Style Hongrois, 13.
[26] Bellman, *The* Style Hongrois, 161.
[27] Daverio, *Crossing Paths*, 240.

in the stakes of their tent in all the countries of Europe, taking centuries to cross them, whereas we covered them within a few years, often, like them, remaining a stranger to the populations we visited, like them seeking the ideal in an incessant absorption in art, if not in nature.[28]

Liszt's professed kinship with Romani musicians placed him squarely within a larger trend among nineteenth-century artists, particularly in France, to self-identify with the existential plight of this people.[29] Moreover, as art historian Marilyn R. Brown has noted, "the notion of the artist as an outcast bohemian was a founding tenet of Western modernism. [...] The concept of avant-garde was predicated on the notion that the artist, as a dissident social outsider, had a clearer vision of the future than conformists."[30] When read in this light, Liszt's celebration of the unique features of Hungarian Romani music—"its system of modulation, based on a kind of complete negation of any sort of system," "its luxuriant ornamentation, eminently Oriental," "its rhythms and their vacillation"—may be understood as a reflection of his own vision of the future of music.[31] In other words, the harmonic, melodic, and rhythmic innovations of Hungarian Romani music would be the core elements of Liszt's renewal of European music.[32]

Liszt's perspective, furthermore, directly informed his comments on Viennese composers of the late eighteenth and early nineteenth centuries. "The eighteenth century," he declared in *Des Bohémiens*, "was the great era of Gypsy music,"[33] and composers "living in Vienna," including Beethoven and Schubert, "had known it enough to be struck by its originality." In the

---

[28] Franz Liszt, *Des Bohémiens et de leur musique en Hongrie* (Paris: Librairie Nouvelle, 1859), 163: "Plus d'un genre de sympathie personnelle nous a depuis bien longtemps rapproché des Bohémiens, et a conduit notre esprit à s'occuper plus particulièrement d'eux et de ce qui pouvait servir comme de glose et de texte explicatif à leur art, auquel nous avons consacré beaucoup d'attention, de soins et d'études. Le souvenir des Zigeuner se lie à ceux de notre enfance et de quelques-unes de ses plus vives impressions. Plus tard nous devînmes virtuose errant, comme eux le sont dans notre patrie. Ils ont planté les pieux de leur tente dans tous les pays de l'Europe, employant des siècles à les traverser, tandis que nous, nous les avons parcourus dans l'espace de quelques années, restant souvent étranger comme eux aux populations que nous visitions, comme eux cherchant l'idéal en une incessante absorption dans l'art, sinon dans la nature."

[29] See Marilyn R. Brown, *Gypsies and Other Bohemians: The Myth of the Artist in Nineteenth-Century France* (Ann Arbor, MI: UMI Research Press, 1985).

[30] Brown, *Gypsies*, 3.

[31] Liszt discusses these features throughout *Des Bohémiens*; see, for instance, his comments on pp. 12, 221 ("son système de modulation, basé sur une sorte de négation totale de tout système à cet égard"), 223 ("sa *fioriture* luxuriante, éminemment orientale"), and 339 ("ses rhythmes et leurs vacillations"). The emphasis is original.

[32] This subject is explored in detail in Loya, *Liszt's Transcultural Modernism*.

[33] Liszt, *Des Bohémiens*, 290: "Le dix-huitième siècle fut la grande ère de la musique bohémienne [...]."

same breath, however, he set himself in opposition to them, dismissing them and their fellow "*civilized* musicians" for "misunderstand[ing] the characteristics essentially inherent in its form."[34] Where Liszt diagnosed a deficit, many subsequent authors have identified opportunities to probe what may have motivated the very composers whom Liszt disparaged. As Bellman has argued, "the key question" has been "*why*—why composers, particularly composers of the greatest artistry, repeatedly found it necessary to use this particular foreign musical language, long associated with the Gypsies themselves and the café milieu in which they most frequently appeared."[35] Bellman's own influential conclusions about composers' identification with the long-suffering but defiant Roma and their adoption of aspects of their music-making, particularly in the nineteenth century, have informed three decades of scholarship, which have elaborated, to use Bellman's phrase, a "poetics of exclusion."[36]

In this book, in contrast, I turn away from the composer-centric approach that has driven studies of the "*style hongrois*," instead investigating music and dance as social activities in which individuals and communities engage. Why were Hungarian dances so prevalent and beloved in Enlightenment Vienna? How were they experienced by inhabitants of the city of different genders and classes? What did these dances and their music *do* within daily eighteenth-century Viennese life? To whom did they matter and why?

Difference and Everyday Music-Making

As these questions imply, much of my study intentionally focuses on the quotidian. Despite musicology's general turn away from "great composer" narratives over the last three decades, embracing or at least accepting studies of the commonplace as an antidote to exegetical investigations of canonical composers and their works, we still know very little about everyday practices of social music-making in the eighteenth century. Important studies by

---

[34] Liszt, *Des Bohémiens*, 331–32: "On peut se convaincre combien peu les musiciens *civilisés* ont pénétré la caractéristique de l'*art bohémien* lorsqu'ils s'en sont occupés, en voyant deux maîtres tels que Beethoven et Schubert se méprendre sur les traits essentiellement inhérents à sa forme. [...] Tous deux, demeurant à Vienne, purent le connaître assez pour être frappés par son originalité." The emphasis is original.

[35] Jonathan Bellman, "The Hungarian Gypsies and the Poetics of Exclusion," in *The Exotic in Western Music*, ed. Jonathan Bellman (Boston: Northeastern University Press, 1998), 94–95. The emphasis is original.

[36] Bellman, "The Hungarian Gypsies and the Poetics of Exclusion."

musicologists Alice Hanson and Leon Botstein, for instance, of what Hanson has termed "the civic environment for music" in Vienna treat a somewhat later time. Readers will find that the scope of my book is thus quite broad, as I provide a detailed account of everyday musicking across multiple contexts as an understudied backdrop for thinking about the performance and reception of Hungarian dances and their music. Furthermore, I attend throughout to Botstein's criticism of Hanson's work, which, while providing "more information about street music, itinerant musicians, popular dance and song than is accessible elsewhere," does not carefully investigate its "social or cultural significance."[37]

To be sure, the question of "how social and cultural identities and differences come to be constructed and articulated in music" is central to editors Georgina Born and David Hesmondhalgh's pathbreaking collection of essays on *Western Music and Its Others*, which extends its area of inquiry to popular as well as art musics.[38] The studies treating popular music in their volume, however, are restricted to the twentieth century. The role of difference in quotidian musical experiences before that time has not been considered in detail. In part this is because, as Born and Hesmondhalgh rightly note, "postcolonial analysis has tended to concentrate on 'official' and high-art discourses at the expense of a systematic account of the prominent role of commercial popular culture [...]."[39] Indeed, postcolonialism has particularly influenced studies of music and difference, especially where they have sought to move beyond questions of borrowing and authenticity, yet regardless of their approach, these studies have focused heavily on concert and stage works, with special attention to the operatic repertoire. As a multimedia genre, opera readily lends itself to what musicologist Ralph P. Locke has termed an "All the Music in Full Context" approach, which expands the focus of study beyond the notes themselves to include extramusical interpretive frames such as words, staging, costuming, and even prevailing ideas and stereotypes.[40] Operas depicting foreign peoples and places have

---

[37] Leon Botstein, review of *Musical Life in Biedermeier Vienna*, by Alice M. Hanson, *Musical Quarterly* 72, no. 4 (1986): 530, 533. The quotation from Hanson's book also appears in Botstein's review.

[38] Georgina Born and David Hesmondhalgh, "Introduction: On Difference, Representation, and Appropriation in Music," in *Western Music and Its Others: Difference, Representation, and Appropriation in Music*, ed. Georgina Born and David Hesmondhalgh (Berkeley: University of California Press, 2000), 2.

[39] Born and Hesmondhalgh, "Introduction," 6–7.

[40] Locke explains the paradigm in detail in his books *Musical Exoticism: Images and Reflections* (Cambridge: Cambridge University Press, 2009) and *Music and the Exotic from the Renaissance to Mozart* (Cambridge: Cambridge University Press, 2015).

provided particularly rich terrain for investigating music's agency in what musicologists Olivia Bloechl and Melanie Lowe have identified as "such longstanding political problematics as freedom, sovereignty, tyranny, legitimacy, belonging, democracy, [and] deliberation."[41] In investigating how experiences of Hungarian dances and their music were imbricated with similar issues of individual and collective identification, I have been inspired by Locke's methodology. I give sustained attention to the frames that shaped cross-cultural encounters in everyday musical life in eighteenth-century Vienna, from texts that provided interpretive clues to amateur musicians to prevailing social dance practices, and from the clienteles of the city's public sites of sociability to the geopolitical struggles of the Habsburgs.

Nonetheless, this study requires an openness to speculation as a valuable scholarly tool; if we reject it, we lose far more than we gain. References to Hungarian dances in Enlightenment Vienna are most often brief and lack detail; contemporary newspapers, for instance, mention them frequently, in articles and particularly in advertisements, but who specifically witnessed performances or bought dance music, and what meanings and uses these events and objects may have had, necessitates much reading between the lines. (The Austrian National Library's "ANNO [AustriaN Newspapers Online] Historische Zeitungen und Zeitschriften" database has been invaluable to me in discovering and accessing these materials.[42]) The experiences of women and of the socioeconomically disadvantaged, two constituencies traditionally silenced by historiography, furthermore, are often particularly difficult to reconstruct. Because the roles and meanings of Hungarian dances within eighteenth-century Viennese life are rarely explicit in historical records, they can only be inferred through careful—and sometimes speculative—interpretation. Some of my arguments may therefore frustrate some readers, but speculation is necessary and unavoidable if we wish to explore private and vernacular music-making. The alternative, the "illusion" of objectivity, as ethnomusicologist Philip V. Bohlman has rightly called it, "is possible only when the questions considered valid are limited to those that can, in fact, be answered without qualification."[43] Such an illusion has contributed to what musicologist Suzanne G. Cusick has called out as "the

---

[41] Olivia Bloechl and Melanie Lowe: "Introduction: Rethinking Difference," in *Rethinking Difference in Music Scholarship*, ed. Olivia Bloechl, Melanie Lowe, and Jeffrey Kallberg (Cambridge: Cambridge University Press, 2015), 25.

[42] https://anno.onb.ac.at.

[43] Philip V. Bohlman, "On the Unremarkable in Music," *19th-Century Music* 16, no. 2 (Autumn 1992): 206.

marginalizing of gender (and the resulting marginalizing of women, women's music-making, 'woman's work,' and the musically 'feminine') within the intellectual microcosm that is musicology [that] helps to sustain the gender system itself, with its intentional devaluing of practices that might be mistaken for 'woman's work.'"[44]

Perhaps ironically, similar intellectual gatekeeping in the eighteenth century was responsible, at least in part, for creating the very documentary vacuum that we now face by devaluing the musical cultures of subordinated groups, including women and the rural and working classes. As Agnew has outlined, some of Burney's contemporaries criticized him for paying undue attention to "the opinions of beer fiddlers and buskers over professional musicians."[45] To a large extent, though, this criticism is unwarranted. Despite Burney's assertion that he "was not contented with hearing music in fine houses, theatres, and palaces, but visited cottages, and garrets, wherever [he] could get scent of a good performer, or a man of genius,"[46] his travelogue, like the writings of his contemporaries with similar inclinations, contains only cursory observations about modest settings and musicians. Burney himself admitted that "vague accounts" are "all I am able to give [...] of performers of a lower order," for "memory seldom assists us in retaining the names of either persons, or things, that are indifferent to us."[47] To judge from the vagueness of Burney's comments about the "band of wind instruments" featured daily at dinner at his inn in Vienna as well as about "the German street-musicians" of the city, he must have been indifferent to all of them, restricting his remarks to musings about why their playing was so out of tune.[48]

Overview

The time period that I consider in this book—spanning the years from approximately 1750 to 1810—begins somewhat before Romani musicians

---

[44] Suzanne G. Cusick, "Gender, Musicology, and Feminism," in *Rethinking Music*, ed. Nicholas Cook and Mark Everist (Oxford: Oxford University Press, 1999), 475.

[45] Agnew, *Enlightenment Orpheus*, 154.

[46] Charles Burney, *Dr. Burney's Musical Tours*, vol. 2, *An Eighteenth-Century Musical Tour in Central Europe and the Netherlands Being Dr. Charles Burney's Account of his Musical Experiences*, ed. Percy A. Scholes (London: Oxford University Press, 1959), "Part IX: The Second Week in Vienna (6–13 September)," 120.

[47] Burney, *Dr. Burney's Musical Tours*, vol. 2, "Part IX: The Second Week in Vienna (6–13 September)," 116.

[48] Burney, *Dr. Burney's Musical Tours*, vol. 2, "Part IX: The Second Week in Vienna (6–13 September)," 114.

emerged as the primary performers of Hungary's national dance music. It starts with the decade during which Hungarians were depicted in nationally themed pantomime ballets at Vienna's court theaters. It encompasses the many years during which Hungarian dances were enjoyed at the keyboard and in social dancing in domestic settings, and it coincides with documented performances by Hungarian dancers and musicians, some of whom were Roma, at the Habsburg court and in public sites of sociability in the Monarchy's capital city. It culminates on the eve of significant changes in music and dance in Hungary, where composers increasingly cultivated unique and individual voices—what musicologist Shay Loya has termed "authorial *verbunkos*"—eventually in service to nascent political nationalism, and in Vienna, where the Congress of Vienna left an enduring stamp on cultural life.[49]

The earliest of the decades I address belong to what musicologist Richard Taruskin has characterized as "something of a historiographical black hole"[50]—the chasm between the generation of J. S. Bach and Handel and that of Haydn and Mozart—but dance music more broadly and the practices in which it is embedded have generally been relegated to the historiographical void. As nineteenth-century critics increasingly valued instrumental music for its aesthetic autonomy, dance music was disparaged for its ties to physicality and functionality. In this regard, musicologist Erica Buurman has drawn attention, for instance, to Eduard Hanslick's important treatise *On the Musically Beautiful* from the mid-nineteenth century, in which the music critic "articulated a theory of listening that distinguished between 'true' listening as an intellectual activity and 'pathological' listening as associated with physical and emotional responses."[51] Until quite recently, as musicologists have gradually begun to investigate and to embrace music as an embodied art form, dance music continued to be considered largely unworthy of attention, relegated to the category of the popular and trivial as opposed to the serious and significant. Scholarship on eighteenth-century Viennese music has privileged, furthermore, the genres with which Haydn, Mozart, and Beethoven are most closely associated—symphony, opera, and string

---

[49] See, for instance, Bence Szabolcsi, *A Concise History of Hungarian Music*, trans. Sára Karig, trans. rev. Florence Knepler (London: Barrie and Rockliff in cooperation with Corvina Press Budapest, 1964), esp. chap. 6; Loya, *Liszt's Transcultural Modernism*, esp. 14, 65, and 78–81; and Buurman, *The Viennese Ballroom*, esp. chap. 7.

[50] Richard Taruskin, *The Oxford History of Western Music*, vol. 2, *Music in the Seventeenth and Eighteenth Centuries* (Oxford: Oxford University Press, 2010), 400.

[51] Buurman, *The Viennese Ballroom*, 4.

quartet—to the detriment of investigations of more quotidian music and attendant practices in the home, ballroom, and church. Admittedly, primary documentation of dance musicians, their activities, and their repertoires is relatively limited. Despite the popularity and importance of dance within the music and culture of Enlightenment Vienna, dance musicians themselves suffered from a relatively low status. (The same was not necessarily true of *composers* of dance music, however.) They received short shrift in otherwise detailed descriptions of the city's musical life, such as Johann Ferdinand Ritter von Schönfeld's *Jahrbuch der Tonkunst von Wien und Prag* of 1796, and dance musicians were excluded, for instance, from the Tonkünstler-Societät, a charitable society that supported the widows and orphans of deceased musicians through the organization of benefit concerts.[52]

Much of the dance music that I explore in this book—from pantomime ballets performed in court theaters to large quantities of music enjoyed by amateurs at home—survives today only in archives, never having been reissued in modern, scholarly editions. (Fortunately, the digitization of much of this archival material has made it increasingly accessible, even during the global COVID-19 pandemic.) Even when extant music has been given new life in such editions, as in the notable cases of two important compilations prepared late in the twentieth century by Hungarian scholars,[53] this music remains for the most part undeniably "occasional," signifying, to borrow musicologist Nicholas Mathew's concise definition, that its "meaning and aesthetic viability remain bound to specific historical periods or events."[54] Its marginalized position in scholarship and its absence from today's stages and music desks, however, mask its popularity, visibility, and significance in its own time.

Each chapter of this book presents a case study of Hungarian dances and their music in a particular setting in eighteenth-century Vienna, with close attention to the mediating and intersecting effects of gender and class

---

[52] Erica Buurman, "The Annual Balls of the Pensionsgesellschaft bildender Künstler, 1792–1832: Music in the Viennese Imperial Ballrooms from Haydn to Lanner," in *Beethoven und andere Hofmusiker seiner Generation: Bericht über den internationalen musikwissenschaftlichen Kongress Bonn, 3. bis 6. Dezember 2015*, ed. Birgit Lodes, Elisabeth Reisinger, and John D. Wilson (Bonn: Beethoven-Haus, 2018), 221–22; and T. C. W. Blanning, *The Culture of Power and the Power of Culture: Old Regime Europe 1660–1789* (Oxford: Oxford University Press, 2003), 176.

[53] Géza Papp, ed., *Hungarian Dances 1784–1810*, Musicalia Danubiana 7 (Budapest: Magyar Tudományos Akadémia, Zenetudományi Intézet, 1986); Ferenc Bónis, ed., *Ungarische Tänze für Klavier/Hungarian Dances for Piano*, Diletto Musicale 662 (Vienna: Doblinger, 1993).

[54] Nicholas Mathew, "Heroic Haydn, the Occasional Work and 'Modern' Political Music," *Eighteenth-Century Music* 4, no. 1 (March 2007): 16.

on individual and collective experiences. The book as a whole contributes to ongoing conversations about the role of music and dance in eighteenth-century cross-cultural encounters, and the importance of such encounters in constructing knowledge, in shaping and reshaping personal and communal identities, and in negotiating hierarchies of power and belonging. It also sheds much-needed light on the intersection of difference with everyday musical experiences. Throughout the study, I privilege the sociality of music, attending at least as much to extramusical frames as to intramusical content. Indeed, the ephemerality of the subject matter of this book necessitates moving away from a text-and-context approach for the simple reason that in many cases—vernacular musicking, choreographies of social dances and of pantomime ballets—texts have not merely vanished over the centuries but likely never existed in the first place. The music of the courtly Hungarian *divertissements*, or presentational dances, I discuss, furthermore, is unknown to us; press reports provide the most information about these dances, but they unfortunately do not identify their music by title or composer.

In chapter 1, I explore diverging representations of Hungary in music and dance at the Habsburg court and its theaters. The inclusion of Hungarians among a host of rustic characters in pantomime ballets of the mid-eighteenth century supports historian Larry Wolff's influential theory of Western Europe's "invention" of Eastern Europe as its less civilized complement during the Enlightenment.[55] But when members of the Russian royal family visited the Viennese court in late 1781, Hungary's nobility presented itself in a particularly elegant light through its performance of Hungarian national dances, underscoring that cultural and political prestige and belonging were by no means incompatible with Hungarian-ness. I argue that careful interpretation of politics, audience, class affinity, aesthetics, and their interrelationships can illuminate why Hungary was staged in such apparently contradictory ways at the Habsburg court. Moreover, I suggest that careful consideration of these same contexts can help refine our understanding of the imaginative construction of Eastern Europe in the eighteenth century.

That music and dance could complicate narratives of political and sociocultural inclusion and exclusion reflects, as Born and Hesmondhalgh have emphasized, "the complexities of authorial agency and practice in relation to wider discursive formations[.]"[56] As performing arts, the execution

---

[55] Larry Wolff, *Inventing Eastern Europe: The Map of Civilization on the Mind of the Enlightenment* (Stanford, CA: Stanford University Press), 1994.
[56] Born and Hesmondhalgh, "Introduction," 7.

and reception of music and dance are constantly in flux, endowing them with varied and changing meanings and with particular agency to challenge hierarchies of power, not least by troubling the boundaries of Self and Other. At the Habsburg court, music and dance played key roles in eighteenth-century definitions of "Hungarian," at times contesting and at others supporting broader discursive definitions of Eastern Europe and its inhabitants during the Enlightenment.

Relative privilege allowed individuals to experience the ballets and, to a certain extent, to participate in the festivities that I discuss in chapter 1. In chapter 2, in contrast, I investigate how socioeconomic privilege intersected with gender-based oppression to exclude elite women from public sites of sociability where Hungarian and other vernacular dance music was played in eighteenth-century Vienna: inns, taverns, beerhouses, wine cellars. Because relatively privileged Viennese women did not patronize such venues, they typically experienced vernacular music secondhand, through written accounts, rather than through direct encounters. At a time when personal experience lent particular authority to descriptions of both the natural and the human worlds, I argue that this mediation further undermined women's power and position within the emerging public sphere.

The accounts of Hungarian music and music-making read by relatively privileged Viennese women were part of the large eighteenth-century literature describing musicians, repertoires, instruments, and performance practices around the world. As I explore in chapter 3, descriptions of Hungarian music were unusual in that they could be consumed in conjunction with an extensive repertoire of keyboard dances for domestic enjoyment ostensibly based on the performances of Romani musicians, almost all of whom were male. I consider in particular how the unique conjunction of these dances and descriptions invited amateur keyboard players—most of whom were women and girls—to imagine and even to identify with Hungarian Romani musicians by adopting some of their performance practices. The great disparities between the two groups—of gender, class, ethnicity, and professional status—suggest that playing Hungarian dances made a variety of subject positions available to amateur female keyboardists, from the culturally obedient to the more resistive: expressing power and authority, developing sympathetic understanding, voicing defiant identification.

In contrast to other foreign national dances—Polish or Scottish, for instance—played by these same amateurs, the performance of Hungarian dances therefore was, or could be, more nearly dialogical, in the sense that literary scholar Ken Hirschkop has proposed in suggesting "a more socially orientated approach to music" that draws on Mikhail Bakhtin's sociolinguistic work.[57] As Hirschkop has argued, because music is immanently social, "to really dialogize music [it is necessary] to bring in not just musical language from popular social contexts but actual institutional elements of those social contexts themselves: forms of performance, reception and composition."[58] Descriptions of Romani music-making that enabled readers to adopt Romani performance practices in their own playing were key to such dialogism, which in turn allowed amateur female keyboardists to enact community with eighteenth-century Europe's perhaps most highly Othered musicians in entirely new social contexts.

Many sets of Hungarian dances for keyboard are preserved in the Austrian National Library's "Kaisersammlung," which brings together Emperor Franz II's music collection as well as the collections of his wives Elisabeth and Marie Therese. These sets were also frequently advertised in eighteenth-century Viennese newspapers, suggesting that playing Hungarian dances provided a point of cultural contact between middle-class amateurs and the imperial family. As I explore in chapter 4, contemporary sources—including extant dance music; writings about dance, music, and aesthetics; and newspaper articles and advertisements—suggest that these dances were also used to accompany simple contredanses in the private, domestic gatherings of individuals and families who owned keyboard instruments. Published descriptions of social dancing in Hungary available to them may well have informed their contredanses, imbuing them with distinctive movements and manners. Social contredanses, however, differed greatly from the extravagant and highly rehearsed presentational contredanses of Vienna's aristocracy. I argue that the somatic enjoyment of Hungarian dances thus magnified the distance separating Vienna's socioeconomic classes, undermining the sense of shared experience suggested by the wide circulation of Hungarian dance music alone. At the same time, the adoption of Hungarian dance practices in the Habsburg capital could forge a cultural connection between the city's middle classes and those of the neighboring Kingdom. This chapter thus underscores both the power and the limits of music and dance to negotiate boundaries of class and culture.

---

[57] Ken Hirschkop, "The Classical and the Popular: Musical Form and Social Context," in *Music and the Politics of Culture*, ed. Christopher Norris (London: Lawrence & Wishart, 1989), 284–85.
[58] Hirschkop, "The Classical and the Popular," 295, as given in Born and Hesmondhalgh, "Introduction," 43.

Hungarian or Romani?

My references throughout this book to "Hungarian" dances and their music are not meant to depreciate the important role and contributions of Romani musicians to their development and dissemination within the Kingdom of Hungary and beyond its borders. Indeed, in a fictitious conversation published in a 1790 issue of the newspaper *Magyar Kurír*, the Romani character Zamántz declared expansively that "we play music for the Hungarian nation."[59] Ironically, Romani musicians attained widespread and rather sudden professional success in the later eighteenth century despite a series of Habsburg decrees issued over many years that aimed to control their lifestyle, in an attempt, as the British physician and medical scientist Richard Bright explained in his travelogue, to "civilize the gypsies, and render them useful to the state."[60] Forcing the Roma to give up their nomadic lifestyle by forbidding their possession of horses and wagons, requiring them to learn and practice a trade, and officially documenting their numbers and occupations facilitated the collection of taxes from a group who previously had lived beyond the reach of the government. In the eighteenth century alone, furthermore, thousands of Romani children were taken from their families and placed in state-run institutions or given to foster parents.[61] Although Bright grossly misrepresented the extent and cruelty of the mistreatment of Hungary's Roma, his account of Habsburg decrees and their motivation is generally correct: the annihilation of Romani culture through forcible assimilation to Catholic, Hungarian society. To this end, not only were Romani children removed from the care of their biological parents, all Roma had to be registered according to an edict issued in 1769. Romani children over the age of ten were compelled to engage in a useful occupation, while male children aged twelve to sixteen years were required to learn a trade; those over

---

[59] *Magyar Kurír*, 13 February 1790, 171: "a' Magyar Nemzetnek musikálúnk [...]." Bálint Sárosi cites this source and provides a German translation of a portion of the text in *Sackpfeifer, Zigeunermusikanten... Die instrumentale ungarische Volksmusik*, trans. Ruth Futaky (Budapest: Corvina, 1999), 22.

[60] Richard Bright, *Travels from Vienna Through Lower Hungary; with Some Remarks on the State of Vienna During the Congress, in the Year 1814* (Edinburgh: Printed for Archibald Constable and Co., 1818), 539–40. The further information I provide on Habsburg measures with respect to Hungary's Romani population is based on David M. Crowe, *A History of the Gypsies of Eastern Europe and Russia* (New York: St. Martin's Press, 1994), 74–76; and Claudia Mayerhofer, *Dorfzigeuner: Kultur und Geschichte der Burgenland-Roma von der Ersten Republik bis zur Gegenwart* (Vienna: Picus, 1987), 23–33.

[61] David Crowe, "The Gypsies in Hungary," in *The Gypsies of Eastern Europe*, ed. David Crowe and John Kolsti (Armonk, NY: M. E. Sharpe, 1991), 117.

sixteen years of age qualified for military service. Unlike her predecessors who legalized and encouraged the persecution of the Roma in order physically to eradicate them from Habsburg lands, Maria Theresa pursued their cultural extermination, prohibiting the use of the Hungarian noun *cigány* ("Gypsy") in 1761 and replacing it with the official epithets "new citizens," "new peasants," and "new Hungarians."

As Bright summarized, Habsburg edicts included provisions limiting the Roma's musical activities; not only were they required to "diligently attend at church, particularly on Sundays and holidays, to give proof of their belief in Christianity" and to "conform to the customs of the country in diet, dress, and language," they were to be "employed particularly in agriculture" and "permitted to amuse themselves with music and other things, only when there is no field-work to be done."[62] Yet Bright noted correctly not only "how little effect" Maria Theresa's assimilatory efforts had had, but also that "no great success attended the attempts of [her son] the Emperor Joseph [II]."[63] Rather, Joseph's pursuit of centralized authority and bureaucratic efficiency ultimately ensured these musicians' success. In 1784, he imposed German as the official administrative language of the Monarchy. In Hungary, the outrage at this proclamation was manifest across class and confessional boundaries; even Protestant Hungarians who had only recently celebrated their newly granted freedom of religion turned against the monarch.[64] In the weeks preceding his death in 1790, the emperor revoked his decrees pertaining to Hungary, with only the proclamations of religious tolerance and the abolition of perpetual serfdom remaining in effect. His retraction, however, came too late, as Bright again concisely summarized:

> The circumstance [...] which called forth all the energy of Hungarian talents in defence of the language, was the attempt made by the Emperor Joseph to annihilate it, by prohibiting its use in all public acts, and substituting German in its place. The national feeling excited upon this occasion shewed itself in numerous publications; and though the ardour of enthusiasm may have passed away, it has left a lasting impression. The minds of the Hungarians have been called to the subject; their national pride is roused; they begin to read with pleasure, in their own tongue,

---

[62] Bright, *Travels from Vienna*, 541–42.
[63] Bright, *Travels from Vienna*, 540.
[64] László Makkai, "Habsburg Absolutism and Hungary (1711–1790)," in *A History of Hungary*, ed. Ervin Pamlényi (Budapest: Corvina, 1973), 203.

biographical accounts of worthies of their own country, and dwell with delight upon the strains of the Hungarian muse.[65]

Hungarian national consciousness was thus awakened in reaction to imperial policies. According to the census conducted in Hungary between 1784 and 1787, although Magyars were the largest ethnic group within the Kingdom, they accounted for no more than half of its population.[66] Not only Roma, but Slovaks, Romanians, Croatians, Serbians, Ruthenians, and Germans, along with other less numerous groups, formed minorities within Hungary,[67] which occupied a large territory including portions of what are now Austria, the Czech Republic, Slovakia, and Romania. The Magyar cultural nationalism that Bright observed in reaction to Joseph's linguistic policy was in large part an effort to maintain Magyar dominance and to counteract similar nationalist inclinations among the Kingdom's many other inhabitants.[68] Until this point, Hungary's elite had taken little interest in the Magyar language, which they regarded as a peasant vernacular. Latin was the traditional official language of business and government in the Kingdom and, as in Vienna, French was the fashionable choice among the aristocracy, who also commonly spoke German.[69]

Within this context, Romani musicians achieved professional success as the primary performers of a newly developed national music. An unsigned article in the *Allgemeine musikalische Zeitung* from 1814 on the history of music in Transylvania succinctly captured the irony of the situation, noting:

> The wise measures adopted by Empress Maria Theresa for the culture of the Hungarians were beneficial in Transylvania as well as in Hungary; regular music found followers and supporters not only among the higher nobility but also in public venues, as for example at balls in Klausenburg [then the capital of Transylvania; now Cluj-Napoca, Romania]. Gypsy music had disappeared until the later, hastier decrees of Joseph II, issued with the same intention, demonstrated here too their reverse effect, and even now

---

[65] Bright, *Travels from Vienna*, 214.
[66] See Lynn M. Hooker, *Redefining Hungarian Music from Liszt to Bartók* (Oxford: Oxford University Press, 2014), 20.
[67] Makkai, "Habsburg Absolutism," 204.
[68] Crowe, *A History of the Gypsies*, 80.
[69] Pieter M. Judson, *The Habsburg Empire: A New History* (Cambridge, MA: Belknap Press of Harvard University Press, 2016), 80; Domokos Kosáry, *Culture and Society in Eighteenth-Century Hungary* (Budapest: Corvina, 1987), 30.

one believes one is acting patriotically when one [...] gives the contract for the Klausenburg balls to the Gypsies.[70]

As the unnamed Pest correspondent to the *Allgemeine musikalische Zeitung* declared in a report from 1810, "the Hungarian dances a lot and likes dancing very much: his national music is first and foremost dance music."[71] The Hungarian national dance music developed in the eighteenth century—often referred to as *verbunk* or *verbunkos*, a noun and an adjective, respectively—melded multiple influences: from folk music, including swineherd and Heyduck dances; from dances such as the *ungaresca* and *saltus hungaricus*, long enjoyed as *Tafelmusik*; and from Romani musical traditions.[72] Homophony, major–minor tonality and its attendant harmony, periodic phrasing, and some facets of *verbunkos* instrumentation—typically performed by an ensemble of male musicians playing two violins, *basso*, and cimbalom (hammered dulcimer)—may also have reflected the influence of contemporary Viennese art music, especially in urban Hungarian centers.[73] The word *verbunk*, a Magyarized version of the German *Werbung*, points to the connection of this music to that used in Habsburg military recruiting in Hungary beginning in 1715. By the late eighteenth century, however, *verbunk* was an integral facet of burgeoning Hungarian cultural nationalism, and it was enjoyed and celebrated as national dance music free of its historical association with military enlistment. When the Hungarian crown was finally returned to the Kingdom from Vienna in 1790, an eyewitness to the celebrations in Győr reported:

---

[70] "Geschichte der Musik in Siebenbürgen," *Allgemeine musikalische Zeitung* 16, no. 46 (16 November 1814): col. 771: "Die zur Cultur der Ungarn ergriffenen, weisen Maassregeln der Kaiserin, Maria Theresia, hatten auch in Siebenbürgen, so wie in Ungarn, ihren wohlthätigen Erfolg, und so fand auch die regelmässige Musik nicht nur bey dem höhern Adel Anhänger und Unterstützer, sondern auch in öffentlichen Orten, als z. B. auf den klausenburger Bällen, war die Zigainermusik bereits verschwunden, bis die spätern, in gleicher Absicht erlassenen, raschern Verfügungen Josephs des 2ten, ihre rückgängige Wirkung auch hierin zeigten, und man auch noch jetzt patriotisch zu handeln glaubt, wenn man, unter einem Vorwand, der eben so gut für die regelmässigen Tonkünstler spricht, die Pächter der klausenburger Bälle contractmässig an die Zigainer binden will."

[71] "Nachrichten: Pest in Ungarn, d. 6ten Febr.," *Allgemeine musikalische Zeitung* 12, no. 24 (14 March 1810): col. 369: "Der Ungar tanzt sehr viel und sehr gern: seine Nationalmusik ist also zunächst Tanzmusik."

[72] See, notably, Papp, *Hungarian Dances*, 27–28; Istvánffy, "All'Ongarese," 18–23; and Benjamin Suchoff, "Editor's Preface," in Béla Bartók, *The Hungarian Folk Song*, ed. Benjamin Suchoff, trans. M. D. Calvocoressi, with annotations by Zoltán Kodály (Albany: State University of New York Press, 1981), xv.

[73] See, for instance, László Dobszay, *A History of Hungarian Music*, trans. Mária Steiner, trans. rev. Paul Merrick (Budapest: Corvina, 1993), 127–28; and Sárosi, *Sackpfeifer*, 59.

The crown itself was followed by violinists picking out Hungarian melodies. [...] It was a pleasure to see how together with the city-dwellers and some of the aristocracy[,] the scurvy peasants from the villages in their shepherds' cloaks took part with timid steps in the Hungarian dances along the wide streets. Various different country wind bands wandered up and down. One in particular, led by the choice members of the Council and citizens, visited the youngsters in their dance-palace, where they danced the verbunkos before them.[74]

The language that I have adopted throughout this book reflects that of eighteenth-century sources, which refer almost exclusively to "Ungarische," "ungarische Tänze," "ungarische Nationaltänze," "hongroises," "danses hongroises," or "magyar tántzok." It also reflects the forced assimilation to which Hungary's Roma were subject, especially during the reign of Maria Theresa, captured in part through their christening as "new Hungarians." Nonetheless, when I am referring specifically to musicians who were ethnically Romani, or to performance practices that were strongly associated with Romani musicians, I have endeavored to make this distinction clear in my writing. Indeed, ambiguities of nomenclature underscore an important thread throughout this study: identities and identifications, individual and collective, are not necessarily single or immutable. They may conflict with one another and/or with wider discursive formulations, expectations, and hierarchies. Experiences and practices of Hungarian music and dance across multiple settings were integral to shaping and expressing personal subjectivities and group affinities in eighteenth-century Vienna, at times marking and at others shifting boundaries of power and belonging.

---

[74] As given and translated in Papp, *Hungarian Dances*, 24, from *Hadi és Más Nevezetes Történetek* 2, no. 14 (26 February 1790): 266 and 269.

1
Staging Hungary at the Habsburg Court

In 1673, the English physician Edward Brown observed that upon traveling only a short distance into Hungary, one "seems to enter upon a new Stage of the world, quite different from that of these Western Countrys: for [one] then bids adieu to hair on the Head, Bands, Cuffes, Hats, Gloves, Beds, Beer: and enters upon Habits, Manners, and course of life: which with no great variety, but under some conformity, extend unto *China*, and the utmost parts of *Asia*."[1] Over a century later, apparently little had changed: Brown's fellow countryman, the naturalist Robert Townson, characterized Hungary as lagging behind the "polished part of Europe."[2] Reports from visitors to Vienna attest that the city's residents, living at Hungary's doorstep, viewed the Kingdom in a similarly negative light. Townson, for example, related:

> Winter had set in when I reached Vienna; and as I was there assured the difficulties the traveler had to encounter in Hungary, the next country I meant to visit, were, for the want of civilization, very great; I thought it prudent to wait here, till the return of fine weather should render the wants of the traveler fewer. [...] I impatiently waited at Vienna for fine weather; and only in fine weather could it be prudent to travel in a country which, according to the accounts current at Vienna, was little better than in a state of nature, and its inhabitants half savage [...]. Indeed so savage was the character of this people drawn by some, that many less accustomed to travel than myself, would have given up their intended tour altogether; and I myself, had I not learned to make deductions from popular accounts, would hardly have ventured without a battalion of grenadiers for protection. If I came back alive I was told I ought to think myself fortunate.[3]

[1] Edward Brown, *A Brief Account of some Travels in Hungaria, Servia, Bulgaria, Macedonia, Thessaly, Austria, Styria, Carinthia, Carniola, and Friuli. As also Some Observations on the Gold, Silver, Copper, Quick-silver Mines, Baths, and Mineral Waters in those parts: With the Figures of some Habits and Remarkable places* (London: Printed by T. R. for Benj. Tooke, 1673), 69. The emphasis is original.

[2] Robert Townson, *Travels in Hungary, with a Short Account of Vienna in the Year 1793* (London: Printed for G. G. and J. Robinson, 1797), 200.

[3] Townson, *Travels in Hungary*, 1 and 32.

Townson's comments echo those of Lady Mary Wortley Montagu several decades earlier. As she prepared to depart Vienna in January 1717 on her way to Constantinople, where her husband would serve as English ambassador, she wrote to her friend Alexander Pope:

> I think I ought to bid adieu to my friends with the same solemnity as if I was going to mount a breach, at least, if I am to believe the information of the people here, who denounce all sort of terrors to me; and indeed the weather is at present such as very few ever set out in. I am threatened at the same time with being froze to death, buried in the snow and taken by the Tartars, who ravage that part of Hungary I am to pass.[4]

As historian Wendy Bracewell has argued, such views of the Kingdom were shared by Eastern and Western Europeans alike. Passing through Hungary on his way back to St. Petersburg from the Adriatic, for instance, the Russian naval officer V. B. Bronevskii commented that "enlightened Europe ceases at the frontiers of Hungary, and ceases very harshly."[5] In demonstrating how Eastern Europeans participated in the construction of the idea of Eastern Europe from the sixteenth through the nineteenth centuries, Bracewell has built upon historian Larry Wolff's seminal work on Western Europe's "invention" of Eastern Europe as its complement during the Enlightenment, a coherent, mediating space between Occident and Orient. Eastern Europe as a whole was characterized as occupying an intermediary stage between civilization and complete barbarism, a stage marked by backwardness and underdevelopment; to travel to Eastern Europe was to take a step back in time.[6] Geography contributed to this perspective, but it was rarely marshaled as the primary basis of assessment. Vienna, notably, lies to the east of Prague but belonged conceptually to the West, while Bohemia was subsumed into the East along with "Poland and Russia [...], Hungary [...], the Balkan lands of Ottoman Europe, and even the Crimea on the Black Sea."[7] Economic, political, social, and cultural considerations outweighed cartography in the Enlightenment's conceptualization of Eastern Europe.

---

[4] Lady Mary Wortley Montagu, *Turkish Embassy Letters*, introduction by Anita Desai, text edited and annotated by Malcolm Jack (Athens: University of Georgia Press, 1993), "Letter XXII, Vienna, 16 January 1717," 44.

[5] As given in Wendy Bracewell, "The Limits of Europe in East European Travel Writing," in *Under Eastern Eyes: A Comparative Introduction to East European Travel Writing on Europe*, ed. Wendy Bracewell and Alex Drace-Francis (Budapest: Central European University Press, 2008), 93. Bracewell quotes Brown and Townson as well.

[6] See Larry Wolff, *Inventing Eastern Europe: The Map of Civilization on the Mind of the Enlightenment* (Stanford, CA: Stanford University Press, 1994).

[7] Wolff, *Inventing Eastern Europe*, 5.

Music and dance were frequently among these considerations. Reporting on his experiences among the Morlacchi of Dalmatia in 1770, for instance, the Italian priest and naturalist Alberto Fortis noted the nasality and monotony of their songs. Although the songs bored him, he reasoned that they moved the Morlacchi, not only because they understood the words better than he did, but because they possessed "artless minds." He characterized their dancing, similarly, as "rude" and "violent." A few years earlier, in Bulgaria in 1762, the Serbian-Italian priest, scientist, and geographer Ruggiero Giuseppe Boscovich encountered "barbarous singing and playing" as well as dancing in the mud; and at a wedding near Kesmark (now Kežmarok, Slovakia), Townson witnessed "some rough school-boys, who danced in the Hungarian style, like the recruiting parties at Pest: and besides the flapping of hands on their breeches and boots, and the jingling of spurs, this was further improved by the dancers throwing themselves on the floor in strange postures, and with such violence as though they were *des possédés* [possessed]: these dances are sometimes called gipsy dances."[8] Traveling through Hungary two decades later, the British physician and medical scientist Richard Bright described a similar scene:

> Walking through the village [of Palota, "a small market-town"], I heard the sound of music in a public-house, and entering, found that it proceeded from three Cyganis [Roma] with their violins and violoncello, who played, whilst a party of half drunken peasants danced. It was the Hungarian irregular and violent dance, which I had before seen, performed by men alone; and in which, without the aid of wine, they become completely frantic.[9]

In these and numerous other passages, observations pertaining explicitly to music and dance in fact reflect travelers' perceptions of the lack of development and civilization of Eastern European societies more generally.

In many descriptions, music not only served as an index of cultivation but also was underscored as an instrument of progress, mitigating otherwise harsh circumstances. In his account of his travels through Bohemia in 1772, for instance, the English musician, composer, and music historian Charles Burney remarked that he "had frequently been told, that the Bohemians

---

[8] Townson, *Travels in Hungary*, 367. The quotations from Fortis and Boscovich are given in Wolff, *Inventing Eastern Europe*, 324–28.

[9] Richard Bright, *Travels from Vienna Through Lower Hungary; with Some Remarks on the State of Vienna During the Congress, in the Year 1814* (Edinburgh: Printed for Archibald Constable and Co., 1818), 619. Bright explained to his readers that "Cygani" [sic] is the Hungarian word for "Gypsy" (p. 109).

were the most musical people of Germany, or, perhaps, of all Europe." Because he "never could suppose effects without a cause," he "crossed the whole kingdom of Bohemia, from south to north; and being very assiduous in [his] enquiries, how the common people learned music, found out at length, that, not only in every large town, but in all villages, where there is a reading and writing school, children of both sexes are taught music." Incongruously, amid the "most melancholy spectacle" of "half-starved people, just recovered from malignant fevers, little less contagious than the plague, occasioned by bad food, and by no food at all," Burney witnessed boys and girls being taught to play "violins, hautbois, bassoons, and other instruments," including clavichords. His meals at the Einhorn Inn in Prague were accompanied by "several minuets and Polonoises" played by "an itinerant band of street-musicians [...] upon the harp, violin, and horn," and in the winter, the city's nobility was "said to have great concerts frequently at their hotels, and palaces, chiefly performed by their own domestics and vassals, who have learned music at country schools."[10]

Crucially, in Burney's description of his experiences in Bohemia, *Western* European music appears as a civilizing force, with street musicians playing aristocratic minuets and sophisticated polonaises. (The gallicization of the latter's name alone points to the distance that separated it from its rustic Polish origins by the eighteenth century.) Not only was this music foreign, it was also elite, but class considerations alone did not necessarily mitigate perceptions of backwardness. To be sure, Eastern Europe's lower classes bore the brunt of negative judgments in the Enlightenment's "philosophic geography,"[11] but its upper classes were typically spared similarly negative

---

[10] Charles Burney, *Dr. Burney's Musical Tours*, vol. 2, *An Eighteenth-Century Musical Tour in Central Europe and the Netherlands Being Dr. Charles Burney's Account of his Musical Experiences*, ed. Percy A. Scholes (London: Oxford University Press, 1959), "Part X: Bohemia and Saxony (14–28 September 1772)—Bohemia," 131–33, 135. James Van Horn Melton, "From Image to Word: Cultural Reform and the Rise of Literate Culture in Eighteenth-Century Austria," *Journal of Modern History* 58, no. 1 (March 1986): 96, notes that Bohemia "had one of the best elementary school networks in Europe" in the late eighteenth century.

[11] The term "philosophic geography" was coined by John Ledyard, an American explorer who traveled across Russia and Siberia in 1787–1788, in reference to the great chasm in "civilization"—itself a new term in the eighteenth century—that he perceived between Eastern and Western Europe. Unfettered by the constraints of conventional geography, the concept of "philosophic geography" allowed him to ascribe "Asiatic & European manners" to Eastern and Western Europe, respectively. See John Ledyard, *John Ledyard's Journey through Russia and Siberia 1787–1788: The Journal and Selected Letters*, ed. Stephen D. Watrous (Madison: University of Wisconsin Press, 2011), 228; Wolff, *Inventing Eastern Europe*, 6; and Larry Wolff, "The Global Perspective of Enlightened Travelers: Philosophic Geography from Siberia to the Pacific Ocean," *European Review of History— Revue européenne d'histoire* 13, no. 3 (September 2006): 437–53.

assessments only when they adopted the manners and fashions of the West. In Warsaw in 1791 as a private tutor to a noble family, for example, the German philosopher Johann Gottlieb Fichte complained that the Polish countess who employed him had a "wild" gaze and "coarse" tone, among a slew of other criticisms ranging from her overuse of makeup to her drunkenness.[12] The German writer Johann Kaspar Riesbeck found Hungary's inhabitants in a similarly "barbarous state," with the exception of "a few of the German colonists only, and the higher nobility, which is modelled after the fashion of the court in Vienna."[13] Townson agreed, juxtaposing the Hungarian dances of the unrefined young men at the wedding near Kesmark to the habits of Hungary's upper classes: "in genteel company French dances are in use."[14] Burney's comments about foreign music in Bohemia, like Townson's assertion of "genteel" Hungarians' preference for French dances, suggest that the perception that Eastern Europeans possessed no national traditions of elite music of their own was operative well before the 1830s, the decade in which musicologist David Gramit has argued that "cultivated music itself bec[ame] a sort of national characteristic, reserved to the central musical cultures, and especially to Germany."[15]

Hungary's staging at the Habsburg court in the second half of the eighteenth century, however, complicates this picture. In *divertissements* performed in honor of a visit from members of the Russian imperial family in late 1781, the music, dance, and dress of Hungary's elite were displayed as exceptionally noble and refined. One unsigned newspaper report noted specifically, furthermore, that their exquisite attire was "truly Hungarian" ("igaz Magyar"),[16] implicitly underscoring that neither cultural prestige nor prominence within the Habsburg Monarchy was at odds with Magyar-ness. The performance of Hungary's aristocracy at court claimed cultural and political power and belonging for the Kingdom of Hungary at a time of geopolitical vulnerability for Joseph II. The Hungarians depicted in pantomime ballets at Vienna's court theaters roughly three decades earlier, on the other hand,

---

[12] As related in Wolff, *Inventing Eastern Europe*, 342.
[13] [Johann Kaspar] Riesbeck, *Travels through Germany, in a Series of Letters; Written in German by the Baron Riesbeck, and Translated by the Rev. Mr. Maty, Late Secretary to the Royal Society, and Under Librarian to the British Museum*, vol. 2 (London: Printed for T. Cadell, in the Strand, 1787; trans. of the original German edition of 1784), 24.
[14] Townson, *Travels in Hungary*, 367.
[15] David Gramit, *Cultivating Music: The Aspirations, Interests, and Limits of German Musical Culture, 1770–1848* (Berkeley: University of California Press, 2002), 56.
[16] "Bétsi víg múlatságok," *Magyar Hírmondó*, 1 December 1781, 739.

were artisans or peasants, like the majority of characters in such ballets, in which naturalness was prized as an antidote to the perceived artificiality or indecency of much contemporary theatrical dance. These Hungarians were thus subsumed into a largely undifferentiated mass of rustic characters on the imperial theatrical stages.

In this chapter, I use the court festivities of 1781 and the ballets of mid-century to explore the multivalence of representations of Hungary's music and dance at the Habsburg court as well as the ambiguity of the term "nation" in the eighteenth century, which was applied just as readily to the elite *natio Hungarica* as to the lower-class characters of the *ballets de nations*. I argue that close attention to immediate contexts—politics, audience, class affinity, aesthetics, and their interplay—can elucidate why Hungary was staged in such divergent and contradictory ways. More broadly, I suggest that careful consideration of these same parameters can help establish the limits of the Enlightenment's conceptual geography of Europe. The contested definition of "Hungarian" at the Viennese court underscores that the construction of Eastern Europe and its inhabitants was hardly monolithic in the eighteenth century. The picture that emerges is thus an ambiguous one, but one in which music and dance played critical roles in establishing boundaries of sociocultural inclusion and exclusion.

Elite Hungarians in Eighteenth-Century Vienna

As the capital of the Habsburg Monarchy, eighteenth-century Vienna welcomed a steady stream of visiting dignitaries and counted numerous nobles among its residents, from princes and counts to barons hailing from throughout the crown lands. They made their homes in Vienna either permanently or for part of the year, in many cases residing in the city during the winter months and returning to their estates in the summer.[17] In his travel memoirs of the late 1770s, the English writer and politician William Wraxall implicitly underscored the relative abundance and diversity of Vienna's upper classes, declaring that in the capital city, "French is indispensable, and

---

[17] See, for instance, Johann Pezzl's description in his *Skizze von Wien* (1786–1790), as translated in H. C. Robbins Landon, *Mozart and Vienna* (New York: Schirmer, 1991), 70–71.

far more useful as well as necessary for a stranger, than German."[18] Wraxall was clearly writing with his readership in mind: individuals with the time and ability to read his *Memoirs* were those for whom French served as a lingua franca as well as a marker of cultivation and status. As an urban hub, Vienna also attracted a variety of businesspeople and professionals, who, like the capital's large underclass of servants, minor artisans, vendors, and laborers of varying stripes, sought to make their fortunes—or eke out their livings—there. Indeed, Riesbeck noted rather harshly that "the facility with which so many foreign families make large fortunes [in Vienna], is a public and striking instance of how much they surpass the natives in activity and understanding."[19]

According to the German writer, editor, and book dealer Friedrich Nicolai, who visited Vienna for several weeks in 1781, Hungarians stood out in this mix. He commented that "one notices especially many Hungarians and Transylvanians, who have drawn nearer to the court in the last forty years but who nevertheless still possess a great degree of national spirit and love of fatherland, one sign of which is that they consistently continue to wear their very beautiful national costume."[20] The precise demographics of Vienna's Hungarian population, like the demographics of the city more generally, are difficult to establish with certainty because Habsburg census-taking in the eighteenth century was limited in scope, recording at most age, sex, and marital status, largely in an effort to facilitate military conscription and taxation. Information on birthplace and occupation was not included, and

---

[18] William Wraxall, *Memoirs of the Courts of Berlin, Dresden, Warsaw and Vienna in the Years 1777, 1778, and 1779*, 2nd ed., vol. 2 (London: Printed by A. Strahan for T. Cadell and W. Davies, 1800), "Letter XXIX, Vienna, 2 February 1779," 291. Wraxall is only one among numerous eighteenth-century commentators who affirmed that French was the language of choice of the upper classes in Vienna. As Bruce Alan Brown has noted, the prestige of French culture in Vienna was no doubt encouraged by the number of francophones in Maria Theresa's husband's, Francis Stephen of Lorraine's, entourage, and by the Monarchy's alliance with France, its long-standing enemy, as of 1756. See Bruce Alan Brown, "Magri in Vienna: The Apprenticeship of a Choreographer," in *The Grotesque Dancer on the Eighteenth-Century Stage: Gennaro Magri and His World*, ed. Rebecca Harris-Warrick and Bruce Alan Brown (Madison: University of Wisconsin Press, 2005), 66.

[19] Riesbeck, *Travels through Germany*, vol. 2, "Letter XXVIII, Vienna," 11.

[20] Friedrich Nicolai, *Beschreibung einer Reise durch Deutschland und die Schweiz, im Jahre 1781. Nebst Bemerkungen über Gelehrsamkeit, Industrie, Religion und Sitten*, vol. 3 (Berlin and Stettin: n.p., 1784), 171: "Besonders bemerkt man viele Ungarn und Siebenbürger; welche sich zwar seit 40 Jahren sehr dem Hofe genähert haben, dennoch aber noch immer Nationalgeist und Liebe zum Vaterlande in hohem Grade besitzen, wovon eines der geringsten Zeichen ist, daß sie ihre ohnedieß so schöne Nationaltracht beständig beybehalten."

women were not necessarily counted.[21] Data on Viennese guilds, in contrast, are somewhat more revealing because they list the geographical origins of craftsmen at all skill levels—apprentices, journeymen, and master artisans—providing a snapshot of a significant subsection of the city's inhabitants.

Artisans accounted for a large percentage of urban populations in the early modern period. They also accounted for a large percentage of individuals on the move. Despite clear differences among trades and skill levels, the majority of those employed in urban crafts were immigrants, and artisans in Vienna were no exception. According to historian Josef Ehmer, only a minority of Viennese craftsmen were born in the city, and "if one includes master artisans' family members and domestic servants in the calculation, one might guess that in the eighteenth century between 40 and 50 per cent of the Viennese population belonged, in one way or another, to the world of the artisans."[22] The surviving data Ehmer presents account only for the artisans themselves, not for their households, but across levels and trades, Hungarians appear to have played a surprisingly negligible role, despite the proximity of Hungary's border to Vienna. Some servants and shopkeepers were undoubtedly Hungarian, as were some of the peasants whom Wraxall encountered in a suburb of Vienna:

> In Lent, it is pleasant on a holiday, to visit "Heren-Haltz," a chapel situated about half a mile to the south of Vienna. Devotion and amusement carry thither multitudes of every rank, and of both sexes. I have met the emperor himself on foot, mixed among the crowd. It is equally curious and entertaining to mingle with the peasants, of whom Sclavonians, Greeks, and Hungarians compose a principal part. They walk, pray, take refreshments, and return in the evening to Vienna.[23]

---

[21] On eighteenth-century Habsburg censuses, see Karl Vocelka, *Glanz und Untergang der höfischen Welt: Repräsentation, Reform und Reaktion im habsburgischen Vielvölkerstaat* (Vienna: Carl Ueberreuter, 2001), 303–7; and Peter Teibenbacher, Diether Kramer, and Wolfgang Göderle, "An Inventory of Austrian Census Materials, 1857–1910. Final Report," Mosaic Working Paper WP2012-007 (December 2012), Max Planck Institute for Demographic Research, https://www.researchgate.net/publication/355145590_An_Inventory_of_Austrian_Census_Materials_1857-1910_Final_Report (accessed 16 January 2025).

[22] Josef Ehmer, "Worlds of Mobility: Migration Patterns of Viennese Artisans in the Eighteenth Century," in *The Artisan and the European Town, 1500–1900*, ed. Geoffrey Crossick (Aldershot: Scolar Press, 1997), 176. See also Annemarie Steidl, "Between Home and Workshop: Regional and Social Mobility of Apprentices in 18th and 19th Centuries [sic] Vienna," *Mélanges de l'École française de Rome—Italie et Méditerranée modernes et contemporaines* (2016), https://journals.openedition.org/mefrim/2491 (accessed 22 March 2020).

[23] Wraxall, *Memoirs*, vol. 2, "Letter XXIX, Vienna, 2 February 1779," 290.

Nicolai, however, seems to have been describing the many Hungarians who were conspicuous in Vienna because of their relatively high status and their correspondingly visible ceremonial, court, and administrative positions in the city, which they carried out in the beautiful dress that he so greatly admired. In 1760, Maria Theresa established the Royal Hungarian Bodyguard, an elite corps of one hundred Hungarian and twenty Transylvanian noblemen; although many members of the Bodyguard belonged to the lesser nobility, the corps was led successively by the magnificent Esterházy princes. The Hungarian Bodyguard not only protected the monarch, but also acted as couriers to foreign powers—and collectors of valuable political information while abroad.[24] As Pezzl described, the Hungarian guards—along with the German and the Galician ones—also played important roles in Vienna's numerous public celebrations and processions on occasions ranging from New Year's Day and Corpus Christi to the bestowing of orders of chivalry. Pezzl noted specifically that the religious nature of many of these events was overshadowed by the secular, with spectators turning out to see the court and the guards in their sumptuous dress. About the Hungarian Bodyguard specifically, he remarked:

> It is possible that somewhere in Europe there are bodyguards with richer uniforms, but this corps is unsurpassed anywhere for general appearance, suitability, dress and withal a martial mien. Man, horse and armour seem to have been made for one another and especially when mounted they have an exceptionally graceful character, no other uniform being lighter, more attractive, manly and martial than that of Hungarian military dress. The young men come from noble families and are specially selected for their build: they ride white Hungarian horses and their shabracks [saddle-cloths] are green with silver edging and bear the monogram of their king. Their uniforms are red with silver, their weapons a large, curved Hungarian sabre; over their shoulders hangs a tiger-skin, on their heads they wear a tall cap of rough fur adorned with a plume of white feathers.[25]

---

[24] On the Royal Hungarian Bodyguard see, for instance, R. J. W. Evans, *Austria, Hungary, and the Habsburgs: Central Europe c. 1683–1867* (Oxford: Oxford University Press, 2006), 31; and Gábor Vermes, *Hungarian Culture and Politics in the Habsburg Monarchy, 1711–1848* (Budapest: Central European University Press, 2014), 33–34.

[25] Pezzl as translated in Landon, *Mozart and Vienna*, 87–88; see also 171–72 and 180–81.

The Hungarian nobility, similarly, were visually arresting in the "very beautiful national costume" to which Nicolai was drawn. Part of its appeal, like that of the Royal Hungarian Bodyguard's uniforms, was no doubt its exotic flair, betraying strong Turkish influences. Men wore a tunic (*dolman*) with twisted sash over slim-fitting pants with braided side seams tucked into short boots; the ensemble was topped with a pelisse (*mente*) lined or edged with fur and fastened with frogs or tassels. Like Turks and Poles, Hungarian men were also notable for their mustaches at a time when facial hair was uncommon in Europe. Noble Hungarian women wore close-fitting dresses fastened either with small, jeweled buttons or—if sleeveless—laced down the front over billowing chemise sleeves. Both female styles were topped with small, embroidered caps and pelisses similar to those worn by noblemen.[26] (See figs. 1.1 and 1.2.)

As fashion historian Aileen Ribeiro has noted, elements of Hungarian dress—fur trimming, notably, and frogged fastenings—became fashionable in many parts of Europe during the eighteenth century, and versions of noble male Hungarian dress were favorites at masquerades, for the everyday attire of boys as well as grown men, and for military uniforms and servants' livery.[27] Several tailors in Vienna specialized in making Hungarian clothing,[28] suggesting the demand for it in the capital city.

The emergence of a centralized Habsburg state in the second half of the eighteenth century and its attendant expansive bureaucracy in Vienna encouraged a concentration of Hungarian nobles there. For educated men from most of the Habsburgs' territories, the numerous positions in the newly centralized administration provided a path to social advancement. Although the highest-ranking state employees were typically noble or aristocratic, middle- and lower-level positions were often filled by educated middle-class men, who increasingly earned patents of nobility in recognition of their civil service. During Maria Theresa's reign, for instance, 40 percent of those who were awarded such patents were bureaucrats. In Hungary, however, state service was restricted to the nobility, who also exclusively filled the Viennese

---

[26] Aileen Ribeiro, *Dress in Eighteenth-Century Europe, 1715–1789* (New Haven, CT: Yale University Press, 2002), 97–99. For further descriptions and examples of Hungarian dress through several centuries, see the catalogue of an exhibition held at the Whitworth Art Gallery, Manchester, August 1979, *Historic Hungarian Costume from Budapest*, foreword by Francis W. Hawcroft (Manchester: Whitworth Art Gallery, 1979).

[27] See Ribeiro, *Dress in Eighteenth-Century Europe*, 98, 150–51, 264.

[28] See, for instance, Pezzl as translated in Landon, *Mozart and Vienna*, 153.

Figure 1.1. Jean-Baptiste Haussard after Jean-Baptiste Vanmour, "Hongrois," in Jacques Le Hay, *Recueil de Cent Estampes Representant differentes Nations du Levant, gravées sur les Tableaux peints d'après Nature en 1707 & 1708 Par les Ordres de M. de Ferriol Ambassadeur du Roi à la Porte; Et mis au jour en 1712 & 1713. Par les soins de M. Le Hay* (Paris: Chez L. Cars, 1714). The Miriam and Ira D. Wallach Division of Art, Prints and Photographs: Art and Architecture Collection, The New York Public Library. From the New York Public Library Digital Collections (https://digitalcollections.nypl.org/items/510d47d9-6a29-a3d9-e040-e00a18064a99/book?parent=372173a0-c6cc-012f-19fd-58d385a7bc34#page/79/mode/2up).

Figure 1.2. Jean-Baptiste Haussard after Jean-Baptiste Vanmour, "Hongroise," in Jacques Le Hay, *Recueil de Cent Estampes Representant differentes Nations du Levant* (Paris: Chez L. Cars, 1714). The Miriam and Ira D. Wallach Division of Art, Prints and Photographs: Art and Architecture Collection, The New York Public Library. From the New York Public Library Digital Collections (https://digitalcollections.nypl.org/items/510d47d9-6a29-a3d9-e040-e00a18064a99/book?parent=372173a0-c6cc-012f-19fd-58d385a7bc34#page/79/mode/2up).

offices that governed Hungarian affairs.[29] Although historian R. J. W. Evans has argued that Hungarians "seem to have remained on the fringes of real power in Vienna," a handful of them acceded to very prominent positions, either at court or as ambassadors representing the court abroad, and many noble Hungarians were educated at the Theresianum, which trained future civil servants.[30]

The *Natio Hungarica* and the Habsburgs

The elite Hungarians whom Nicolai observed during his stay in Vienna in 1781 "ha[d] drawn nearer to the court in the last forty years" belonged to the *natio Hungarica*, the community of nobles who possessed political rights in Hungary, electing and serving as representatives in the Kingdom's diet as well as in county governments. Although Hungary's nobility was relatively large—roughly 4 to 5 percent of its population—the definition of the *natio Hungarica* as the noble estate excluded the vast majority of the inhabitants of the Kingdom, who remained subservient to it. And while this class-based interpretation of the term "nation" was very exclusive, from an ethnic and cultural perspective it was entirely inclusive. As historian Tofik Islamov has so aptly put it, the *natio Hungarica* was "the nation of Hungary—but not a Hungarian (Magyar) nation." It denoted a particular estate (the nobility) of a common political territory (the Kingdom of Hungary), regardless of ethnicity (Magyar, German, Slovak, Serbian, Croatian, etc.), and regardless of whether the members of that estate had assimilated to the culture of the dominant Magyars, the largest ethnic group in the Kingdom, accounting for roughly half of its population.[31] In any case, most of Hungary's ruling class did not speak Hungarian, which was regarded in the eighteenth century as a peasant language.[32] Latin was the traditional official language of business and government in Hungary; French was the fashionable language of choice of the elite, a reflection of cultivation and status just as it was in Vienna.[33] An

---

[29] This paragraph is based on Pieter M. Judson, *The Habsburg Empire: A New History* (Cambridge, MA: Belknap Press of Harvard University Press, 2016), chap. 1.
[30] Evans, *Austria, Hungary, and the Habsburgs*, 29.
[31] Tofik M. Islamov, "From *Natio Hungarica* to Hungarian Nation," in *Nationalism and Empire: The Habsburg Empire and the Soviet Union*, ed. Richard L. Rudolph and David F. Good (New York: St. Martin's Press, 1992), 166–67 (quotation at p. 166).
[32] Judson, *The Habsburg Empire*, 80.
[33] As Domokos Kosáry has observed, Hungarian aristocrats were exposed to the French language and theater in the Habsburg capital, which acted as a "mediator of French influence in Hungary." See Domokos Kosáry, *Culture and Society in Eighteenth-Century Hungary* (Budapest: Corvina, 1987), 30.

interest in the Hungarian language among the Kingdom's aristocracy—and a gradual redefinition of the "nation" to encompass the population at large, or at least the Magyar part of it—did not manifest itself until after Joseph II's decree of 1784, which, in an effort at greater bureaucratic efficiency, imposed German as the administrative language of all Habsburg lands. The resulting Magyarizing spirit, moreover, was as much an effort to counteract similar nationalist inclinations among the Kingdom's other ethnic groups and to maintain Magyar dominance as it was a reaction to Joseph's policy.

The *rapprochement* that Nicolai noted between the *natio Hungarica* and the court in Vienna forty years before his visit to the city was due to their support of a very beleaguered Maria Theresa in 1741. In the early eighteenth century, her father, Charles VI, and grandfather, Leopold I, passed a series of laws collectively known as the Pragmatic Sanction, forbidding the Monarchy's division and establishing the right of female succession in the absence of a male Habsburg heir. Although the Pragmatic Sanction was ratified by regional governments within the Monarchy, who thereby hoped to safeguard peace and stability, it was not recognized by several rival European powers, despite Charles VI's efforts. When he died, the Monarchy was immediately under attack: Frederick II of Prussia invaded Silesia; and Elector Charles Albert of Bavaria, supported by France and a portion of the Bohemian diet, seized Bohemia and succeeded in being elected Holy Roman Emperor as Charles VII over Francis Stephen of Lorraine, Maria Theresa's husband. Finding herself in desperate need of financial and military support, Maria Theresa—attired in the Hungarian colors of white, blue, and gold—made an emotional appeal to the Hungarian diet in Pressburg (Pozsony in Hungarian, and now Bratislava, the capital of Slovakia): "The very existence of the kingdom of Hungary, of our own person, of our children and of our crown are now at stake. Now that we are forsaken by all, our sole resource is the fidelity, arms, and long-tried valor of the Hungarians. In regard to ourself, the faithful Estates and Orders of Hungary will enjoy our hearty cooperation." In response, the *natio Hungarica* pledged "life and blood to our king Maria Theresa."[34]

Maria Theresa's gratitude toward the Hungarian nobility—and her need for their enduring support—meant that they continued to enjoy special privileges during her reign (1740–1780) even as the elites of other Habsburg lands did not. Although agrarian reforms improved conditions—and productivity—for

---

[34] Both quotations are from the translations in Judson, *The Habsburg Empire*, 25. My summary of the outbreak of the War of the Austrian Succession and the events leading up to it is based on Judson's very lucid account (pp. 22–27).

Hungarian peasants at the expense of the nobility, in many other respects the *natio Hungarica* was exempt from Maria Theresa's centralizing efforts. The Bohemian Chancellery, for instance, was merged with that of the hereditary lands (the territory corresponding roughly to Austria and Slovenia today), while the Hungarian Chancellery remained a separate entity. Despite the size of the Kingdom of Hungary, furthermore, its contributions to the Habsburg military budget were relatively small, especially in comparison to those of Bohemia and the hereditary lands, whose payments were fixed for ten-year periods, drastically reducing these regions' bargaining power with the central government in Vienna. Perhaps most notably, the *natio Hungarica* remained exempt from taxation, which Maria Theresa had imposed on the nobility of Bohemia and the hereditary lands beginning in 1748.

In addition to official measures that favored Hungary's nobility, Maria Theresa also exercised various forms of soft power to win and maintain their loyalty—or to reduce them gently to subservience. Riesbeck, for instance, observed:

> The plan which the court [in Vienna] has followed for a long time, to reduce this overgrown [Hungarian] nobility, promises much more success than any extraordinary acts of severity, which only serve to irritate the minds of men, and set them more upon their guard. The court of Vienna, conscious of the influence, luxury and pleasure have over the minds of men, allured the proud Hungarians from the freeholds to the court, or to the city. By distinguished places, titles, and marriages, they gave them opportunities to spend their money in a brilliant way, to contract debts, and finally, by the seizure of their lands for the payment, to surrender at discretion. The deceived Hungarian looked upon it as an honour, to connect himself with the Austrian, who made a greater figure than himself at court, and took a greater share in the government of the country. For this purpose he chose his wife at Vienna, and fettered himself by this means. The lady too, by introducing the court manners into his house, finished corrupting him, and made him entirely dependant. There is hardly an Hungarian noble, at this time of day, that is either free from debt, or that does not, like the Austrian one, look upon his debts as an honour. The court has consequently no further commotions to fear in this country, as the discontented people will not easily find a leader with power and consequence enough to make their risings dangerous.[35]

---

[35] Riesbeck, *Travels through Germany*, vol. 2, "Letter XXX, Vienna," 32–33.

Beyond such schemes, the Habsburgs also aligned themselves sartorially with the *natio Hungarica*, spearheading the eventual fashionability of noble Hungarian dress well beyond the borders of the Monarchy. Maria Theresa's father occasionally appeared in Hungarian costume on ceremonial occasions in Hungary, and he unofficially permitted Hungarian dress as attire for the Hungarian nobility at the Viennese court. Contemporary visual art attests that Maria Theresa went much further, often wearing Hungarian dress herself or clothing her children in it—including the crown prince, the future Joseph II (r. 1765–1790; see fig. 1.3).[36] Maria Theresa thus united herself and her family in a very visible way with the Hungarian nobility, encouraging their goodwill toward her and her administration more generally.

As I explore below, however, the *natio Hungarica* also shaped its own image and claimed its place within the Monarchy and Europe's wider aristocracy through soft power. At lavish court festivities of late 1781, only one year after Maria Theresa's death, representatives of the *natio Hungarica* asserted their cultural belonging and political significance at a time of geopolitical turmoil through their performance of Hungarian music and dance, pushing against the notional boundary of civilization dividing Eastern from Western Europe.

A Snapshot from 1781

On 21 November 1781, the Viennese court welcomed distinguished guests: Grand Duke Paul of Russia (son of Catherine the Great and heir to the Russian throne) and his wife, Grand Duchess Maria Feodorovna (née Sophia Dorothea of Württemberg), whose visit afforded her, among other diversions and delights, the opportunity to see members of her Württemberg family, who were also guests at court at this time. Throughout their stay, the visitors were treated to excursions around Vienna to take in the city's sights, as well as to numerous banquets and entertainments, including several operas, a keyboard-playing competition between Mozart and Clementi, and a Christmas-day performance of Haydn's Opus 33 string quartets.[37] On

---

[36] See Katalin Dózsa, "Court and City Costume, 18th to 20th Centuries," in *Historic Hungarian Costume*, 16–17; and Katalin Földi-Dózsa, "Die ungarische Nationaltracht als Hofkleidung," in *Kaiser und König, 1526–1918*, ed. István Fazekas and Gábor Ujváry (Vienna: Collegium Hungaricum, 2001), 25.

[37] On the visit see, for instance, Larry Wolff, *The Singing Turk: Ottoman Power and Operatic Emotions on the European Stage from the Siege of Vienna to the Age of Napoleon* (Stanford, CA: Stanford University Press, 2016), 157.

Figure 1.3. Martin van Meytens, *Joseph II. als Kronprinz mit sechs Geschwistern*, ca. 1750. Wien Museum Inv.-Nr. 61011, CC BY 4.0, Photo: Birgit and Peter Kainz, Wien Museum (https://sammlung.wienmuseum.at/en/object/29/). The princes are dressed in Hungarian style.

25 November, the guests enjoyed a sumptuous midday meal at Schönbrunn palace and a performance of Gluck's *Alceste*, after which they took part in a grand masked ball and lavish supper at the castle, where the revelry lasted into the early morning hours. An extensive article in the *Wiener Zeitung*

outlining the eminent guests' daily activities while in Vienna mentions only the presence of large numbers of the high nobility at the ball,[38] but we know that Mozart—along with roughly 4,000 others—was also in attendance. In a letter to his father, he reported that owing to the disorganized distribution of tickets, which were free and available to the public, "the ball was full of friseurs and housemaids."[39]

The festivities of 25 November included *divertissements*, or entertainments presented for the enjoyment of revelers, consisting on this particular occasion of groups of dancers performing national dances, as described in the *Wiener Zeitung*:

> In the first small dance hall, eight couples danced a quadrille, in the most splendid Roman clothing, with their arms-bearers; among them was his Highness Prince Ferdinand von Württemberg, whose splendor was admired by everyone. Afterward, the dignitaries proceeded into the large hall, where there were six couples in Hungarian national costume, with their own national music. The splendor of their attire and their delight in the performance of their national dance so pleased the dignitaries that [the dancers] received loud applause. In the third dance hall was a troop of twenty-four couples, in Tartar national dress, who also performed their contredanses to the best of their ability in the manner of the Tartars. Since they were also exceptionally splendid, they delighted [the audience] as much as the previous [dancers]. This [dance] was followed by [that of] eight couples in the dress of Strasbourg, whose appeal is such [...] that their dancing was all the more striking. The final [dance] was performed by twelve couples dressed as sailors, who received similarly high approval from the dignitaries[.][40]

---

[38] "Wien den 28. Wintermon.," *Anhang zur Wiener Zeitung Nro. 95*, 28 November 1781, col. 2.

[39] Mozart to his father, Vienna, 5 December 1781, in *The Letters of Mozart and His Family*, ed. Emily Anderson (New York: W. W. Norton, 1985), 781 (letter 435). Mozart indicated that there were about 3,000 ball-goers, but the *Wiener Zeitung* reported the number as 4,000.

[40] "Wien den 28. Wintermon.," cols. 2-3: "In dem ersten kleinen Tanzsaale befand sich eine Quadrille von 8 paar, in prächtigster römischer Kleidung, mit ihren Waffenträgern, unter deren ersten sich des Prinzen Ferdinand von Würtemberg Durchl. befanden, deren Pracht von jedermann bewundert wurde. Nachdem selbe ihre Tänze vollend[e]t hatten, erhoben Sich die allerhöchste und höchste Herrschaften in den grossen Saal: hier befand sich ein Trupp von 6 Paar in hungarischer Nazionaltracht, mit ihrer eigenen Landmusik; der Pracht ihres Anzugs, die Nettigkeit, und reizende Ergötzung in Vorstellung ihres landesüblichen Tanzes vergnügte die höchste Herrschaften so ausnehmend, daß Sie ihnen Dero lauten Beyfalle zusicherten. In dem dritten Tanzsaale war eine Trupp von 24 Paar, in tartarischer Landestracht, welche ebenfalls nach Art der Tartarn ihre Contratänze auf das fertigste vorstellten; und da ihre Pracht ebenfalls ausnehmend gewesen, so ergötzten sie so sehr als die vorigen. Auf diese folgten 8 Paar in Straßburgertracht, dessen

As was common in the eighteenth century, this colorful report was reproduced word-for-word or in translation in several other newspapers as well: the *Pressburger Zeitung*, the *Ephemerides Vindobonenses*, and the *Magyar Hírmondó*.[41] The article in the *Magyar Hírmondó*, however, added to the report from the *Wiener Zeitung*. Written from the perspective of an eyewitness—"a Viennese well-wisher"—the additional text includes detailed information about the dress and identities of the Hungarian dancers and musicians:

> The Hungarian counts and countesses of high nobility appeared in our national costume, tailored in the way of the old Hungarians, short and martial, in their pelisses [*mentéjek*] and tunics [*dolmányjok*], among other nationally costumed dignitaries for a very courtly, cheerful entertainment held at Schönbrunn. The men's clothing was prepared from very refined, beautiful sea- or sky-colored cloth, adorned with pure gold piping and gold fringes on the piping; the belts from braided cordons of pure silver with gold buttons; boots worked with yellow and gold; shakos covered with black velvet and gold piping, and adorned very richly with needlework of the same kind. In addition, the shakos were studded with expensive diamonds, so many that each one might have had stones worth 30,000 to 40,000 forints. Similarly, our nation's noblewomen all glittered in true Hungarian clothing, with robes so richly made of similarly colored silk material; the value of the stones on each one's head and clothing might have been 100,000 forints. [...] The acquisition and handsome construction of all the ornate costumes was entrusted to the Hungarian master tailor József Szalai living in Vienna, who by way of great industry found favor with every great dignitary.

Niedlichkeit ohnehin bekannt, und da an der Pracht nichts verabschäumt wurde, so fiele die Kunst und das Angenehme in Tanzen um so mehr in die Augen. Den Beschluß machten 12 Paar als Matelots gekleidet, die nicht minder als die übrigen allen Beyfall der allerhöchst- und höchsten Herrschaften erhielten; wie dann überhaupt nicht nur an diesen, sondern auch an den meisten übrigen Masquen, nebst dem billigst zu bewundernden Pracht, an den kostbaresten Geschmucke, auch die Nettigkeit und Zierde allen Vorzug vor andern derley Festen verdiente."

[41] Maria Domokos, "Kiegészítések a verbunkos zene es tánc bécsi adataihoz," *Zenetudományi Dolgozatok* (1985): 97. On the pirating practices of the eighteenth-century press, see Alex Balisch, "The *Wiener Zeitung* Reports on the French Revolution," in *Austria in the Age of the French Revolution, 1789–1815*, ed. Kinley Brauer and William E. Wright (Minneapolis: Center for Austrian Studies, University of Minnesota, 1990), 185–92.

On this occasion at Schönbrunn the dances of the Hungarian recruiting soldiers (*verbungus*) were demonstrated as well. The gentlemen officers of the Royal Hungarian Bodyguard danced, together with Lieutenant Potyondi, in the dress of a guardsman, Lieutenant Rédi, in the dress of a corporal, Lieutenants Dóczi, Batskádi, Czírjék, Doloviczényi, Ambrus Berzeviczi, Bacsák and Rédei, all dancing; Lieutenants Poturnyai, Barcsai and Baron Vécsey and Captain Malocsányi played the music.[42]

When the *divertissements* were presented once more a few days later at a much smaller ball at the Hofburg on 4 December, the *Wiener Zeitung* and the *Magyar Hírmondó* again both reported on the occasion, but this time only briefly and without further details in the latter publication:

In the evening, in the most splendidly illuminated large hall of the palace, the emperor, the Russian royalty, and the dignitaries from Württemberg appeared at a small ball. Three hundred members of the high nobility were invited, among whom were [the dancers who had performed] the five quadrilles that had given so much pleasure at Schönbrunn. They presented the dances [again] with the same great splendor and skill, followed by a grand supper.[43]

---

[42] "Bétsi víg múlatságok," *Magyar Hírmondó*, 1 December 1781, 739–40. The original Hungarian text is also given in Domokos, "Kiegészítések a verbunkos zene," 98: "A Sönbrunnban tartatott nagy udvari víg mulatságra, egyéb nemzeti álöltözetű méltóságok között, megjelenének a magyar nagyméltóságú gróf urak s asszonyok is, nemzetünk öltözetében, úgy mint a régi magyarok módjára szabott rövid és katonás mentéjek s dolmányjokban. A férjfiak öltözete szép tenger-, vagyis égszínű igen finom posztóból készíttetett, tiszta arany paszomány s azon aranyrojtokkal ékesíttetve, az övök tiszta ezüst sinórokból aranygombokkal, csizmájok sárga és arannyal kivarrott, csákós süvegek fekete bársonnyal borított és aranypaszománytal s azonnemű varrással igen gazdagon ékesíttetett vala. Azonkívül a csákó-süvegek drága gyémántokkal ugyannyira ki volt rakva, hogy egyik-egyiken 30–40 ezer forint ára kövek is lehettek. Hasonlatosképpen a nemzetünkféle úri asszonyságok mind igaz magyar viselettel, hasonló színű selyem matériából oly gazdagon készült köntössel fényeskedének, hogy egynémelyiknek fején és ruháján százezer forint ára kövek is látszottak. [...] Mindezen ékes öltözeteknek megszerzése és csinosan való mindennémű elkészíttetése egyáltaljában Szalai József Bécsben lakozó magyar szabó mesteremberre volt bízattatva, ki is nagy iparkodás által mindenik méltóság előtt nagy kedvet talála.
Ugyanott Sönbrunnban ez alkalmatossággal a magyar katonafogadóknak (verbungusoknak) a táncok is előmutattatott. Ezt pedig a cs. k. testőrző tiszt-urak járták, úgymint Potyondi hadnagy úr, strázsamester képében, Rédi hadnagy úr káplár képében, Dóczi, Batskádi, Czírjék, Doloviczényi, Berzeviczi Ambrus, Bacsák és Rédei hadnagy urak táncolva; Poturnyai, Barcsai s báró Vécsey hadnagy urak és Malocsányi kapitány úr muzsikálva." A short excerpt of this passage is translated in Géza Papp, ed., *Hungarian Dances 1784–1810*, Musicalia Danubiana 7 (Budapest: Magyar Tudományos Akadémia, Zenetudományi Intézet, 1986), 25.

[43] "Wien den 1. Christmonat," *Anhang zur Wiener Zeitung Nro. 97*, 5 December 1781, col. 3: "Dagegen war Abends in der Burg in dem dasigen auf das prächtigste beleuchten grossen Saale, Kammerball, bey welchem Se. röm. kais. Majest. nebst den russisch-kaiserl. Hoheiten, dann den Durchl. Herzogl. Württembergischen Herrschaften erschienen; vom hohen Adel wurden 300 an der Zahl dazu geladen: unter diesen befanden sich vorzüglich die 5 Quadrillen, die zu Schönbrunn

An article about the 4 December festivities in the *Ephemerides Vindobonenses* included one additional sentence about the Hungarian dancers: "About the Hungarian group we must also mention that members of the Royal Hungarian Bodyguard performed as military recruiters with amazing skill, and they were from the same noble company of guards who accompanied the Hungarian dances on violin."[44]

The descriptions of these events in the local and regional press attest to their significance, which was undoubtedly enhanced by the newspaper articles themselves, as they not only documented the festivities but made them widely known to the reading public. On a general level, the lavish spectacle offered by the *divertissements* heightened the splendor of the two occasions, which abundantly displayed the wealth and magnificence of the Habsburg court to their distinguished visitors. But a closer examination of the *divertissements* suggests specific political overtones as well. Even without knowing Joseph II's precise role in selecting or approving such entertainments, we can assume that they were interpreted—by the guests in attendance as well as by newspaper readers after the fact—as embodying and reflecting his authority and objectives.[45] In speculating about how these *divertissements* affected perceptions of the Habsburgs and their priorities, considering what was presented to the audience is key: a series of national dances—from Rome, Hungary, Tartary, and Strasbourg—followed by a dance for sailors of indeterminate origin. *Divertissements* featuring national dances were common interpolations in balls during the eighteenth and nineteenth centuries, and in this particular case, the panorama may have been particularly apt, mirroring the great variety of cultures that the Russian royalty and their entourage were experiencing on their fifteen-month European tour. But given the importance of the occasions on which the *divertissements*

---

den höchsten und hohen Fremden so grosses Vergnügen schaften; welche in ihrem nämlichen grossen Prachte, und gezeigten besondern Geschicklichkeit, die Tänze so, wie zu Schönbrunn bey dem letzthin alldort gehaltenen grossen, und prächtigsten Ballfeste vorstellten; hierauf erfolgte ein grosses Soupee an verschiedenen Tafeln." The Hungarian text appearing in the *Magyar Hírmondó*, 12 December 1781, 765, is given in Domokos, "Kiegészítések a verbunkos zene," 99.

[44] The Latin text of the report appearing in the 7 December 1781 issue of the *Ephemerides Vindobonenses* and a Hungarian translation of it are given in Domokos, "Kiegészítések a verbunkos zene," 99. The original Latin reads: "De Hungarica turma illud etiam commemorandum est, quosdam de Hungarica nobili cohorte praetoriana conquisitores militum mira dexteritate egisse, et de eadem nobili cohorte fuisse, qui choreas Hungaricas fidibus animarunt."

[45] Michael Yonan has explored similar dynamics with respect to visual art and architecture in *Empress Maria Theresa and the Politics of Habsburg Imperial Art* (University Park: Pennsylvania State University Press, 2011)—see, for instance, his summary of his interpretive approach on pp. 10–11.

were performed—as part of a visit from the future Russian tsar—and the political circumstances of the time, they take on special significance.

As art historian Michael Yonan has explored with particular attention to visual art and architecture, the Habsburg court was similar to others throughout Europe in its long tradition of representation of far-flung lands and peoples as a means of self-glorification. As rulers of a monarchy comprising such a multiplicity of cultures and ethnicities, moreover, Habsburg representations of the world's diversity were perhaps even more meaningful, reinforcing their dynastic right to govern various peoples.[46] Of the groups represented in the *divertissements* of late 1781, only the Hungarians were under Habsburg rule, but Joseph II established notional dominion over all those on display. Of particular significance in this respect is the inclusion of a Tartar dance. "Tartar" (or "Tatar") was a term used in the eighteenth century to refer indiscriminately to the various peoples of a broad swath of Eurasia, from the Crimea to Siberia. Because the term was ambiguous, and because the geographical area inhabited by Tartars in the eighteenth century was so vast, different groups of Tartars lived under different rulers—Chinese, Russian, Ottoman. The *divertissements* may have subtly alluded to Joseph II's recent attempt to address the Habsburgs' "eastern question": how to respond to Russia's increasing influence in southeastern Europe, along the coasts of the Black Sea and in the Balkans, as Ottoman power waned. After protracted negotiations with Catherine the Great, Joseph had allied himself with Russia against the Ottomans, but he had required in return his share of any territory that was gained from the Turks, with nothing going to his arch-enemy, Prussia (whose lands the Russian Grand Duke and Duchess pointedly did not visit on their tour of Europe).[47] The Tartar dance at the 1781 festivities in honor of the visiting Russians may well have functioned as an implicit reference to (and reminder of) the terms of the alliance, which had the potential to grant the Habsburgs more than merely symbolic dominion over regions inhabited by Tartars.

As Joseph II attempted to govern amid such a precarious geopolitical situation, he could ill afford unnecessary strife within his own territories, and

---

[46] Michael E. Yonan, "Veneers of Authority: Chinese Lacquers in Maria Theresa's Vienna," *Eighteenth-Century Studies* 37, no. 4 (Summer 2004): 652–72. See also Andrew Wheatcroft, *The Habsburgs: Embodying Empire* (London: Viking, 1995), chap. 6.

[47] On the Austro-Russian Treaty of 1781 and the secretive negotiations that led to it, see Karl A. Roider, Jr., *Austria's Eastern Question, 1700–1790* (Princeton, NJ: Princeton University Press, 1982), chap. 9; and A. Wess Mitchell, *The Grand Strategy of the Habsburg Empire* (Princeton, NJ: Princeton University Press, 2018), chap. 5.

this may explain how Hungary was represented in the *divertissements*. We know from the newspaper reports that the entertainments included two different kinds of Hungarian dances: military recruiting dances performed by members of the Royal Hungarian Bodyguard and a dance for couples performed by six pairs of dancers. The *Magyar Hírmondó*, the first Hungarian-language newspaper, understandably dwelt in particular on the brilliance of the latter group of dancers, who were from Hungary's highest nobility. The description of their attire, made for the occasion by a Hungarian tailor in Vienna, but adorned with jewels so precious and costly that, as musicologist Maria Domokos has observed, they must have come from the dancers' own coffers, suggests their exceptional wealth and high rank.[48] Moreover, unlike the other national dances featured in the *divertissements*, which were performed by nobles costumed to represent the groups in question—like Duke Ferdinand of Württemberg, Maria Feodorovna's brother, who took part in the Roman weapon dance—the Hungarian dances were performed by the Hungarian nobility themselves to the accompaniment of Hungarian national music. The brilliance of their dress and performances claimed their cultural prestige and prominent status within the Monarchy, all the while maintaining a distinctly Hungarian identity.

The staging of the *natio Hungarica* in such a favorable light may be read as part of the Habsburgs' ongoing strategy of appeasement toward them, all the more necessary in times of transition or turmoil, which the Hungarian nobility frequently exploited by leveraging their support for Viennese rule to maintain their privileges within the Monarchy. Hungary did not occupy the special place in Joseph II's heart that it had in his mother's, although some of his early policies after her death—greater governmental control of the Catholic Church and religious toleration, for instance—did garner substantial support from the *natio Hungarica*. Despite Joseph's refusal to be crowned in Hungary, which would have given its elite an opportunity to voice their complaints and demands at a coronation diet, his policies with respect to the Kingdom that most infuriated its elite were not enacted until the mid- to late 1780s.[49] But regardless of what Joseph's actual feelings toward the *natio Hungarica* may have been in 1781, what was most important at the court festivities held late that year was how his relationship to Hungary would be *perceived* by those in attendance. Any hint of internal discord could be used

---

[48] Domokos, "Kiegészítések a verbunkos zene," 99.
[49] For a summary of Joseph II's reforms and Hungarian opposition to them, see Judson, *The Habsburg Empire*, esp. 63–71 and 79–85.

against the Monarchy, and this must have been an issue of particular concern at a time when the Habsburgs' control over their eastern holdings was potentially threatened by Russian aggrandizement. Conveying the strength and unity of the Monarchy as well as at least the appearance of good relations between Vienna and Hungary's often recalcitrant nobility was key.[50]

Russia's expansionist ambitions may also have lent increased urgency to the inclusion of the *natio Hungarica* among powerful, civilized Europeans, a status that was in doubt in the eighteenth century, when Hungary was still sometimes considered part of "Turkey in Europe."[51] The strength of the Kingdom's elite was suggested through the men's martial dress and the display of military dances in the *divertissements*, insinuating that they were not merely pawns at the mercy of competing imperial powers. Although their music, dance, and dress established that they were not simply a mirror of Western Europe's manners and styles, their performances also made plain that they were neither weak nor "culturally backwards," as the Bohemian aristocrat and intellectual Kaspar Sternberg, for instance, had characterized Hungary and its nobles when he witnessed them participating in a wolf hunt, aided by fur-clad beaters, during his travels through the Kingdom in the 1780s.[52] The elegance of Hungary's elite at the 1781 court festivities showed off their wealth and aristocratic status and confirmed that their music and dance were not only unique but highly civilized. Through their performance in the *divertissements*, the *natio Hungarica* thus claimed notional kinship and belonging with nobility across Europe, even while the *Magyar Hírmondó*'s description privileged their Magyar-ness. The newspaper's extensive description of their dress and characterization of it as "truly Hungarian"—according to the newspaper article, the nobles were turned out "mind igaz magyar viselettel," literally "all in true Hungarian wear"[53]— implies the precedence and pride accorded to Magyar-ness within the *natio*

---

[50] Appeasement and the avoidance of internal rifts are two of the "broad principles of Habsburg strategic statecraft" described in Mitchell, *The Grand Strategy of the Habsburg Empire* (quotation from p. 317).

[51] See, for instance, the discussion in Wolff, *Inventing Eastern Europe*, 160–66.

[52] Kaspar Sternberg, *Leben des Grafen Kaspar Sternberg von ihm selbst beschrieben*, ed. Franz Palacký (Prague: Friedrich Tempsky, 1868), 21: "Nach dem, was ich in Italien gesehen, kam mir der Aufenthalt in diesem wenig bevölkerten, in der Cultur, besonders auf dem flachen Lande, gegen andere Nationen weit zurückstehenden Lande, sehr sonderbar vor. [...] Unter die Lustbarkeiten unseres Landlebens gehörte eine Wolfsjagd, zu welcher an 300 Treiber aus der ganzen Umgegend und fünf nobiles Hungariae als des Magnaten Vasallen zu Pferde erschienen, die Treiber in schwarze kurze Pelze (Guba) gekleidet und mit Knitteln bewaffnet."

[53] As given in Domokos, "Kiegészítések a verbunkos zene," 98.

Hungarica as well as the consonance of this identity with high social status. Their sumptuous attire, furthermore, clearly distinguished Hungary's elite from the vast impoverished population with whom they shared their territory. Through their participation in Habsburg festivities, Hungary's nobility thus positioned themselves as the true embodiment of the Kingdom, claiming precedence over the lower classes as its rightful cultural representatives, in strong contrast to Hungary's staging in Viennese ballets from the mid-eighteenth century.

A Snapshot from Mid-Century

In the 1750s and 1760s, ballets featuring all the peoples represented in the *divertissements* of the 1781 festivities were performed on the stages of Vienna's court theaters: Romans in *La pace fralle due nazioni ristabilita* (Burgtheater, 27 April 1762), Hungarians in *L'Hongrois* (Burgtheater, 1754–1755 season), Tartars in *Le Tartare triomphant* (Kärntnertortheater, 1754–1755 season), and Alsatians in *Les Noces de Strasbourg* (Kärntnertortheater, 28 October 1758), for example.[54] The first of these works was performed as part of Hasse's opera seria *Il trionfo di Clelia*, but the others were independent pantomime ballets put on between plays or operas as part of lengthy entertainments. Pantomime ballet, a genre combining dance and gesture, flourished in Vienna in the second half of the eighteenth century, initially as a result of the Viennese dancer and choreographer Franz Hilverding's work. When Vienna's theaters came under court control in 1752, Hilverding was appointed choreographer of both the Kärntnertortheater and the Burgtheater, but his heavy load was lightened through the assistance of several other choreographers over the years. Of the ballets named above, for instance, Hilverding choreographed only *L'Hongrois*; Giuseppe Salomone and Charles Bernardi choreographed *Le Tartare triomphant* and *Les Noces de Strasbourg*, respectively, while Hilverding's erstwhile student and eventual successor in Vienna, Gasparo Angiolini, was responsible for *La pace fralle due nazioni ristabilita*.

[54] Bruce Alan Brown, "'... les danses confédérées': Multinational Ballets on the Viennese Stages, 1740–1776" (paper presented at the 75th annual meeting of the American Musicological Society, Philadelphia, PA, November 2009). Brown's handout gives information about dozens of ballets performed in Vienna between 1752 and 1775. Seasons ran from after Easter through Carnaval of the following calendar year. I thank Professor Brown for generously sharing his handout with me.

When Hilverding began dancing, and soon thereafter choreographing, at the Habsburg court in 1737, theatrical dance in Vienna consisted of two diametrically opposed styles: the serious French style and the low Italian comic style, widely condemned as crude and trivial.[55] As later recounted by Angiolini, who not only carried on his master's vision through numerous ballets of his own, but expounded and defended Hilverding's principles against his detractors (the elder choreographer having committed nothing to writing himself), Hilverding used the period of mourning following Emperor Charles VI's death in 1740, when Vienna's stages went dark, to contemplate a reform of theatrical dance:

> In this theatrical inactivity M. Hilverding ... began to reflect that the indecent comic business should be driven out of the theatre, so that upright persons might enter without blushing.... [H]e knew that the sublime in the liberal arts lay in the imitation of beautiful and simple nature, that the most refined of artists is he who knows better than the others how to arrive at this imitation, and that the greatest [artist] is he who joins imitation to the sublime part of invention. This, and many other ideas, united with a deep, sound, and methodical study of literature, in a mind that was poetic, musical, and picturesque, eventually produced new ideas—small at first, to be sure, but which he was able to enlarge upon with his own forces ...
>
> In 1742, when the theatres of Vienna reopened ... in place of the *pas de deux* of Harlequins, of Pulcinellas, of Giangurgolos, etc., he substituted the natural characters of threshers, colliers, Hungarian gypsies, Tyroleans, Moravians, etc., and in each of these ballets there was represented a small action suited to the habits, customs, and stations of the aforesaid personages. [...] Step by step, and by himself, he managed to conceive, combine, and produce a complete pantomimic action with a beginning, a middle, and an end.[56]

To be sure, Hilverding was only one of several eighteenth-century choreographers whose ballets integrated—or at least incorporated—both dance and gesture in their depictions of peasants and artisans of various nationalities. Sailors and shoemakers peopled stages across Europe

---

[55] Bruce Alan Brown, *Gluck and the French Theatre in Vienna* (Oxford: Clarendon Press, 1991), 152–53.

[56] As given and translated in Brown, *Gluck and the French Theatre in Vienna*, 153–54, from Gasparo Angiolini, *Lettere di Gasparo Angiolini a Monsieur Noverre sopra i balli pantomimi* (Milan: G. B. Bianchi, 1773), 11–14.

alongside rustic villagers and pirates of every stripe.[57] But while Turks, Spaniards, Savoyards, and Netherlanders, among many other characters, were equally fashionable in Naples, Paris, and Vienna, only Hilverding and his fellow choreographers in the Habsburg capital routinely depicted the inhabitants of Central and Eastern Europe.[58] Roughly 10 percent of the *ballets de nations* created in Vienna between 1752 and 1764, the period during which information about titles and performances is most complete, were on Central or Eastern European themes.[59] Along with the Hungarians, Roma, Tyroleans, and Moravians whom Angiolini underscored in his description of Hilverding's accomplishments, Poles, Carinthians, Styrians, and Cossacks were all represented on Vienna's stages.

Regardless of the provenance of their characters, however, the "small actions" portrayed in mid-century Viennese ballets tended to be quite similar to one another, not least because they were held together by only the thinnest of narrative threads. Although the ballets were performed without printed programs or sung or spoken text, synopses of several of them survive in accounts published in the widely read *Journal encyclopédique* and *Journal étranger*, as well as in Hilverding's assistant Philipp Gumpenhuber's chronicles of performances at the court theaters in the late 1750s and early 1760s.[60] The extant scenarios document that these ballets were generally light-hearted and presented a loose sequence of events that essentially provided a pretense for entertaining dance and pantomime performed by picturesque characters against the backdrop of locales that would delight spectators. Markets, fairs, and ports were all common settings, easily lending themselves to scenes featuring numerous dancers depicting the variety of characters so typical of mid-century pantomime ballets. In his painstaking research into Viennese ballets of Hilverding's era, musicologist Bruce Alan Brown has uncovered numerous stereotypical phrases that recur time and again in surviving descriptions of these works, underscoring their creators'

[57] See, for instance, the numerous ballets discussed in Harris-Warrick and Brown, eds., *The Grotesque Dancer on the Eighteenth-Century Stage*.

[58] Ralph P. Locke explores this phenomenon briefly in *Music and the Exotic from the Renaissance to Mozart* (Cambridge: Cambridge University Press, 2015), 278.

[59] The year 1752 marks the beginning of court control over Viennese theaters and 1764 the departure of their director, Count Giacomo Durazzo. See Brown, "... les danses confédérées," 2. I thank Professor Brown for generously sharing the unpublished typescript of his talk with me.

[60] Brown has noted that the level of detail in the newspaper articles raises questions about their putative status as eyewitness reports provided by the publications' Vienna correspondents. Gumpenhuber's accounts may have been produced in an effort to convince Durazzo of the ballets' respectability. See Brown, *Gluck and the French Theatre in Vienna*, 172–75.

overriding concern to entertain their audiences. As the three representative scenarios given in table 1.1 show, appeals to incidents, activities, and events "typical for these sorts of places," as well as to "brilliance," "charm," "agreeableness," and "variety," define the ballet synopses and are strongly reminiscent of Angiolini's summary of Hilverding's achievements. Despite claims to "verisimilitude" in many of the descriptions, as Brown has astutely noted, the conclusion of the synopsis of *Un Port de mer dans la Provençe*, which is to "en[d] as merrily as possible, with the accompaniment of instruments appropriate to the country one aims to represent," suggests that this—and undoubtedly other scenarios as well—are "really more of a template for *any* sort of national ballet one might wish to stage."[61]

Although we have no synopses for the two mid-century Viennese ballets that make explicit reference to Hungarians in their titles—*L'Hongrois* and *Les Polonois à la foire hongroise*—their faint storylines were undoubtedly very similar to those of the dozens of other nationally themed ballets with which they are contemporary.[62] *Les Polonois à la foire hongroise* is known to us only by its inclusion in the anonymous *Répertoire des théâtres de la ville de Vienne depuis l'année 1752 jusqu'à l'année 1757*, where it is listed as having been performed at the Kärntnertortheater during the 1755–1756 season.[63] *L'Hongrois*, however, not only is referenced in the *Répertoire* and in the *Wienerisches Diarium* as having been performed at the Burgtheater the

---

[61] Brown, "... les danses confédérées," 6.

[62] A third ballet, *Les Hussards au marché aux chevaux*, may refer to Hungarians, but the word "hussard" (or "hussart," "houssard," or even "housard"), although acknowledged to be a gallicization of a Hungarian word, was used variously in the eighteenth century to refer to Hungarians as well as to Poles, or even to cavalry more generally. See, for instance, Antoine Furetière, *Dictionnaire universel, contenant generalement tous les mots françois, tant vieux que modernes, et les termes des sciences et des arts*, vol. 2 (The Hague: chez Pierre Husson, Thomas Johnson, Jean Swart, Jean van Duren, Charles le Vier, la Veuve van Dole, 1727), "Hussart." Searching The ARTFL Project's database "Dictionnaires d'autrefois" also yields numerous illuminating results (https://artfl-project.uchicago.edu/content/dictionnaires-dautrefois, accessed 13 January 2022). According to a report ("Verzeichnuß") in the 12 February 1755 issue of the *Wienerisches Diarium*, a ballet called *Der Pferdmarkt* was performed in the Kärntnertortheater during the 1754–1755 season, the same time period during which the *Répertoire des théâtres de la ville de Vienne depuis l'année 1752 jusqu'à l'année 1757* (Vienna: Johann Leopold van Ghelen, 1757) identifies *Les Hussards au marché aux chevaux* ("de Mr. Hilwerdin"; entry 36) as having been performed at the German theater. Rudolf Graf Khevenhüller-Metsch, and Dr. Hanns Schlitter, eds., *Aus der Zeit Maria Theresias. Tagebuch des Fürsten Johann Joseph Khevenhüller-Metsch, kaiserlichen Obersthofmeisters 1742–1776*, vol. 3 (1752–1755) (Vienna: Adolf Holzhausen and Leipzig: Wilhelm Engelmann, 1910), 176, gives 19 May 1754 as the date of performance of "*La Surprise de la haine* [a comedy by Louis de Boissy] mit einem neuen grotesque Ballet von Hussaren."

[63] *Répertoire des théâtres de la ville de Vienne*, entry 51 in the catalogue of ballets performed at the Kärntnertortheater. Brown, *Gluck and the French Theatre in Vienna*, 6, indicates that the *Répertoire* was undoubtedly compiled at Durazzo's prompting.

Table 1.1. Descriptions of three representative mid-century Viennese pantomime ballets.

La Foire de Zamoysck, ou Le Cosaque jaloux (comp. J. Starzer; chor. F. Hilverding Burgtheater, 15 Oct. 1757)	*Le Marché aux poissons* (comp. C. Gluck; chor. C. Bernardi Kärntnertortheater, 3 Oct. 1759)	*Un Port de mer dans la Provençe* (comp.?; chor. G. Salomone, Kärntnertortheater, 16 Aug. 1763)
"Every year a fur fair is held in the town of Zamoysk [Zamość]. The stage shows the square of this town: the decoration of it is elegant. All the shops seem to have displayed all the most beautiful and rare furs. The colors of the costumes, the bonnets, the sleeves, &c. form a varied and novel perspective, which recedes in various streets, the shops of which are decorated in the same manner, and full of a multitude of merchants and customers. One sees among the latter several Poles, who are amusing themselves in different activities typical for these sorts of places. There are three little Jewesses who quarrel over the sale of their merchandise; there is also a Cossack whose mistress people pretend to carry off, in order to amuse a Polish nobleman. His anger amuses the crowd: he is pacified by the gift of some fur, and he is made to dance in the manner of his country. In this ballet one admired the verisimilitude and the customs, which are very well observed; but that is not its only merit; in it one found an infinite variety in the characters, and everything brilliant that choreography has to offer."[a]	"This ballet represents the fish market in Holland. The theatrical décor is most agreeable, and will charm the eyes of the spectators. Some young men dance with girls in the manner of that country, which is very entertaining. The events that ordinarily happen in such places cause several entertaining changes that are expressed in the dance. The invention of this finale is completely novel, very lively, and well thought out."[b]	"In the decoration of this ballet one sees several vessels at the shore, and many people busy unloading a number of bales of merchandise. Several women are in their boutiques situated on the land to one or the other side, in order to buy or sell, which makes for a pretty view. After having worked, the ones and the others [the buyers and sellers] are taken with a desire to divert themselves, and form a general dance which is the start of this completely merry and diverting ballet [i.e., the start of the danced portion of the work]. As seaports are always teeming with people of every nationality, [in this] ballet one will have the charm of variety of several characters who will appear in it. A sailor of the country, wishing to amuse himself, plays some tricks on an unsuspecting young girl. After a minor quarrel they are soon reconciled, and this ballet ends as merrily as possible, with the accompaniment of instruments appropriate to the country one aims to represent."[c]

(continued)

Table 1.1. Continued.

[a] As given and translated in Bruce Alan Brown, "Of Caricatures and Contexts: Some Representations of Jews (Real and Imagined) in the Habsburg Monarchy during the Eighteenth Century" (PowerPoint presentation, STIMU-Symposium: "Reinventing a Usable Past," Festival Oude Muziek, Utrecht, August 2016). I thank Professor Brown for generously sharing this unpublished material with me. The original description appearing in the *Journal encyclopédique*, 15 January 1758, 118–19, is given in Professor Brown's presentation as well as in Brown, *Gluck and the French Theatre in Vienna*, 173: "On tient tous les ans dans la Ville de Zamoysck une Foire de Pelleteries. Le Théâtre represente la Place de cette Ville: la Décoration en est élegante. Toutes les Boutiques paroissent avoir étalé tout ce qu'il y a de plus beau, & de plus rare en Pelleterië. Les couleurs des habits, des bonnets, des manchons &c. forment une perspective variée & nouvelle, qui se perd dans differentes ruës, dont les Boutiques sont ornées de même, & remplies d'une multitude de Marchands, & d'acheteurs. On voit parmi ceux-ci plusieurs Polonois, qui se rejouissent de differents incidens ordinaires dans ces sortes d'endroits. [I]l y a trois petites Juives qui se querelent pour le debit de leur Marchandise: il y a encore un Cosaque auquel, pour amuser un Seigneur Polonois, on fait semblant de vouloir enlever la maitresse. Sa colere divertit la compagnie: on l'apaise en lui donnant quelque Pelleterie, & on l'oblige de danser à la mode de son Pays. On a admiré dans ce Ballet la verité & le costume qui y sont très bien observés; mais ce n'est pas son seul merite; on y a trouvé une varieté infinie dans les caractères, & tout ce que la Chorégraphie a de plus brillant."

[b] As given and translated by Bruce Alan Brown, "Appendix 3: Gumpenhuber's Descriptions of Ballets Performed in the Kärntnertortheater during 1759 (Excluding End of 1758–59 Season)," in *The Grotesque Dancer on the Eighteenth-Century Stage*, 316. Gumpenhuber's description is transcribed on the same page: "Ce Ballet represente le marché aux poissons en Hollande. La Decoration theatrale est fort agreable, et cha[r]mera les yeux des Spectateurs. De jeunes gens dansent avec les filles à la mode du Païs, la quelle est fort divertissante. Les accidents qui arrivent ordinairement en tels endroits causent plusieurs changements divertissants qui seront exprimés dans la danse. L'invention de ce final est toute neuve, fort vive, et bien pensée."

[c] As given and translated in the PowerPoint presentation accompanying Brown, "… les danses confédérées." I thank Professor Brown for kindly sharing this presentation with me. The original description is in Philipp Gumpenhuber, *Repertoire de Tous les Spectacles, qui ont été donné au Theatre de la Ville*, Kärntnertortheater 1763 volume, US-CAt, MS Thr 248.3: 1763, seq. 409–410: "On voit dans la Decoration de çe Ballet plusieurs vaisseaux au Rivage, et beaucoup de monde occupé à débarquer nombre de balots de marchandises. Plusieurs fem[m]es sont à leurs boutiques situées à terre de l'un, et de l'autre coté pour acheter, où vendre, çe qui fait un beaucoup [sic] d'œil. Àpres avoir travaillé les uns et les autres, l'envie de se divertir les prend, et forment une danse generale qui fait le comencement de çe Ballet tout à fait gai, et divertissant. Comme les Ports de Mer abordent toujours de Personnes de toutes les Nations, on aura l'agrement, çe Ballet de la variete de plusieurs Caracteures, qui y paroitront un matelot du Païs voulant s'amuser joue quelques tours à une jeune Personne qui ne s'en doutoit pas[.] Àpres une legere querelle bientôt ils se raccomodent, et çe Ballet se termine gaiement autant que possible, avec l'accompagnment des Instruments propres au Païs qu'on veut representer."

---

year before *Les Polonois à la foire hongroise* (that is, during the 1754–1755 season), but its music survives, both in rehearsal and in full performance parts.[64] The rehearsal parts, scored for two violins and *basso*, were compiled at theater director Count Giacomo Durazzo's behest by his assistant,

---

[64] "Verzeichnuß," *Wienerisches Diarium*, 12 February 1755; *Répertoire des théâtres de la ville de Vienne*, entry 27 in the catalogue of ballets performed at the Burgtheater.

Giuseppe Maria Varese, and are now among the *ballets de nations* preserved in partbooks in Turin (see fig. 1.4).[65]

Varese's annotation identifies Hilverding as the choreographer of the ballets (see fig. 1.4); payment records confirm Joseph Starzer as the composer of all ballet music for the court theaters from 1754 (the year of the earliest extant complete records) through the 1758–1759 season, after which he followed Hilverding to the Russian court. The finished performance parts for *L'Hongrois*, scored for strings and winds, are among the more than 180 orchestral partbooks prepared by copyists of the Viennese court theaters now housed in the archives at Český Krumlov castle in the Czech Republic, in the eighteenth century the seat of the powerful Schwarzenberg family.[66] The performance parts show that the ballet unfolded across a series of ten brief numbers following an opening instrumental sinfonia (see table 1.2). Depending on tempi and choices with respect to repeats, the ballet likely would have taken between ten and fifteen minutes to perform.[67]

The highly evocative music of *L'Hongrois* establishes a strong contrast between the eponymous character, danced by Angiolini, and the first soloist to take the stage, Louise Joffroy-Bodin. Both dancers were stars at the Burgtheater, and they are the focus of attention in *L'Hongrois*. Following the sinfonia—a lively gigue—Bodin appears to the strains of a graceful minuet (no. 1), marked *sempre dolce* and replete with sighing appoggiaturas (see ex. 1.1).

The subsequent number, a "concerto" or group dance for the *figurants* (no. 2), returns to the meter and affect of the opening sinfonia. The gaiety of the scene seems to influence the female soloist, for she then dances to the music of a very quick and cheerful contredanse (no. 3). Taken together, the

---

[65] I-Tn, Fondo Foà 102, 103, 104; the library dates the bound parts to 1760, but they preserve ballets from the previous decade. Brown ("... les danses confédérées," 4) has identified the compiler of the partbooks, and he speculates that they made their way to Italy when Durazzo became ambassador to the Venetian Republic (*Gluck and the French Theatre*, 144).

[66] Brown, *Gluck and the French Theatre*, 144. The performance parts for *L'Hongrois* are preserved in CZ-K, No. 25, K-II.

[67] Comparing the rehearsal parts to the finished performance ones shows that some material was cut during the preparation of the ballet for performance. Twelve measures of repeated material were eliminated from the end of no. 5; the indication to play no. 8 twice (in addition to the marked repeats) was removed; the original no. 9, which was a repeat of the music of no. 7 with sixteen additional measures of music, was replaced with an indication simply to play no. 7 da capo; and twenty measures of repeated material were cut from the final number. Beyond these cuts and the addition of wind parts, the only other differences between the rehearsal and the performance parts are a handful of small changes in articulation and dynamics.

Table 1.2 is based on similar tables providing overviews of contemporaneous ballets in Brown, *Gluck and the French Theatre*.

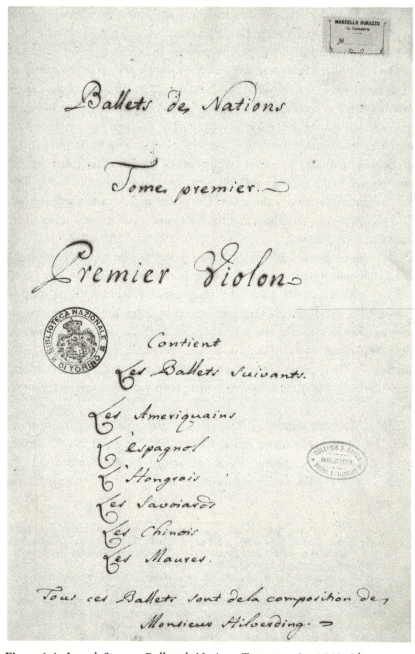

Figure 1.4. Joseph Starzer, *Ballets de Nations, Tome premier*, 1760, title page of the first violin part. Reproduced with permission of the Italian Ministry of Culture, National University Library of Turin from I-Tn, Fondo Foà 102. Reproduction forbidden.

Table 1.2. Joseph Starzer and Franz Hilverding, *L'Hongrois* (1754/1755).

No.	Title	Marking	Meter	Key	No. of mm.	Instrumentation
	Sinfonia	Allegro	6/8	G major	26	2 ob., 2 hn., 2 vln., *basso*
1	Mad: Bodin	Andante	3/4	D major	34	2 ob., 2 hn., 2 vln., *basso*
2	Concerto	Allegro	6/8	D major	24	2 vln., *basso*
3	Mad: Bodin	Allegro molto	2/4	G major	40	2 fl., 2 hn., 2 vln., *basso*
4	Sig:re Angiolini	Allegro	3/4	D major	20	2 ob., 2 hn., 2 vln., *basso*
5		Allegro moderato	2/4	D major	16	2 hn., 2 vln., *basso*
6		Andante	3/4	G major	10	2 vln., *basso*
7		Allegro	2/4	G major	24	2 ob., 2 hn., 2 vln., *basso*
8		Minor	2/4	G minor	12	2 vln., *basso*
7 da capo						
9	Finale	Allegro assai	2/4	G major	10	2 hn., 2 vln., *basso*
10		Dolce	2/4	G major	16	2 hn., 2 vln., *basso*

sinfonia and the opening three danced numbers of the ballet form a tonally closed group, moving from tonic to dominant and back again. Bodin's dances would have been the highlights of this group, but their music—and, by extension, presumably their choreography as well, which does not survive—is unmarked as anything other than generically Western European. Angiolini's appearance, therefore, must have been all the more striking because it is accompanied by a completely different soundworld. No. 4 opens with a full measure exclusively comprising Hungarian *bokázó* ("heel-clicking" or, literally translated, "ankling") figures in the oboes and violins, recognizable from their distinctive melodic and rhythmic profiles, supported by leaping octaves in the *basso* part (see ex. 1.2).

This number ultimately ends on a half cadence, linking it strongly to the following one (no. 5), in which the opening phrase brings back the *bokázó* figure once again. In no. 6, as in Bodin's opening number, the music suggests a minuet through its triple time, but now the melody is noodling and angular, with constant comical alternations between *forte* and *piano* dynamics—as if the Hungarian were trying to dance a dignified minuet but not quite succeeding (see ex. 1.3).

Example 1.1. Joseph Starzer, *L'Hongrois*, no. 1, "Mad: Bodin," mm. 1–8 (1754/1755). Transcribed with permission of the State Regional Archives, Třeboň, from CZ-K, No. 25, K-II.

The contrast with Bodin's elegant music in no. 1 hints at a difference in status between the two characters, beyond the difference in nationality and ethnicity already suggested by their music. This Hungarian, unlike those who would perform in the *divertissements* of 1781, almost certainly did not belong to the *natio Hungarica*. The remaining numbers of the ballet resume the lively contredanse affect heard previously, but they retain the Hungarian coloring introduced with Angiolini's appearance—including in the finale, in which the *figurants* would have participated—through numerous trills and grace notes, frequent alternations between *piano* and *forte* dynamics, sharpened fourth scale degrees, and *bokázó* figures. The final number of the ballet brings all these elements together for a rousing, colorful close that differs conspicuously from the music that accompanied Bodin's entrance in no. 1, despite sharing its *dolce* marking (see ex. 1.4).

The strong contrasts that define *L'Hongrois*'s music, and presumably its gestures and choreography as well, are typical of contemporary Viennese pantomime ballets. Brown has described, for instance, how vividly the music reflects the conflicting passions of the characters in *La Force du sang* (1757) and how clearly it delineates the European from the Turkish characters in *Le Turc généreux* (1758).[68] These contrasts added to the "charm of variety" (per the scenario of *Un Port de mer dans la Provençe*) that was at the heart of the entertainment these ballets provided. Considering the whole ensemble of pieces—ballets, typically performed in pairs; operas; and/or spoken plays—performed on any given evening in Vienna's court theaters gives a yet better sense of the heterogeneous spectacles they offered audiences. Although we do not know the exact date(s) on which *L'Hongrois* was performed at the Burgtheater during the 1754–1755 season, the *Répertoire des théâtres de la ville de Vienne depuis l'année 1752 jusqu'à l'année 1757* identifies fourteen ballets presented at that theater alone during that season, depicting themes and characters drawn from Classical antiquity to sailors, hunters, woodcutters, harvesters, shepherds, and Spaniards, in addition to Hungarians.[69] The *Répertoire* lists plays and operas with less precision than ballets with respect to dates of performance, but the number and variety of such offerings underscore the emphasis on diversity that characterized Viennese theatrical spectacle in the mid-eighteenth century.

---

[68] Brown, *Gluck and the French Theatre*, 182–83, 189.
[69] *Répertoire des théâtres de la ville de Vienne*, entries 22–35 in the catalogue of ballets performed at the Burgtheater. The Spanish-themed ballet was Starzer and Hilverding's *La Sérénade espagnole* (entry 28). The "Verzeichnuß" published in the *Wienerisches Diarium*, 12 February 1755, gives the title of this ballet as "*L'Espagnol*."

Example 1.2. Joseph Starzer, *L'Hongrois*, no. 4, "Sig:^re Angiolini," mm. 1–4 (1754/1755). Transcribed with permission of the State Regional Archives, Třeboň, from CZ-K, No. 25, K-II.

Example 1.3. Joseph Starzer, *L'Hongrois*, no. 6, complete (1754/1755). Transcribed with permission of the State Regional Archives, Třeboň, from CZ-K, No. 25, K-II.

Example 1.4. Joseph Starzer, *L'Hongrois*, no. 10, mm. 1–8 (1754/1755). Transcribed with permission of the State Regional Archives, Třeboň, from CZ-K, No. 25, K-II.

While ballets drawing on familiar subjects—particular occupations, nationalities, ancient myths—may have rendered characters' actions easier for the Burgtheater's audiences to understand without the help of spoken or sung text or a program, spectators undoubtedly perceived the characters who typically peopled the ballets as quite different from themselves. With some exceptions—Classical heroes or the merciful pasha in *Le Turc généreux*, for example—Viennese pantomime ballets featured, in Angiolini's words, "natural characters." These artisans and pastoral types contrasted sharply with the theater's primarily aristocratic audiences, although Brown has noted the parallel between the diverse provenance of the spectators—not only the Viennese aristocracy, but nobles from throughout the Habsburg Monarchy and ambassadors from yet farther afield—and the foreign settings of many ballets.[70] Nonetheless, it is highly unlikely that a Hungarian aristocrat would have identified with the title character of *L'Hongrois* any more than with any other relatively rustic character, in spite of their shared homeland. As musicologist Richard Taruskin has observed, throughout most of the eighteenth century "class associations rather than national ones determined a sense of community among the cosmopolitan [...] 'cultivated circles.'"[71] Given the typical difference in social station between audience members and characters on stage, spectators inhabited the position of the Polish nobleman in *La Foire de Zamoysck* (see table 1.1), whose status excuses him from active participation in the unfolding of the ballet, affording him instead the position of onlooker for whose entertainment it is performed.

***

Viennese pantomime ballets of mid-century and the *divertissements* of 1781 capitalized on the popularity of character dance in the eighteenth century (and beyond), a broad category encompassing "national dances, [...] rustic dances, dances by older characters, and dances that show a character's occupation (e.g., dances of shoemakers, bakers, sailors)," as dance and music historians Lisa C. Arkin and Marian Smith have explained.[72] In 1781, Hungarian dances were presented together with Roman, Tartar, Alsatian, and maritime ones, while in the mid-eighteenth century, *L'Hongrois* and other *ballets de nations* were performed alongside *ballets de métiers*, *ballets de fables*, and *ballets d'invention*, or pantomime ballets depicting occupations, myths, and original stories, respectively.[73] Despite these similarities of subject matter and the emphasis on variety, entertainment, and spectacle evident in both the *divertissements* of 1781 and mid-century ballets, Hungary's staging in these distinct performances at the Habsburg court could hardly have been more divergent, presenting two entirely different conceptions of the Hungarian "nation." The Hungarian in *L'Hongrois*—along with his brethren in *Les Polonois à la foire hongroise*, presumably, and most of the characters peopling the *ballets de nations*—belonged to the working or peasant classes. The Hungarians who performed in 1781, however, were

---

[70] Brown, "... les danses confédérées," 3. On the Burgtheater's audiences, see also Brown, *Gluck and the French Theatre*, 104–7; and my discussion in the following chapter.

[71] Richard Taruskin, "Nationalism," in *Grove Music Online*, www.oxfordmusiconline.com (accessed 18 March 2022).

[72] Lisa C. Arkin and Marian Smith, "National Dance in the Romantic Ballet," in *Rethinking the Sylph: New Perspectives on the Romantic Ballet*, ed. Lynn Garafola (Hanover, NH: University Press of New England, 1997), 57n4.

[73] Brown, *Gluck and the French Theatre*, 161–63.

among the Kingdom's most elite, and they claimed for their "nation of Hungary," as well as for its music and dance, a cultural status equivalent to that of their primary audience, the Habsburg and Russian imperial families. As Mozart's account of the 25 November ball at Schönbrunn makes clear, members of these families were physically closest to the performers, with the general populace behind them; at one point, as Mozart related to his father, "the Viennese mob [...] pushed [...] so roughly that they forced [the Grand Duchess to let go] the [Emperor's] arm, and shoved her forward among the dancers. [The Emperor] began to stamp furiously, cursed like a lazzarone, pushed back a crowd of people and dealt blows right and left."[74] The letter paints a vivid picture of a scene unlike any at the Burgtheater, where more homogeneous audiences were entertained by depictions of Hungarians taking their place among the host of plebeian characters who regularly appeared on stage.

Viennese pantomime ballets belong to the vast eighteenth-century repertoire overshadowed today by the accomplishments of the century's musical giants. Practically none of these ballets is available in modern editions or recordings, and they have only relatively recently begun to emerge from outright scholarly oblivion or to be acknowledged as anything more than precursors to Gluck's theatrical reforms. Similarly, the *divertissements* of 1781 are known to us primarily—if at all—thanks to Mozart's mention of them in his personal correspondence; his description, however, alludes only to "two sets of contredanses—Romans and Tartars," omitting any reference whatsoever to the Hungarian dancers. One must turn to contemporary newspaper reports for descriptions of their performances. Interpreting Hungary's staging at the Habsburg court in the immediate context of the grand Russian visit of 1781 demonstrates how pressing current affairs could loosen the grip of the Enlightenment's conceptual geography and how music and dance could contest the notional boundary separating East from West. To be sure, any entertainment presented at the Viennese court or one of its theaters ultimately reflected Habsburg hegemony, but the Hungarian performances of 1781 suggest that Eastern European music and dance could function as more than mere diversion for a condescending West. In contrast, *L'Hongrois* and many of its contemporary *ballets de nations* instantiate what

---

[74] Mozart to his father, Vienna, 5 December 1781, in *The Letters of Mozart and His Family*, 781 (letter 435). A reading of the class implications of this event is also given in Erica Buurman, *The Viennese Ballroom in the Age of Beethoven* (Cambridge: Cambridge University Press, 2022), 87–88; I discuss Buurman's reading briefly in chapter 4.

Wolff has identified as the Enlightenment's "idea of Eastern Europe as a folkloric domain of song and dance."[75] It would thus be easy to dismiss them at best as nothing more than confirmations of the sway of the imaginative geography of the time and at worst as superficial representations or grossly distorted appropriations of poorly understood cultures. Yet Hilverding and his Viennese contemporaries' innovative work was in fact critical to eighteenth-century developments in theatrical dance. As Angiolini reminds us, provincial characters including "Hungarian gypsies, Tyroleans, [and] Moravians" were at the conceptual heart of his master's reform, and the pantomime ballets that resulted from Hilverding's reimagining of theatrical dance helped make the stages of the Habsburgs' court theaters among the most important and innovative of their time.

---

[75] Wolff, *Inventing Eastern Europe*, 331. For an exploration of this idea in relation to the music market of the late eighteenth and early nineteenth centuries, see Catherine Mayes, "Eastern European National Music as Concept and Commodity at the Turn of the Nineteenth Century," *Music & Letters* 95, no. 1 (February 2014): 70–91.

2
Experiencing Vernacular Music

Shortly after she acceded to the throne, Maria Theresa ordered the transformation of a small building next to the Hofburg housing a tennis court into the Burgtheater, the theater in which *L'Hongrois* (discussed in chapter 1) was premiered in the mid-1750s. Although the Burgtheater was a court theater, it was open to anyone who could afford to attend performances there. This accessibility marked a notable departure from the new empress's father's protocol at the preceding court theater, the Bibiena, where performances were enjoyed only by those who were invited to attend them. In describing the founding of the Burgtheater, musicologist Daniel Heartz has noted that "with this penetration of a wider public into the middle of hitherto exclusively aristocratic precincts [...] there is evident a general leveling between classes with respect to the arts."[1] This leveling, however, extended only to the most socioeconomically privileged individuals in Vienna, as well as to the artists most closely connected to the theater. As theater historian Otto G. Schindler's detailed research has revealed, the yearly audience of the Burgtheater in the mid-1770s was never more than 12,000 of Vienna's roughly 200,000 residents—only 6 to 7 percent of the city's inhabitants made up 90 percent of the theater's audience.[2] Even as venues such as the Burgtheater bridged the gap between noble and non-noble, they created a new elite defined by wealth, education, and taste rather than birth.

Ample research and evidence have demonstrated that an individual's access to many kinds of music in the eighteenth century was correlated to other forms of privilege, as it continues to be today. Just like the Burgtheater, most public opera houses and concert venues were within reach only of socioeconomically advantaged individuals, as were domestic musical instruments, notated music, and the time and resources necessary to learn how to read

---

[1] Daniel Heartz, *Haydn, Mozart and the Viennese School, 1740–1780* (New York: W. W. Norton, 1995), 41.

[2] Otto G. Schindler, "Das Publikum des Burgtheaters in der josephinischen Ära," in *Das Burgtheater und sein Publikum: Festgabe zur 200-Jahr-Feier der Erhebung des Burgtheaters zum Nationaltheater*, ed. Margret Dietrich (Vienna: Veröffentlichungen des Instituts für Publikumsforschung, 1976), 89 and 92.

and play or sing it. As musicologist David Gramit has explored, eighteenth-century efforts to define music considered elite depended on establishing it as the exclusive purview of individuals of a particular nation, class, gender, or level of education.[3] In contrast, the broad accessibility of vernacular music is an integral part of its definition. As ethnomusicologist Philip V. Bohlman has explained:

> Classifications and ontologies of music that distinguish between musical practices in which few or many participate give rise to the concept of vernacular music. Unlike musics known and practised by a socio-cultural and professional élite, vernacular music is accessible to the majority of people because of their familiarity with its forms and functions and because they are able to acquire knowledge of it through everyday practice, that is, without any specialized skills.[4]

In this chapter, I explore how class and gender in fact intersected to *limit* access to venues featuring Hungarian Romani and other vernacular musics in Enlightenment Vienna—inns, taverns, beerhouses, wine cellars. A report in the 13 June 1787 issue of the *Magyar Kurír* recounted, for instance, that "not long ago a band of five musicians, with black hair and white teeth, arrived in Vienna from Galánta, whose music-making, without the printed music, was listened to with amazement. [...] This is the second music-making Gypsý band [*musikáló Tzigánybanda*] in Vienna, who play with such great proficiency that the inn [*vendég-fogadó*] where these people perform is full with people gathered in amazement, and they do the innkeeper a lot of good."[5] Who were the "people gathered in amazement"? The report provides

---

[3] David Gramit, *Cultivating Music: The Aspirations, Interests, and Limits of German Musical Culture, 1770–1848* (Berkeley: University of California Press, 2002). For a sustained discussion of eighteenth-century classifications of music, see Matthew Gelbart, *The Invention of "Folk Music" and "Art Music": Emerging Categories from Ossian to Wagner* (Cambridge: Cambridge University Press, 2007). For a twentieth-century classification see, for example, H. Wiley Hitchcock, *Music in the United States: A Historical Introduction*, 3rd ed. (Englewood Cliffs, NJ: Prentice Hall, 1988), 54. For Hitchcock, the "cultivated tradition" is "to be approached with some effort and to be appreciated for its edification—its moral, spiritual, or aesthetic values," whereas the "vernacular tradition" is "understood and appreciated simply for its utilitarian or entertainment value."

[4] Philip V. Bohlman, "Vernacular Music," in *Grove Music Online*, www.oxfordmusiconline.com (accessed 13 February 2020).

[5] As translated in Bálint Sárosi, *Gypsy Music*, trans. Fred Macnicol (Budapest: Corvina, 1978), 68–69, from an unsigned article in the first section, "Mind itt van," of the *Magyar Kurír*, 13 June 1787, 378–79. Galánta is a small town approximately 100 kilometers east of Vienna, near what is now Bratislava, the capital of Slovakia; until 1918, this area was the western part of the Kingdom of Hungary. According to Robert Townson, *Travels in Hungary, with a Short Account of Vienna in the Year 1793* (London: Printed for G. G. and J. Robinson, 1797), "A List of Home and Foreign

no details about the inn or its patrons, but women with the time and ability to read the newspaper account were unlikely to have been in attendance, as the setting of the event was incompatible with eighteenth-century ideals of respectable femininity, which were themselves inseparable from class.

I argue that socioeconomically privileged Viennese women routinely experienced vernacular music through written accounts rather than personal encounters and that this mediation contributed to their circumscribed position in the nascent public sphere. One of the main concerns of the Enlightenment was a fuller understanding of humanity by means of the same detailed observations used to study the natural world. Scientific travel led to the birth of anthropology as a discipline, but in Vienna, firsthand encounters with various cultures and their musics were potentially at one's doorstep, as was the authority that personal experience conferred upon written descriptions. Yet literate Viennese women were routinely denied that authority and rendered passive recipients of knowledge, reinforcing and justifying their limited participation in the emerging public sphere.

Class, Gender, and Sites of Sociability

When the English musician, composer, and music historian Charles Burney visited Vienna in 1772, he attended a performance of Gotthold Ephraim Lessing's play *Emilia Galotti* at the Kärntnertortheater, just east of the imperial palace. Like the Burgtheater, the Kärntnertortheater was open to the paying public, and Burney noted that the least expensive seats cost only sixteen kreuzers. But despite Burney's declaration that "the admission to this theatre is at a very easy rate," the most affordable places were roughly equivalent to what the writer and civil servant Johann Pezzl identified as the daily wage of "the ordinary man" ("der gemeine Mann") in the capital city in which he lived over a decade later—about seventeen kreuzers in 1787. Pezzl himself equated these earnings to the lowest cost of a bath in Vienna, which he recognized was out of reach for many residents. They undoubtedly went to the theater even less frequently than they bathed, and they certainly would not have participated in the masked balls held in the Hofburg during carnival season each year (from 7 January until Ash Wednesday) and nominally

---

Newspapers and Journals, which are to be had at the General Post-Office at Vienna, postage free, with their prices," 30, the *Magyar Kurír* was available for eleven florins per year in Vienna.

open to the public—with the exception of liveried servants—since the early 1770s. According to the English writer and politician William Wraxall's travel *Memoirs* of the late 1770s, the price of admission to these was "only" two florins, or 120 kreuzers.[6]

Social and economic constraints, both implicit and explicit, routinely curbed official freedom in Enlightenment Vienna. Even measures such as Joseph II's opening of the Prater in 1766 "during all times of the year and every hour of the day for everyone without exception" and in 1775 of the Augarten, "a place of recreation dedicated to all people by one who values them," were only ambivalently successful.[7] Many residents seem to have enjoyed spending time in parks and gardens that had previously been off-limits to all but the nobility, but classes still generally did not mix. As Pezzl described, each green space in Vienna had its own public, which also varied by day of the week and by time of the day.[8] About the Augarten specifically, he commented that "because the rabble [*der Pöbel*] would look so wretched next to the countless rich and beautifully groomed men and women, it stays away of its own accord."[9] Even those whom Pezzl deemed "ordinary" individuals— the lower middle class—and who did frequent parks and gardens made use

---

[6] Charles Burney, *Dr. Burney's Musical Tours*, vol. 2, *An Eighteenth-Century Musical Tour in Central Europe and the Netherlands Being Dr. Charles Burney's Account of his Musical Experiences*, ed. Percy A. Scholes (London: Oxford University Press, 1959), "Part VIII: The First Week in Vienna (30 August–5 September 1772)—Salieri's 'Il Barone'," 85; Johann Pezzl, *Skizze von Wien*, part 4 (Vienna and Leipzig: In der kraussischen Buchhandlung, 1787), "Bäder," 600; William Wraxall, *Memoirs of the Courts of Berlin, Dresden, Warsaw and Vienna in the Years 1777, 1778, and 1779*, 2nd ed., vol. 2 (London: Printed by A. Strahan for T. Cadell and W. Davies, 1800), "Letter XXIX, Vienna, 2 February 1779," 283. In comparison, Schindler, "Das Publikum des Burgtheaters," 40–41, gives twenty kreuzers as the lowest cost of admission to the Burgtheater until 1776, when the court took over the theater's management from impresarios to whom it had previously been leased. Schindler documents much lower prices immediately after the takeover (as low as seven kreuzers in the fourth-floor gallery), but these had risen again to seventeen kreuzers by 1787—see Ignaz de Luca, *Wiens gegenwärtiger Zustand unter Josephs Regierung* (Vienna: Wucherer, 1787), "Theater," 362. De Luca (pp. 362–63) also provides admission prices for various sections of the Kärntnertortheater and the Marinelli Theater, some of which were lower than those at the Burgtheater.

[7] The imperial "Avertissement" on the opening of the Prater from 7 April 1766 was printed in the *Wienerisches Diarium* on 9, 12, and 16 April 1766: "von nun an zu allen Zeiten des Jahrs und zu allen Stunden des Tags, ohne Unterschied jedermann in den Bratter sowohl als auch in das Stadtgut frey spazieren zu gehen, zu reiten und zu fahren." The dedication of the Augarten is inscribed on its main gate: "Allen Menschen gewidmeter Erlustigungs-Ort von ihrem Schaetzer."

[8] Johann Pezzl, *Neue Skizze von Wien*, part 1 (Vienna: J. V. Degen, 1805), "Sonntags-Publicum," 130. Pezzl goes on to discuss the different publics of Vienna's theaters. He and many other contemporary commentators decried another popular Viennese pastime: animal-baiting. As they did at the theater, members of different socioeconomic classes sat in different areas of the suburban amphitheater in which the gruesome spectacles took place; see Gerhard Tanzer, *Spectacle müssen seyn: Die Freizeit der Wiener im 18. Jahrhundert* (Vienna: Böhlau, 1992), 141.

[9] Pezzl, *Skizze von Wien*, part 5 (Vienna and Leipzig: In der kraussischen Buchhandlung, 1788), "Der Augarten," 699: "Da der Pöbel aber neben den unzähligen reich und schön geputzten Weibern und Männern eine gar elende Figur machen würde, so bleibt er von selbst weg."

of them in different ways than did wealthier Viennese: the former enjoyed walking and picnicking there while the latter could also afford the fireworks (with an entrance fee of twenty kreuzers in the Prater according to Pezzl) and the concerts they offered. The timing of concerts, furthermore—like restaurateur Ignaz Jahn's famous morning ones in the Augarten, which featured Mozart and later Beethoven, among others—was often such that the working classes were excluded de facto, sending a clear message about the audience for whom these events were intended. Similarly, the popular St. Brigitta fair attracted thousands of visitors each year, but Vienna's different socioeconomic classes enjoyed it on different days: Sunday for the lower classes and Monday for the more elite.[10]

Despite Joseph II's reforms, Vienna thus remained a city openly divided by class. Pezzl's "nobility of the first rank"—princes, counts, and barons—followed by his "nobility of the second rank"—"councilors, commissioners, doctors, also bankers and business people [...] honourable but non-titled sons of the earth"—were at the top of the hierarchy.[11] At its bottom was a large underclass of liveried servants, minor artisans, vendors, and workers of varying skill levels and incomes. A suburban seamstress, for instance, earned only three and a half kreuzers for "a long day's work," while a servant in a bourgeois household made approximately seven florins (420 kreuzers) per month, or roughly the daily wage of Pezzl's "ordinary man."[12] This lowest class accounted for the vast majority of Vienna's population—192,000 to 193,000 of the capital's just over 206,000 inhabitants in the Austrian statistician Ignaz de Luca's tabulation of 1782, roughly 40,000 of whom were domestic servants.[13] Between this "rabble" and the nobility were middle-class individuals, whom Pezzl described as "bourgeois [*Bürger*] or, to put it more precisely, professional men, tradesmen, lower-ranking court servants and servants of the nobility, shopkeepers, in short, the usual kind of people

---

[10] Gertraud Pressler, "Brigittakirtag," in *Oesterreichisches Musiklexicon Online*, ed. Rudolf Flotzinger and Barbara Boisits, https://www.musiklexikon.ac.at/ml/musik_B/Brigittakirtag.xml (accessed 23 January 2024).

[11] Pezzl, *Skizze von Wien*, as translated in H. C. Robbins Landon, *Mozart and Vienna* (New York: Schirmer, 1991), 70, 72.

[12] Pezzl as translated in Landon, *Mozart and Vienna*, 74; and Pezzl, *Skizze von Wien*, part 5, "Lakeien," 705.

[13] De Luca, *Wiens gegenwärtiger Zustand unter Josephs Regierung*, "Volksmenge," 393, gives the population of Vienna and its suburbs in 1782 as 206,120, specifying: "Darunter waren: Adeliche 2,611; Geistliche 1,979; Beamte 3,123; Bürger 5,890; Hauer (Winzer) 1." It is unclear how the 474 Jews whom de Luca listed separately fit into these categories. On the number of domestic servants, see Pezzl, *Skizze von Wien*, part 5, "Lakeien," 704.

between the nobility and domestic servants."[14] Social standing and financial success were variable in this class; Pezzl recognized that there was not a *single* middle class but middle class*es* ("Mittelstände"), from the moneyed bourgeoisie ("vermögende bourgeoisie") down to lowly legal clerks ("subalterne Kanzleimänner").[15] Taken together, the nobility, clerics, civil servants, and bourgeoisie made up less than 7 percent of Vienna's population, according to de Luca. His figure is perhaps unsurprisingly nearly identical to the proportion of the city's residents whom Schindler estimated patronized the Burgtheater.[16]

More and less affluent Viennese often frequented different sites of sociability even though they enjoyed many of the same types of recreation, including games, eating, drinking, listening to music, and dancing to it. Many suburban gardens, theaters, and fairs attracted the middle and lower classes, while the wealthy were more likely to be found in the gardens and galleries of the Belvedere, on sleigh rides, or at lemonade stalls, where lemonade itself was the least expensive treat at seven kreuzers per glass, and flavored ices cost up to thirty kreuzers per bowl. The enjoyment of these delicacies purveyed in tents set up in public squares was often augmented by *Harmoniemusik* (wind band music) supplied at the stall owners' expense. Similarly, a sleigh ride afforded multisensory pleasures for partakers and spectacles for onlookers, as it was replete with furs, torches, sleigh bells, and the martial music of trumpets and drums.[17] The event culminated in "a grand supper at which [the participants] dance, joke and laugh, whiling away the hours until daybreak at the celebration ball."[18] Such parties or assemblies were common among Vienna's upper classes, who had the money, time, and space for them. Wraxall noted that "besides the houses of Prince Kaunitz and Co[l]loredo, there are others, in which, during winter, assemblies are held once a week, or more frequently. [...] Ices and lemonades are offered to the company, but there is never any supper except by particular invitation. Play is general" except among some ladies who preferred conversation to cards.[19] Pezzl concurred that "parties are given by all classes, from the nobility of the first rank down to well-to-do middle-class people [*bemittelte Bürger*]. [...] They

---

[14] Pezzl as translated in Landon, *Mozart and Vienna*, 72.
[15] Pezzl, *Skizze von Wien*, part 5, "Lakeien," 705.
[16] De Luca, *Wiens gegenwärtiger Zustand*, "Volksmenge," 393.
[17] Pezzl's descriptions of sleigh rides, the Belvedere, and lemonade stalls are translated in Landon, *Mozart and Vienna*, 134–35, 139, and 182–83, respectively.
[18] Pezzl as translated in Landon, *Mozart and Vienna*, 135.
[19] Wraxall, *Memoirs*, vol. 2, "Letter XXIX, Vienna, 2 February 1779," 242.

vary greatly: at some, everybody must gamble, at others you may gamble if you wish; at some there is music; at others there is dancing; at others, people simply spend the evening in friendly conversation."[20] Especially during Lent, when the theaters were closed, affluent residents often held private concerts in their homes, and guests enjoyed food, drink, and card games in addition to music, which ran the gamut from solo keyboard to orchestral.[21]

Outside private homes, beginning in the 1780s casinos provided entertainment and refreshments for Vienna's well-heeled: "the nobility, foreigners, officers, civil servants, doctors, clerics—in short, for anyone with education and good manners."[22] Casinos were open from early in the morning until late at night, providing members with a comfortable space in which to converse, read newspapers, play cards and billiards, and make music. Access to newspapers, musical instruments, sheet music, music stands and lighting for them, and entry to concerts and balls were all included in the cost of membership—six ducats for a year, four for a half-year, or one ducat for a month. Meals were served at fixed times and paid for separately. Casino members also had the right to reserve the space for their own private "musical events, picnics, card parties, dinners, etc.—since all the necessary facilities and comforts are available."[23] Men who could not afford membership in such exclusive establishments could take part in their balls by paying an entrance fee of one florin (sixty kreuzers); women could obtain a ball ticket free of charge.

The numerous dance halls dotting Vienna and its suburbs provided a relatively more affordable alternative, with entry free for women and usually set at twenty kreuzers for men. The German writer, editor, and book dealer Friedrich Nicolai, who visited Vienna for several weeks in 1781, described these halls as catering primarily to the middle classes, with liveried servants expressly forbidden.[24] These were respectable establishments, whose reputations and even

---

[20] Pezzl as translated in Landon, *Mozart and Vienna*, 179.
[21] See, for example, the description in Friedrich Nicolai, *Beschreibung einer Reise durch Deutschland und die Schweiz, im Jahre 1781. Nebst Bemerkungen über Gelehrsamkeit, Industrie, Religion und Sitten*, vol. 4 (Berlin and Stettin: n.p., 1784), "Von der Musik in Wien," 552.
[22] Pezzl, *Skizze von Wien*, part 6 (Vienna and Leipzig: In der kraussischen Buchhandlung, 1790), "Casinen," 880.
[23] Pezzl as translated in Landon, *Mozart and Vienna*, 183. See also the descriptions of casinos in Nicolai, *Beschreibung einer Reise*, vol. 5 (Berlin and Stettin: n.p., 1785), "Einige Anmerkungen über Sitten, Gewohnheiten, Charakter, und Sprache der Einwohner von Wien," 245; and de Luca, *Wiens gegenwärtiger Zustand*, "Casino," 39–40.
[24] Nicolai, *Beschreibung einer Reise*, vol. 5, "Einige Anmerkungen," 244; Pezzl, *Skizze von Wien*, part 5, "Lakeien," 709–10. Pezzl recognized that a second set of clothes was often all that was needed to circumvent this rule.

survival depended on their exclusion of the lowest socioeconomic classes. Nicolai made a point of describing the aesthetic appeal and respectability of one of the most famous Viennese dance halls, the suburban Mondenschein auf der Wieden: "It is a very beautiful hall extending through two floors, illuminated with various glass candelabra. On Sundays one sees here many merchants, well-to-do young citizens, and lower-ranking civil servants with their wives, daughters, and sisters. Everything is respectable."[25]

Food and drink were included in the price of admission to dance halls and were for sale in innumerable establishments operating under a bewildering variety of names: *traiteurs*, inns, taverns, wine cellars, beerhouses, coffeehouses.[26] Their clienteles and the refreshments they purveyed varied as greatly as their nomenclature, and there was often considerable overlap between seemingly different establishments; some coffeehouses, for instance, served beer and wine.[27] Nonetheless, it is possible to draw general distinctions about what was available and for whom. *Traiteurs* served a range of fixed-price meals from eight to eighteen kreuzers in different rooms of the same restaurant; again, classes generally did not mix. Pezzl explained that "liveried servants make up the majority of the customers at [the eight-kreuzer] tables. The ten-kreuzer meal consists of roughly the same food, but is served in a separate room, where every guest has a napkin, an individual white roll and his own drinking glass. The clientele is of a better class— artists, clerics, government officials."[28] Other *traiteurs* were much more upscale and offered meals from thirty kreuzers up to one florin.[29] Similarly, taverns and inns served wine as well as midday and evening meals, and prices varied from ten kreuzers to over one florin. (Some inns also offered travelers a place to stay as well as fodder and stabling for their horses.) Wine cellars

---

[25] Nicolai, *Beschreibung einer Reise*, vol. 5, "Einige Anmerkungen," 257: "Daselbst ist ein sehr schöner durch zwey Geschosse gehender Saal mit verschiedenen gläsernen Kronen erleuchtet. Hier kann man Sonntags viele Kaufleute, wohlhabende junge Bürger, und Civilbedienten unterer Klasse mit ihren Frauen, Töchtern und Schwestern sehen. Alles geht anständig zu."

[26] Some German terms for these establishments often encountered in primary sources (with variable spellings) include *Gasthöfe, Gasthäuser, Wirtshäuser, Trakteurs, Speisehäuser, Specereibuden, Kaffeegewölber, Kaffehäuser, Bierhäuser, Bierschänke, Weinkeller, Weinhäuser, Weinschänke*. On the innumerable quantity of such establishments in eighteenth-century Vienna see, for instance, Friedrich Wilhelm Weiskern, *Beschreibung der k.k. Haupt und Residenzstadt Wien, als der dritte Theil zur österreichischen Topographie* (Vienna: Kurzböcken, 1770), 9.

[27] See, for instance, de Luca's annotation of the coffeehouse "Untern Weißgärbern" in *Wiens gegenwärtiger Zustand*, "Caffeehäuser," 38.

[28] Pezzl as translated in Landon, *Mozart and Vienna*, 139.

[29] See de Luca, *Wiens gegenwärtiger Zustand*, "Speisehäuser," 336–37.

offered much more limited options: wine itself for as little as six kreuzers, served with a piece of bread and cheese, cold fish or meat, or radishes. Those who could not afford a warm meal often ate in wine cellars or beerhouses, many of which offered the same inexpensive fare.[30] Other beerhouses—or separate rooms within beerhouses—were more upscale and patronized by wealthier individuals. They served beer as well as more varied dishes than wine cellars—Nicolai mentioned specifically snails, eggs, roast lungs, and crescent rolls—in comfortably furnished and beautifully decorated rooms.[31]

Like the taste for beer, that for coffee—or a stand-in for it—was shared across classes. Pezzl described how "in all the suburbs until noon there are wooden stalls where a drinking bowl and a little crescent roll can be purchased by any passerby for one kreuzer: except that it is not real coffee, but roasted barley sweetened with syrup." For day laborers and market-women, "this is—at one kreuzer—the best [and most warming] breakfast they can obtain." Bachelors of limited means as well as "humble servant girls, [...] their lovers, the coachmen, stable-boys, hussars and porters [*Hausknechte*]" ate quick breakfasts and warmed themselves in Vienna's many modest coffeehouses.[32] By mid-morning, coffeehouses filled up with those who could afford to be idle. Like upscale beerhouses, many coffeehouses were well appointed with beautiful furniture, lighting, mirrors, and artwork; de Luca specifically annotated his list of coffeehouses to indicate to his readers which had the best views, the most noteworthy paintings, which also served beer and wine, and which attracted the most distinguished clientele.[33] In addition to enjoying coffee, tea, chocolate, and other treats, patrons spent their time in such coffeehouses reading newspapers and discussing their contents, as well as politics and business; playing billiards and other games; and smoking

---

[30] On wine cellars and beerhouses, see de Luca, *Wiens gegenwärtiger Zustand*, "Weinschank," 408–9; and Pezzl, *Skizze von Wien*, part 2 (Vienna and Leipzig: In der kraussischen Buchhandlung, 1789), "Weinkeller," 276–78, and "Bierhäuser," 279–82. Pezzl maintained that the poor were more likely to choose a beerhouse since the quality of the beer surpassed that of the wine at the same price point and beer was more filling.

[31] Nicolai, *Beschreibung einer Reise*, vol. 5, "Einige Anmerkungen," 221. Nicolai (pp. 219–20) described beerhouses patronized by a "wohlhabender Bürger" hung with silk wallpaper and illuminated with glass candelabra and sconces. Similarly, de Luca (*Wiens gegenwärtiger Zustand*, "Bierschenken," 22) described "Personen von Unterscheidung" in "Zimmer [die] ganz artig meublirt sind."

[32] Based on the translations of Pezzl in Landon, *Mozart and Vienna*, 155 and 81, respectively. See also Arnold [the satirist Johann Rautenstrauch], *Schwachheiten der Wiener. Aus dem Manuskript eines Reisenden*, vol. 3 (Vienna and Leipzig: August Hartmann, 1786), "Kaffee," 41–43.

[33] De Luca, *Wiens gegenwärtiger Zustand*, "Caffeehäuser," 35–38.

(see fig. 2.1). As figure 2.2 shows, these same pastimes were common in other establishments that purveyed food and drink as well.

Vocal and instrumental music were common in many Viennese coffeehouses, and many other establishments that served food and drink also offered concert or dance music for their patrons, encouraging them to spend more time and money there. According to de Luca's annotations, the coffeehouse in the suburb of Leopoldstadt near the Prater (conscription number 396) had a dance hall on the first floor above ground level where music was played on Sundays and holidays. Similarly, Nicolai quoted newspaper advertisements from winter 1783 for dancing to occur at a tavern ("Wirthshaus") and a *traiteur*, respectively.[34] Like the food and drink themselves, the music varied according to the clientele. More upscale coffeehouses, for instance, often featured chamber music or *Harmoniemusik*, and Burney noted with displeasure that the meals he took at the inn where he lodged in Vienna were accompanied by a "band of wind instruments [...] all so miserably out of tune, that I wished them a hundred miles off."[35]

Vernacular music was the staple of establishments catering to the less affluent. (Compare the patrons and furnishings in fig. 2.3 to those in figs. 2.1 and 2.2, for instance.) During Vienna's carnival season, for example, Pezzl noted that "the rabble [*der Pöbel*] flock to any place sporting a wine bottle and a dulcimer [*Hackbrett*]."[36] In addition to dulcimers, harps, bagpipes, guitars, violins, and voices provided the soundtrack to socializing, dancing, eating, and drinking for the lower classes, whether played by professional musicians who passed the hat or by patrons themselves who used instruments hung on the walls at their disposal.[37] Similarly, while elite visitors to the popular

---

[34] Nicolai, *Beschreibung einer Reise*, vol. 5, "Einige Anmerkungen," 244–45. The numerous laws and decrees governing music and dance in eighteenth-century Vienna confirm how widespread these activities were in a variety of establishments; for a summary of these regulations, see Reingard Witzmann, *Der Ländler in Wien: Ein Beitrag zur Entwicklungsgeschichte des Wiener Walzers bis in die Zeit des Wiener Kongresses* (Vienna: Arbeitsstelle für den Volkskundeatlas in Österreich, 1976), 96–104.

[35] Burney, *Dr. Burney's Musical Tours*, vol. 2, "Part IX: The Second Week in Vienna (6–13 September 1772)—Mealtime music," 114. See also the discussions in Gerhard H. Oberzill, *Ins Kaffeehaus! Geschichte einer Wiener Institution* (Vienna: Jugend und Volk, 1983), 63–64, 154–55; and Ulla Heise, *Kaffee und Kaffeehaus: Eine Kulturgeschichte* (Hildesheim: Olms, 1987), 128.

[36] Based on the translation of Pezzl in Landon, *Mozart and Vienna*, 141.

[37] Herbert Zotti and Susanne Schedtler, "'Vom Trübsalblasen gar ka Spur': Musik im Wirtshaus," in *Im Wirtshaus: Eine Geschichte der Wiener Geselligkeit*, ed. Ulrike Spring, Wolfgang Kos, and Wolfgang Freitag (Vienna: Czernin Verlag, 2007), 216. For examples of music from Vienna's taverns, beerhouses, and wine cellars, see Gertraud Schaller-Pressler, "Volksmusik und Volkslied in Wien," in *Wien Musikgeschichte*, vol. 1, *Volksmusik und Wienerlied*, ed. Elisabeth Theresia Fritz and Helmut Kretschmer (Vienna: Lit, 2006), esp. 41–102; and Alice M. Hanson, *Musical Life in Biedermeier Vienna* (Cambridge: Cambridge University Press, 1985), 169–76.

Figure 2.1. *Im Café Seidl—Neujahrskarte mit Empfehlungen des Besitzers des griechischen Kaffeehauses, Jakob Seidl*, artist unknown, 1794. Wien Museum Inv.-Nr. 21829, CC0 (https://sammlung.wienmuseum.at/en/object/58831/).

Figure 2.2. *Gaststube des Wirtshauses "Zur Schnecke" im Prater*, artist unknown, 1772. Wien Museum Inv.-Nr. 31714, CC0 (https://sammlung.wienmuseum.at/en/object/61130/).

Figure 2.3. Georg Emanuel Opitz (also Opiz), *Altwiener Kellerwirtshaus*, 1803. Wien Museum Inv.-Nr. 61033, CC0 (https://sammlung.wienmuseum.at/en/object/403962/).

St. Brigitta fair dined and danced in elegant tents to the strains of orchestral music, Vienna's lower classes were entertained in the open or in huts by singers, zither and barrel organ players, bagpipers, violinists, clarinetists, trumpeters, and harpists, playing alone or in small groups. Carl Rabl, an Austrian miracle doctor, reported in 1807 that at the fair, "to the sounds of pipes, violins, lyres, shawms, and bagpipes, [they] danced in country, German, Hungarian, and Bohemian styles."[38]

In recounting his nine-month journey to Sicily, likewise, the German writer Johann Gottfried Seume told of soldiers drinking wine, playing cards, singing, arguing, and dancing to the strains of a bagpipe-like instrument in a village inn ("Wirthsstube") not far from Vienna. Seume's account is interesting in part because it offers a glimpse of the types of music and dance enjoyed in establishments often excluded from contemporary and more recent writings about eighteenth-century life. Moreover, it also provides insight into the patrons who socialized in such venues: mostly men. Seume described how as the bagpiper started to play, two infantrymen held each other under the arms and began to waltz. Others then joined in the dancing, clasping young women and even the old innkeeper herself; solo Cossack (Ukrainian) and Styrian dances were then performed, as well as a very lascivious one, possibly of Greek origin (a "Kordax"), so wild and rude that the women ran from it and even the bagpiper stopped playing.[39] Within a heteronormative social context, that the soldiers danced with each other and even with the unappealing innkeeper suggests not only their drunkenness but the small number of women at the inn that night.

Contemporary accounts make clear that gender ordered daily life and sociability practices in late eighteenth-century Vienna as much as class did. On a typical weekday, servant girls made their way to church between six and six-thirty in the morning, at the same time that the women who sold their wares in markets set up their stalls to be ready for middle-class wives and daughters to make their purchases around eight o'clock. "Ladies

---

[38] As given in Pressler, "Brigittakirtag": "'bei Pfeifen, Geigen, Leyer, Schallmeyen und Dudelsack landlerisch, deutsch, hungarisch und böhmisch getanzt' wurde." The quotation is from Gottfried Roth, ed., *Vom Baderlehrling zum Wundarzt: Carl Rabl, ein Mediziner im Biedermeier* (Linz: Oberösterreichischer Landesverlag, 1971), 27.

[39] I. G. [Johann Gottfried] Seume, *Spaziergang nach Syrakus im Jahre 1802* (Braunschweig and Leipzig: n.p., 1803), 45: "Bey dem sechsten [Takte] fassten ein Paar Grenadiere einander unter die Arme und fingen an zu walzen. Der Ball vermehrte sich, als ob Hüons Horn geblasen würde; man ergriff die Mädchen und sogar die alte dicke Wirthin, und aller Zank war vergessen. Dann traten Solotänzer auf und tanzten steyerisch, dann kosakisch, und dann den ausgelassensten ungezogensten Kordax, dass die Mädchen davon liefen und selbst der Sackpfeifer aufhörte."

of distinction," wrote Pezzl, did not venture out until midday, when they were driven in their carriages toward "the Prater with their friends or children, so as to enjoy the spring air and to provide a break in their interminable sitting-about." Meanwhile, "the ladies of the middle class use this time of day to take the air on the Bastei [city fortifications]."[40] In the evening, their husbands might have joined them for a stroll, at the theater, or in a private home, whether their own or someone else's. Men across classes, in contrast, were much more likely to work and to socialize outside private homes than were women. Wraxall observed that "women of fashion rarely stir out in a morning, except to hear mass, or on particular occasions," while their husbands—"chancellors, vice-chancellors, presidents, vice-presidents, archivists, judges, etc."—were on their way to work before mid-morning, where they usually remained until six o'clock in the evening.[41] With the exception of some aristocratic men who continued to work from home, bureaucratic work in eighteenth-century Vienna typically entailed working in an office outside the home during specific hours.[42]

If they were not at home, men who were not bound by such externally imposed work schedules were likely to be reading newspapers, socializing, or doing business in a casino or coffeehouse, both spaces that were gendered male. Although women took part in the special balls and parties hosted periodically in casinos, casino membership itself was only available to men, and typically the only woman in an upscale coffeehouse was the cashier. As Ulla Heise has noted in her cultural historical study of coffee and coffeehouses, until about 1840, with the spread of coffee gardens and coffeehouses devoted to concert music, the only public coffee establishments relatively privileged Austrian women could patronize without jeopardizing their reputations were those set up outdoors in tents and pavilions during the summer months.[43]

Similarly, the gendered language used to describe the clienteles of Viennese wine cellars and beerhouses in eighteenth-century sources suggests that women were largely absent there also. After many days of hard work in his attic—where "nestle the poorest types of tailors, copyists, gilders,

---

[40] Pezzl as translated in Landon, *Mozart and Vienna*, 81–85.

[41] Wraxall, *Memoirs*, vol. 2, "Letter XXIX, Vienna, 2 February 1779," 241; and Pezzl as translated in Landon, *Mozart and Vienna*, 82. Home is where elite women would have been exposed to—or would have made—certain kinds of utilitarian vernacular music, such as lullabies and tunes sung or hummed by servants as they worked.

[42] On the strong trend toward separating home and workplace in eighteenth-century Vienna, see Pieter M. Judson, *The Habsburg Empire: A New History* (Cambridge, MA: Belknap Press of Harvard University Press, 2016), 60.

[43] Heise, *Kaffee und Kaffeehaus*, 128; see also Oberzill, *Ins Kaffeehaus!*, 47–50.

music copyists, wood-carvers, painters, and so on"—with "only his wife and children for company," Pezzl described a poor man scraping together enough money that "he climbs down in the evening from his tower to the street, stands for a while under the street door watching the passing crowd and then descends another thirty steps to a wine-cellar below street level."[44] His wife, meanwhile, presumably remained occupied in the couple's garret, tending to children and household chores. And whereas a bourgeois man ("Bürgersmann") often went to a beerhouse when his workday came to an end, his wife was unlikely to have joined him; she was even less likely to have gone to a beerhouse unaccompanied.[45] In his satirical description of such an establishment, the popular local dramatist, actor, and pamphleteer Joachim Perinet confirmed how unusual this would have been. After poking fun at the large appetites of his fellow Viennese, enumerating the variety of dishes ingested by the men patronizing the iconic Lothringer Bierhaus, Perinet continued: "Every mouth is busy, every stomach takes part, and every throat covets [the food]; even our beauties now and then come to this place that they otherwise consider so disreputable to admonish their leaders that they are united with them in spirit—and in stomach."[46] De Luca identified the Lothringer Bierhaus as one of Vienna's best known, and Nicolai described it specifically as aesthetically pleasing, with rooms hung with red silk wallpaper and illuminated with glass candelabra and sconces, patronized by people of good standing ("ganz angesehene Leute").[47] That the wives and daughters of the commissioners, doctors, theologians, and impresarios whom Perinet placed there typically disdained it suggests a perceived unseemliness masked by the beautiful décor.

Whether the suspicion of clandestine prostitution in coffeehouses, taverns, beerhouses, and wine cellars was the cause or the result of their overwhelmingly male clientele is inscrutable, but coupled with the availability of alcohol and games of chance, it lent these establishments an unsavory quality (see fig. 2.4 as well as fig. 2.3, in which the attire of the woman

---

[44] Pezzl as translated in Landon, *Mozart and Vienna*, 118.
[45] Pezzl as translated in Landon, *Mozart and Vienna*, 84.
[46] Joachim Perinet, *Annehmlichkeiten in Wien* (Vienna: Lukas Hochenleitter, 1788), "Das Lothringer-Bierhaus," 13: "Jeder Mund ist thätig, jeder Magen theilnehmend, und jede Gurgel begehrlich; selbst unsere Schönen besuchen dann und wann den sonst bei ihnen so verruffenen Ort, um ihren Führern zu beweisen, daß sie mit ihnen nur eine Seele und ein—Bauch sind."
[47] De Luca, *Wiens gegenwärtiger Zustand*, "Bierschenken," 22; and Nicolai, *Beschreibung einer Reise*, vol. 5, "Einige Anmerkungen," 220.

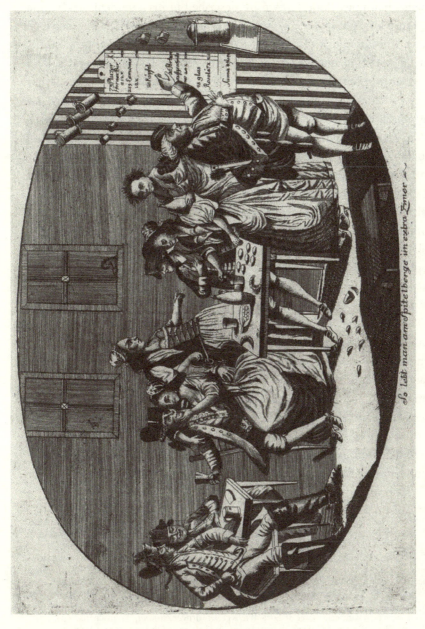

Figure 2.4. Johann Hieronymus Löschenkohl, *Am Spittelberg im Extrazimmer*, 1783. Wien Museum Inv.-Nr. 108472, CC0 (https://sammlung.wienmuseum.at/en/object/185727/).

on the right of the painting identifies her as a prostitute).[48] Perhaps even the most stylish of these venues were not really so different from what the English naturalist Robert Townson described in his comments on Vienna as "those kinds of resorts, which serve as places of relaxation and debauch to the inferior ranks of life, and to those of grosser taste; where music, dancing, feasting, and women of the town are to be had at cheap rates, [and in which] this city and its suburbs abound."[49] The prolific Viennese writer Joseph Richter's biting social critique *Taschenbuch für Grabennymphen auf das Jahr 1787* concludes, after all, with an annotated list of several taverns where the prostitutes to whom the pamphlet is putatively addressed could profitably ply their trade among elegant gentlemen.[50] The prohibition on female servers in Vienna's wine cellars discouraged covert prostitution in these establishments, in tandem with harsher—and ultimately unsuccessful—Habsburg policies and practices to eradicate prostitution from the city, including Maria Theresa's Chastity Commission (Keuschheitskommission) as well as public shaming, forced labor, and deportation.[51] Even in the absence of prostitution, real or imagined, establishments patronized so heavily by men were simply not deemed appropriate sites of sociability for women who desired or needed to preserve at least a façade of respectability.[52]

The Enlightenment ideal of femininity, which prized domesticity, idleness, sensibility, and conspicuous consumption, moreover, was a construction dependent on socioeconomic privilege. It was inseparable from class in a way that standards of male conduct and sociability were not, or at least not to the same extent, due in part to a prevailing double standard of sexual morality. Men of different classes were much more likely to mix outside the home than were women of different social standing. The separation of women, moreover, increased in tandem with privilege. By the second half of the eighteenth century, for instance, aristocratic men took part in salons that were

---

[48] See the description of the painting (reproduced here as figure 2.3) in Beatrix Beneder, "Mädchenbedienung im Männerort: Geschlechter-Inszenierungen im Wirtshaus," in *Im Wirtshaus*, ed. Spring, Kos, and Freitag, 246.

[49] Townson, *Travels in Hungary*, 16. Pezzl concurred that "brutal whores [...] haunt the beerhouses of the suburbs, get drunk on mugs of beer and then lie in wild thrashings with soldiers, coachmen and rough manual workers." Pezzl as translated in Landon, *Mozart and Vienna*, 151.

[50] [Joseph Richter], *Taschenbuch für Grabennymphen auf das Jahr 1787* (Vienna: n.p., 1787), 74–76.

[51] On servers in wine cellars, see de Luca, *Wiens gegenwärtiger Zustand*, "Weinschank," 409.

[52] Lady Mary Wortley Montagu observed early in the eighteenth century that Viennese ladies commonly had both husbands and lovers; see Lady Mary Wortley Montagu, *Turkish Embassy Letters*, introduction by Anita Desai, text edited and annotated by Malcolm Jack (Athens: University of Georgia Press, 1993), "Letter X, Vienna, 20 September 1716," 21–23.

not exclusively frequented by the nobility, but according to the German composer and writer Johann Friedrich Reichardt, as late as 1809, when he was in Vienna, with the exception of major public events, women of the high nobility very rarely—if ever—mixed with women of other social classes.[53] One of the engravings in Richter's *Taschenbuch*, in contrast, depicts an encounter between a gentleman and his servant on the steps leading to their shared prostitute's quarters, one arriving, the other departing; Richter noted in his caption that "the servant and the gentleman are both startled to find out that they are brothers-in-law" (see fig. 2.5).[54] The same gentleman might also occasionally have patronized a tavern where the "young sons and daughters of minor artisans [*niedrigen Handwerksleute*]" courted—and where they celebrated weddings, baptisms, and funerals—while a woman of his same social standing would not: her reputation and position were constructed on her absence from such establishments.[55] This absence set her apart from men, as well as from women who were not her socioeconomic equals, but it also prevented her from hearing vernacular music that was common in taverns and other similar venues, such as that played by the "band of five musicians, with black hair and white teeth" who visited Vienna in 1787.

Hungarian Romani Music-Making in Eighteenth-Century Vienna

The Hungarian Romani musicians discussed in the June 1787 report in the *Magyar Kurír* (cited in this chapter's introduction) seem to have remained in Vienna for several days, judging from the tone of the article:

---

[53] Johann Friedrich Reichardt, *Vertraute Briefe geschrieben auf einer Reise nach Wien und den Oesterreichischen Staaten zu Ende des Jahres 1808 und zu Anfang 1809*, vol. 1 (Amsterdam: Im Kunst- und Industrie-Comtoir, 1810), "Vier und zwanzigster Brief, Wien, den 7. Febr. 1809," 397–98: "Die Damen des hohen Adels mischen sich aber, außer den großen öffentlichen Veranstaltungen, gar nicht, oder doch sehr selten, mit denen anderer Stände, und das scheint mir auch sehr anständig und zweckmäßig." On the mixing of classes in salons, see Tanzer, *Spectacle müssen seyn*, 206–8.

[54] Richter, *Taschenbuch*, caption of engraving 9: "Ein Kavalier will einer Grabennymphe eine Visite machen, und begegnet seinem Bedienten, der eben von der nämlichen Nymphe die Treppe herab kömmt. Der Bediente erschrickt, und sein Herr erstaunet nicht weniger, daß er und sein Lakey Schwäger seyen."

[55] The quotation is from Pezzl as translated in Landon, *Mozart and Vienna*, 111. On celebrations commonly held in taverns catering to the masses, see Martin Scheutz, "Von den 'höchst-verbottenen Zusammenkünften': Das Wirtshaus der frühen Neuzeit," in *Im Wirtshaus*, ed. Spring, Kos, and Freitag, 78.

Figure 2.5. Joseph Richter, *Taschenbuch für Grabennymphen auf das Jahr 1787* (Vienna: n.p., 1787), engraving 9. Reproduced with permission of the Wienbibliothek im Rathaus from A-Wst, Secr-A 761.

Someone asked them one day: "How in God's name did you dare to come here? You know, Gypsies are not allowed to frequent this place." "Oh, sir!" answered one of them. "But we aren't Gypsies! The king has made *new citizens* of us! He wants us to be people, too, now! We came to serve the Hungarian gentlemen!" [...] In the time of our departed mother, Maria Theresa, His Excellency Count B. D. [Dénes Bánffy] had a band of Gypsy musicians brought up from Transylvania, and dressing them in German outfit, gained favour for them. This is the second music-making Gypsy band in Vienna, who play with such great proficiency that the inn where these people perform is full with people gathered in amazement, and they do the innkeeper a lot of good.[56]

Several pieces of information may be gleaned from this brief article: Romani musicians were not necessarily welcome as entertainers in Vienna; perhaps as a result, the anonymous author of the report contended that only two groups of them had performed in Vienna by 1787; and the first group went there under the patronage of Count Dénes Bánffy (b. 1723), Master of the Horse to Maria Theresa, sometime before the count and the empress both died in 1780.

Despite a general trend away from open persecution (mutilation, forced labor, execution) toward more economically pragmatic Habsburg policies of forced settlement in the eighteenth century, the Roma remained highly stigmatized. Along with Jews, beggars, journeymen, day laborers and other itinerant workers, as well as physically and mentally disabled persons, Romani individuals and communities were often marginalized, mistreated, and criminalized.[57] Romani musicians, specifically, were viewed as part of a larger undesirable category of itinerant musicians, actors, magicians, fortune tellers, and circus performers whose activities and movements were impeded by a variety of laws and decrees. The traveling passes required to enter or move from one part of the Monarchy to another were often difficult or impossible for them to acquire because their occupations and lifestyles

---

[56] As translated in Sárosi, *Gypsy Music*, 68–69. The emphasis is original. As I discussed in the introduction to this book, "new citizens" is a reference to one of Maria Theresa's decrees aimed at the forced assimilation of Hungary's Roma, whereby she prohibited the use of the Hungarian noun *cigány* ("Gypsy") in reference to this people, who were instead to be known as "new citizens," "new peasants," or "new Hungarians."

[57] For further discussion see, for instance, Karl Vocelka, *Glanz und Untergang der höfischen Welt: Repräsentation, Reform und Reaktion im habsburgischen Vielvölkerstaat* (Vienna: Carl Ueberreuter, 2001), 337–50.

were incompatible with the utilitarian work ethic promoted by the government.[58] Entry into Vienna itself was even more strictly controlled, restricted to those in possession of the necessary passes and barring individuals who had slipped by previous checkpoints from entering the capital city.[59] Additionally, innkeepers as well as anyone offering accommodation to strangers in their own homes were required to check their traveling passes and to record and report all pertinent information about them: name, occupation, status, and duration of stay.[60]

The patron's astonishment that Romani musicians would perform in a Viennese tavern, as recorded in the 1787 account, undoubtedly reflected this state of affairs. Yet a decree of 1821, stipulating that "foreign musicians, particularly those from the mountain towns of Bohemia and Hungary, who appear in Vienna from time to time, are allowed to remain [in the city] for a short period of time as long as they are in possession of the required passes,"[61] suggests that Hungarian Romani musicians were likely occasionally—and legally—heard in Vienna. It remains impossible, however, to evaluate the claim that the "Gypsy band" of 1787 was only the second one to make an appearance in the city; the presence of others may simply not have been documented or commented upon, or evidence of it may no longer be extant. What *is* certain is that authorities did their best to limit the activities of itinerant musicians as a whole, especially pursuant to an imperial decree of 10 December 1765, which ruled that they should not make their livings solely from playing music. In addition to restrictions on their movements, musicians were also required to obtain licenses to perform, which were difficult to get, and their incomes were heavily taxed.[62] The very scant evidence of Hungarian Romani musicians' activities in Vienna undoubtedly reflects this whole nexus of circumstances and makes the 1787 newspaper article all the more valuable.

---

[58] See the discussions in Hannelore Burger, "Pässe für Fremde" and Zdenka Stokláskova, "Der Reisepass als Voraussetzung für den Eintritt von Fremden nach Österreich," both in *Grenze und Staat: Paßwesen, Staatsbürgerschaft, Heimatrecht und Fremdengesetzgebung in der österreichischen Monarchie, 1750–1867*, ed. Waltraud Heindl, Edith Saurer, Hannelore Burger, and Harald Wendelin (Vienna: Böhlau, 2000), 76–87 and 632–47, respectively.

[59] Stokláskova, "Der Reisepass," 638.

[60] The decree is given in Burger, "Pässe für Fremde," 78n237.

[61] As given in Witzmann, *Der Ländler in Wien*, 103: "9. Mai 1821: Fremden Musikanten, besonders jenen aus den Bergstädten Böhmens und Ungarns, die in Wien von Zeit zu Zeit auftauchen, ist, wenn sie mit ordentlichen Pässen versehen sind, der Aufenthalt für eine kurze Zeit gestattet."

[62] See Witzmann, *Der Ländler in Wien*, 18–20, 103; and Schaller-Pressler, "Volksmusik und Volkslied in Wien," 115.

The article specifies that the Romani musicians' "music-making, without the printed music, was listened to with amazement." Many other contemporary accounts attest that the majority of Romani musicians were not musically literate, and the virtuosity of their improvisatory music-making delighted and astounded their audiences.[63] The image conjured by these descriptions is difficult to reconcile with the information given about the group who had accompanied Count Dénes Bánffy to Vienna sometime before 1780. As musicologist Bálint Sárosi has argued, if an eighteenth-century nobleman brought musicians from what is now central Romania as far as Vienna and "dress[ed] them in German outfit," it was almost certainly because they were trained as literate musicians familiar with current art music and its practices.[64] Corroborating this contention is an unsigned article in the 13 March 1784 issue of the *Preßburger Zeitung*. After noting that the Roma were naturally skillful at music, the author explained: "The Galánta Gypsies are excellent musicians in Hungary, and, what is more, they are also employable musical artists. They frequently take their places in aristocratic orchestras, too, and never play without the music. Apart from dance music they also perform concertos and symphonies and are in fact shaped more by art than by nature."[65] It is unclear whether the group of musicians from Galánta who played at the Viennese inn in 1787 were in fact musically literate but simply chose to play without notated music in this particular setting. Patrons in lower-class taverns, beerhouses, and wine cellars were accustomed to vernacular music played from memory or improvised; musicologist Walter Salmen has argued that it was precisely the ability to read music and to perform it with the necessary gallantry that separated musicians who were employed in more distinguished establishments from those who were not considered fit for them.[66] It is possible that along with the "Hungarian gentlemen" whom the Romani musicians reportedly identified as the motivation for their trip to the capital in 1787, they also entertained Viennese ladies—of Hungarian origin or not—as well, playing concertos or symphonies or accompanying their dances. But while gentlemen may have

---

[63] I consider such accounts in detail in the following chapter.
[64] Sárosi, *Gypsy Music*, 69.
[65] As partially translated in Sárosi, *Gypsy Music*, 68, from "Aus Siebenbürgen, vom 26 Febr.," *Preßburger Zeitung*, 13 March 1784, 3: "Die Galanther Zigeuner in Ungarn sind vortrefliche Musikanten und was noch mehr auch brauchbare Tonkünstler. Sie besetzen öfters herrschaftliche Orchester, und spielen nie ohne Noten. Ausser den Tänzen, führen sie auch Concerte und Symphonien auf, sind aber freylich mehr nach Kunst als von Natur gebildete Musici."
[66] Walter Salmen, "Spielleute und Ballmusiker," in *Mozart in der Tanzkultur seiner Zeit*, ed. Walter Salmen (Innsbruck: Helbling, 1990), 52.

witnessed their performance of vernacular music at the inn, relatively privileged women would not have been there to experience it firsthand; instead, they may well have read about it.

Reading Women

Historical literacy rates are difficult to establish because literacy itself is not a single skill but many, each of which was learned separately in the eighteenth century. An individual who could sign her name may not have been able to read, and many women who could read did not know how to write. Before Maria Theresa's school reform of 1774, schools in rural areas of the Habsburg Monarchy provided little more than religious and musical education via oral instruction delivered by the parish sacristan, who was eager to put his pupils' newly acquired musical skills to use in the Catholic Church's numerous masses and processions. Reading, writing, and arithmetic—subjects considered fundamental today—were not typically part of the curriculum; most of a pupil's time was spent memorizing and reciting the catechism. Schools located in towns and cities, and especially those catering to the more privileged classes, were much more likely to include instruction in reading and writing, because these skills were more necessary in their students' daily lives. Merchants, clerks, and professionals whose employment required literacy were also more likely to live in urban than in rural areas, and towns and cities afforded greater access to print culture. For all these reasons, rates of literacy were higher in urban areas than in rural ones. Men overall had higher literacy rates than women, especially in terms of their ability to write, a skill deemed less essential for women than for men.

Maria Theresa's General School Ordinance of 1774 professionalized teaching, standardized textbooks and curricula, and prioritized basic literacy. It made schooling compulsory for children aged six through twelve years old and mandated instruction in at least reading, writing, arithmetic, and religion; schools in urban areas included a wider range of subjects at more advanced levels. In spite of the Ordinance, in rural areas only a minority of elementary-school-aged children actually went to school, and although the Ordinance applied equally to children of both sexes, families were more likely to send their sons than their daughters to school. Despite some gains in the eighteenth century, in practice, compliance with compulsory schooling and its effects on literacy were not broadly felt until well into the nineteenth century.

Overall, the greatest predictors of literacy in the eighteenth century were wealth and social standing. School fees and textbooks, which were sometimes waived or offered free of charge for the neediest students, were significant financial burdens on many families, as was the loss of labor when children were in school instead of working alongside their parents.[67] In the eighteenth century as now, a family's ability to pay for school often determined the kind and quality of education—if any—their children would receive. According to Pezzl, annual tuition at Viennese elementary schools (*Trivialschulen*) was three florins in 1805; at high schools (*Gymnasienschulen*) it was twelve florins.[68] The sons and daughters of wealthy families did not attend these public schools; instead, they were typically educated at home by private tutors. Relatively privileged girls were also frequently sent to convent schools; as Pezzl explained with respect to Vienna, "the Ursulines in the city educate bourgeois girls; and the Salesian Sisters on the Rennweg run a boarding school for daughters of the nobility."[69] By 1805, in addition to the Ursuline Convent, two other Viennese schools educated middle-class girls ("Töchter aus dem Bürgerstande und den übrigen mittleren Ständen"), one located in the city itself and the other in the suburb of Leopoldstadt. Although these were public schools, with teachers paid by the state, the cost of attendance would have been prohibitive for many Viennese families: tuition was thirty kreuzers per month, with an extra forty kreuzers due in the winter to cover the cost of wood for heating. The education a girl received there, however, exceeded what she would learn in a *Trivialschule*, where she would be schooled only in religion, basic literacy, and simple arithmetic. At a *Mädchenschule*, because she was educated only with her socioeconomic

---

[67] The information on literacy is summarized from James Van Horn Melton, *The Rise of the Public in Enlightenment Europe* (Cambridge: Cambridge University Press, 2001), 81–86; James Van Horn Melton, "School, Stage, Salon: Musical Cultures in Haydn's Vienna," in *Haydn and the Performance of Rhetoric*, ed. Tom Beghin and Sander M. Goldberg (Chicago: University of Chicago Press, 2007), 80–108; and James Van Horn Melton, *Absolutism and the Eighteenth-Century Origins of Compulsory Schooling in Prussia and Austria* (Cambridge: Cambridge University Press, 1988), chaps. 1 and 8. On school reform and literacy, see also Mary Jo Maynes, *Schooling in Western Europe: A Social History* (Albany: State University of New York Press, 1985). For figures on school attendance in Vienna in the 1770s, see István György Tóth, *Literacy and Written Culture in Early Modern Central Europe* (Budapest: Central European University Press, 2000), 37. Tóth's study documents the generally paltry state of literacy in early modern Central Europe, in many parts of which illiteracy rates remained very high until the twentieth century.

[68] Pezzl, *Neue Skizze von Wien*, "Schulgelder," 277.

[69] Pezzl as translated in Landon, *Mozart and Vienna*, 164–65.

peers and only with other girls, a pupil's studies also involved calligraphy, German, and knitting. For an extra fee of one florin per month, she received additional tutelage in more refined knitting skills as well as in French—the international language of the upper classes throughout Europe. Private girls' schools, where boarding was also available, offered a yet wider range of instruction. At a cost of 370 florins per year for room, board, and schooling at the renowned institution of Madame Klement ("die Schule der Madame Klement auf dem neuen Markt"), for instance, a girl from a socioeconomically privileged family was taught all the usual subjects ("die gewöhnlichen Unterrichtsgegenstände") as well as music, dance, drawing, embroidery, and foreign languages.[70]

These accomplishments, much like reading, were pastimes suited to the socioeconomic position of Madame Klement's charges; wealth afforded these young women time to pursue leisure activities. When Pezzl declared that in order for a book to be a success, it must appeal to women, he was quick to specify that "women who can give themselves over to reading are normally affluent girls and young women who want for nothing, from whom all cares and work are taken away, and who consequently have sufficient leisure and desire to give free rein to their imaginations."[71] Women read a variety of literature, from novels and moral weeklies to travelogues and newspapers; these materials provided personal enjoyment and edification as well as fodder for discussion. Pezzl opined that the wives of professionals and business people (his "nobility of the second rank") were particularly fond of reading and the sociability it engendered. "In their houses," he described, "one does not yawn with boredom over miserable card parties. Intimate musical entertainment, good conversation among friends, literary novelties, discussions about books, travels, works of art, theatre, interesting pieces of news, daily events, all related with spice, judged and illuminated—such are the entertainments that shorten the winter evenings of such a familiar circle."[72]

---

[70] Information on the education of girls in Vienna is from Pezzl, *Neue Skizze von Wien*, "Mädchenschulen," 304–8. For further details on eighteenth-century Viennese schools, see Ignaz de Luca, *Topographie von Wien*, vol. 1 (Vienna: In Kommission bey Thad. Edlen v. Schmidbauer und Komp. am Graben zur blauen Krone, 1794), "Gymnasien" and "Volksschulen," 239–42.

[71] Pezzl, *Neue Skizze von Wien*, "Einfluß der Weiber auf die Lectüre," 116–17: "Wenn heut zu Tage ein Buch in Wien sein Glück machen soll, das heißt, wenn es stark gekauft oder doch gelesen werden will, so muß es die Weiber interessiren. [...] Die weiblichen Geschöpfe, welche sich mit Lectüre abgeben können, sind in der Regel die Mädchen und jüngeren Weiber aus der wohlhabenden Classe, denen es an nichts gebricht, was zur Lebens- und Leibesnotdurft gehört, die folglich aller Sorgen und Arbeiten überhoben sind, und somit Muße genug, ja sogar den Drang haben, bloß ihre Phantasie arbeiten zu lassen."

[72] Pezzl as translated in Landon, *Mozart and Vienna*, 72.

One can well imagine these women reading and discussing descriptions of Hungarian Romani music and music-making that appeared particularly in newspapers, periodicals, and as prefaces to collections of keyboard dances published for domestic enjoyment.[73] That such descriptions were included in the collections themselves underscores the presumption that the women who were the primary players of these dances were generally unfamiliar with the vernacular music on which they were ostensibly based.[74]

Travel Writing, Mediation, and the Enlightened Public Sphere

Descriptions of Hungarian Romani music and music-making may be construed as part of the broad category of eighteenth-century travel literature, which encompassed an expansive spectrum from fiction (Jonathan Swift's *Gulliver's Travels* and Montesquieu's *Lettres persanes*, for instance) to chronicles of actual voyages (most notably Captain James Cook's expeditions in the Pacific) and everything in between. Across genres, travel writing provided opportunities for critical comparisons of peoples, places, and customs; self-reflection and introspection; and dissemination of newly acquired knowledge about the world and its inhabitants. These perspectives, which historian Larry Wolff has characterized as philosophical, sentimental, and scientific, respectively, were often brought to bear in conjunction with one another, resulting in the "uniquely modern perspective of the 'civilized traveler,' passing judgment on lands and peoples with reference to the newly articulated standard of civilization."[75]

---

[73] I discuss the content of these descriptions and well as Hungarian dances for keyboard in the following chapter.

[74] The literature on women and girls as the primary performers of domestic keyboard music in the eighteenth and early nineteenth centuries is quite large; see, notably, Bianca Maria Antolini, "Publishers and Buyers," in *Music Publishing in Europe 1600–1900: Concepts and Issues, Bibliography*, ed. Rudolf Rasch (Berlin: Berliner Wissenschafts-Verlag, 2005), 234–35; William Weber, *Music and the Middle Class: The Social Structure of Concert Life in London, Paris and Vienna* (New York: Holmes & Meier, 1975), 35–36; Jeffrey Kallberg, *Chopin at the Boundaries: Sex, History, and Musical Genre* (Cambridge, MA: Harvard University Press, 1996), 35–38; Richard Leppert, "Music, Domestic Life, and Cultural Chauvinism: Images of British Subjects at Home in India," in *Music and Society: The Politics of Composition, Performance, and Reception*, ed. Richard Leppert and Susan McClary (Cambridge: Cambridge University Press, 1987), 85; and Arthur Loesser, *Men, Women & Pianos: A Social History* (New York: Simon & Schuster, 1954), esp. 64–67.

[75] Larry Wolff, "Travel Literature," in *Encyclopedia of the Enlightenment*, ed. Alan Charles Kors, vol. 4 (Oxford: Oxford University Press, 2003), 188. The blurring of genres in travel literature is addressed in Michel-Rolph Trouillot, *Global Transformations: Anthropology and the Modern World* (New York: Palgrave Macmillan, 2003), 14–16.

Only novels outstripped travel literature in popularity in the eighteenth century; the published account of Cook's first Pacific voyage, for example, was a bestseller. Like novels, travel literature had the potential both to edify and to entertain readers, as the editor of Lady Mary Wortley Montagu's *Turkish Embassy Letters* stated explicitly by way of advertisement when the correspondence from Lady Mary's voyage to Constantinople in 1716–1717, where her husband had been appointed English ambassador, was published in 1763, the year after her death:

> The letters from Ratisbon [Regensburg], Vienna, Dresden, Peterwaradin [Petrovaradin], Belgrade, Adrianople [Edirne], Constantinople [Istanbul], Pera [Beyoğlu], Tunis, Genoa, Lyons, and Paris, are, certainly, the most curious and interesting part of this publication, and both in point of *matter* and *form*, are, to say no more of them, singularly worthy of the curiosity and attention of all *men of taste*, and even of all *women of fashion*. As to those female readers, who read for improvement, and think their beauty an insipid thing, if it is not seasoned by intellectual charms, they will find in these Letters what they seek for, and will behold in their author, an ornament and model to their sex.[76]

To make accounts more enticing to the reading public, fictive passages were often introduced into otherwise scientific writing. John Hawkesworth, for example, fabricated sexual material to include in his published narrative of Cook's sojourn in Tahiti, greatly angering the explorer who had entrusted Hawkesworth with the task of turning his notes into a cohesive, readable account.[77] Lady Mary herself confirmed readers' expectation, to a certain degree, of fantastic tales of incredible places and beings when she complained in a letter to her sister that another unnamed correspondent (Elisabeth Griffin, Lady Rich), was "angry that I won't lie like other travellers. I verily believe she expects I should tell her of the anthropophagi [cannibals], and men whose heads grow below their shoulders."[78]

---

[76] "Advertisement of the Editor," *Letters of the Right Honourable Lady M- -y W- - -y M- - - -e: Written, during her Travels in Europe, Asia and Africa, to Persons of Distinction, Men of Letters, &c. in different Parts of Europe. Which Contain, among other curious Relations, Accounts of the Policy and Manners of the Turks; Drawn from Sources that have been inaccessible to other Travellers*, vol. 1 (London: Printed for T. Becket and P. A. De Hondt, 1763). The emphasis is original. On the popularity of travel literature as a genre in the eighteenth century, see Dorinda Outram, *The Enlightenment*, 4th ed. (Cambridge: Cambridge University Press, 2019), 67.

[77] Outram, *The Enlightenment*, 66.

[78] Montagu, *Turkish Embassy Letters*, "Letter XXI, Vienna, 16 January 1717," 44.

As a result, much eighteenth-century travel writing not only insisted on its value—both educational and recreational—but linked this value to the truth of the account at hand. William Smith, an early missionary to Tahiti, for example, argued that the appeal of explorers' "authentic narratives" lay in the fact that they led readers to "empathize with the travelers' adventures and be entertained and morally improved in the process."[79] Burney began the introduction to his *Present State of Music in Germany, the Netherlands, and United Provinces, or the Journal of a Tour through Those Countries* by acknowledging these precepts at length:

It is well known that such merchandize as is capable of adulteration, is seldom genuine after passing through many hands; and this principle is still more generally allowed with respect to intelligence, which is, perhaps, never pure but at the source.

Music has, through life, been the favourite object of my pursuit, not only with respect to the practice of it as a profession, but the history of it as an art; and that my knowledge might be free from such falsehood and error as the plainest and simplest facts are known to gather up in successive relations, I have made a second tour on the continent, taking nothing upon report, of which I could procure better testimony, and, accumulating the most authentic memorials of the times that are past; and as I have, in a late publication, endeavoured to do justice to the talents and attainments of the present musicians of France and Italy, I shall now make the same attempt with respect to those of Germany, hoping that the testimony of one who has himself been witness of the particulars he relates, will have a weight which integrity itself cannot give to hear-say evidence, and that the mind of the reader will be more entertained, in proportion as it is more satisfied of the truth of what is written. For if *knowledge* be *medicine for the soul*, according to the famous inscription on the Egyptian Library, it seems as

---

[79] As given in Vanessa Agnew, "Encounter Music in Oceania: Cross-Cultural Musical Exchange in Eighteenth- and Early Nineteenth-Century Voyage Accounts," in *The Cambridge History of World Music*, ed. Philip V. Bohlman (Cambridge: Cambridge University Press, 2013), 194, from William Smith, *Journal of a Voyage in the Missionary Ship Duff, to the Pacific Ocean in the Years 1796, 7, 8, 9, 1800, 1, 2, &c.: Comprehending Authentic and Circumstantial Narratives of the Disasters which Attended the First Effort of the "London Missionary Society." With an Appendix; Containing Interesting Circumstances in the Life of Captain James Wilson, the Commander of the Duff, when he was Engaged in the Wars in the East Indies, and taken Prisoner by Hyder Ally's troops,—his bold attempt to escape, and subsequent difficulties* (New York: Collins, 1813), iii.

much to concern us to obtain it genuine, as to procure unadulterated medicine for the body.[80]

In his introduction to his account of his earlier travels through France and Italy, Burney expressed largely the same sentiments. After lamenting that existing books had not provided him with the information he sought, not least because "these books are, in general, such faithful copies of each other, that he who reads two or three, has the substance of as many hundred," Burney declared: "In hopes, therefore, of stamping on my intended History some marks of originality, or at least of novelty, I determined to allay my thirst of knowledge at the source, and take such draughts in Italy, as England cannot supply. It was there I determined to hear with my *own* ears, and to see with my *own* eyes: and, if possible, to *hear* and *see* nothing but *music*."[81]

This insistence on firsthand knowledge is unsurprising given that much eighteenth-century travel literature was penned by authors who did not themselves travel; they were poets, novelists, or philosophers who voyaged only imaginatively or relied on the accounts of others. As historical geographer Charles Withers has observed, scientific travel writing typically set itself apart through its emphasis on personal experience and empirical observation rather than secondhand authority.[82] These qualities, moreover, marked scientific travel literature—in its own right or as a constitutive element of the broader narratives of philosophical, sentimental, or civilized travelers—as critical to the Enlightenment and to the new discipline of anthropology—the "science of man"—to which it gave rise. Like knowledge of the natural world, new anthropological knowledge was to be arrived at through firsthand encounter and scientific study. Notwithstanding ongoing imperialistic and religious motivations, exploration in the eighteenth century was for the first time fundamentally concerned with gathering data, on humans and their societies as well as on nature, throughout the world.[83]

---

[80] Burney, *Dr. Burney's Musical Tours*, vol. 2, "The Introduction," xi. The emphasis is original.

[81] Charles Burney, *Dr. Burney's Musical Tours*, vol. 1, *An Eighteenth-Century Musical Tour in France and Italy Being Dr. Charles Burney's Account of his Musical Experiences As It Appears in His Published Volume with Which Are Incorporated His Travel Experiences According to His Original Intention*, ed. Percy A. Scholes (London: Oxford University Press, 1959), "Burney's Introduction to His Book As Published," xxvii. The emphasis is original.

[82] See Charles W. J. Withers, *Placing the Enlightenment: Thinking Geographically about the Age of Reason* (Chicago: University of Chicago Press, 2007), 110.

[83] On the Enlightenment's anthropological orientation, see esp. Larry Wolff and Marco Cipolloni, eds., *The Anthropology of the Enlightenment* (Stanford, CA: Stanford University Press, 2007). See also Withers, *Placing the Enlightenment*, and Outram, *The Enlightenment*, esp. chap. 5.

In eighteenth-century accounts of world musics, writers often underscored their status as earwitnesses, as it were, by emphasizing their presence and by providing very specific details about what they had experienced. Burney, for instance, was not content simply to note that the music he heard in the streets of Naples was "totally different, both in melody and in modulation, from all that I have heard elsewhere," but proceeded to outline the modulations in painstaking—and seemingly superfluous—detail not once but twice. "The modulation surprised me very much: from the key of A natural, to that of C and F, was not difficult or new; but from that of A, with a sharp third, to E flat, was astonishing; and the more so, as the return to the original key was always so insensibly managed, as neither to shock the ear, nor to be easily discovered by what road or relations it was brought about." And again a few pages later:

> In the canzone of to-night they began in A natural, and, without well knowing how, they got into the most extraneous keys it is possible to imagine, yet without offending the ear. After the instruments have played a long symphony in A, the singer begins in F, and stops in C, which is not uncommon or difficult; but, after another ritornel, from F, he gets into E flat, then closes in A natural, after this there were transitions even into B flat, and D flat, without giving offence, returning, or rather *sliding* always into the original key of A natural, the instruments moving the whole time in quick notes, without the least intermission.[84]

Similarly, many accounts of Hungarian Romani music and music-making go beyond the minimal description given in the 1787 *Magyar Kurír* article previously discussed, betraying a desire to suggest close personal observation *in situ*. Following a rather poetic description of Hungarian Romani music and musicians published in 1810, for example, the anonymous Pest correspondent to the *Allgemeine musikalische Zeitung* noted that "their [preferred] modes are mostly aeolian, hyperdorian, hyperaeolian, and hyperphrygian. They play in A-flat, B-flat, E-flat, and A minor," some of which are not the most likely key choices for ensembles of string instruments.[85] Likewise,

---

[84] Burney, *Dr. Burney's Musical Tours*, vol. 1, 244 and 254, respectively. The emphasis is original.
[85] "Nachrichten: Pest in Ungarn, d. 6ten Febr.," *Allgemeine musikalische Zeitung* 12, no. 24 (14 March 1810): col. 371: "Ihre Modulationen in etwas zu bezeichnen, würd' ich sagen, dass ihre Tonarten meist aeolisch, hyperdorisch, hypoaolisch, und hyperphrygisch sind. Sie spielen aus dem As, B, Es, und A moll. Ihre Instrumente sind gewöhnlich die Violin, das Violoncell und der Cymbal oder das Hackbret."

the first of a four-volume set of *Originelle Ungarische Nationaltänze* was prefaced with a few lines about the Hungarian preference for striking modulations, emphasis on downbeats, and trills in thirds, fourths, and fifths by its self-styled "collector" ("der Sammler"), who both effaced his agency in the composition of the published music and claimed firsthand experience of its authentic performance by so designating himself.[86] Although Percy Scholes, the twentieth-century editor of Burney's accounts, notes that "it says a good deal for the keenness of Burney's ear that he could quickly recognise and record the incidents of [a] passage over such a rocky road,"[87] the level of detail Burney and others provided their readers says just as much about the credibility and authority eighteenth-century travel writers garnered precisely by emphasizing the lack of mediation of their accounts.[88]

Such accounts, unless they were fictive or borrowed from other writings, depended on firsthand experiences and therefore privileged men, who were much more likely to travel—and to travel farther—than women in the eighteenth century. Young men of means toured Europe as part of their education; while such a "Grand Tour," especially of France and Italy, is often associated with young Englishmen, Wraxall noted that young Viennese men "like us, commonly travel; that is from Vienna to Paris, through Italy and home."[89] But some men also traveled farther afield, along three routes that Wolff has identified as delineating Eastern Europe in the eighteenth century: through Poland to St. Petersburg, from St. Petersburg to Constantinople, and from Constantinople through southeastern Europe.[90] In contrast, as the prolific writer and traveler Lady Elizabeth Craven neared the end of this last route

---

[86] As given in Géza Papp, ed., *Hungarian Dances 1784–1810*, Musicalia Danubiana 7 (Budapest: Magyar Tudományos Akadémia, Zenetudományi Intézet, 1986), 356. I have transcribed the collection's foreword as text C in the appendix. The entire set was published in Vienna between 1806/1807 and 1812.

[87] Burney, *Dr. Burney's Musical Tours*, vol. 1, 254n1.

[88] On the importance of presence and listening in eighteenth-century accounts of Eastern European music, see also Kevin C. Karnes, "Inventing Eastern Europe in the Ear of the Enlightenment," *Journal of the American Musicological Society* 71, no. 1 (Spring 2018): 75–108. As Karnes notes (p. 83), despite the emphasis on direct encounter in much travel writing, "we must remember that all such encounters were episodic, and all written accounts selective. [...] All such accounts were produced by elite, literate authors, writing from an etic (or outsider's) perspective. [...] For these reasons these travelers' recollections of sounds and sights cannot necessarily be taken as representative of the experiences or practices of those who inhabited the spaces traversed." In other words, even scientific travel writing was highly mediated, despite its claims to the contrary; references to keys and modes indeed emphasize writers' tendency to approach foreign music through the Western parameters with which they were familiar.

[89] Wraxall, *Memoirs*, vol. 2, "Letter XXIX, Vienna, 2 February 1779," 251.

[90] Larry Wolff, *Inventing Eastern Europe: The Map of Civilization on the Mind of the Enlightenment* (Stanford, CA: Stanford University Press, 1994), 122. Accounts of men's journeys constitute the majority of the documents on which Wolff's study is based.

and re-entered Habsburg territory in the late 1780s, she related that the customs agent commented the she was "the first lady he had seen or heard of passing that frontier."[91] Lady Elizabeth herself admitted that "most women would be frightened with the journey I am taking."[92] Similarly, as Lady Mary Wortley Montagu prepared to leave Vienna for Constantinople, eastward-bound through the same terrain that Lady Elizabeth had traversed in the opposite direction, she wrote to her sister that "the ladies of my acquaintance have so much goodness for me, they cry whenever they see me since I have determined to undertake this journey; and, indeed, I am not very easy when I reflect on what I am going to suffer. Almost everybody I see frights me with some new difficulty."[93] Lady Mary embarked on the journey nonetheless, in order to accompany her husband in his new post, but Lady Elizabeth's travel was not undertaken to fulfill familial or professional obligations (as a singer, actor, governess, or other domestic servant, for example), the two most common reasons eighteenth-century women traveled. Unusually, Lady Elizabeth was traveling for the same reasons that men of high socioeconomic standing commonly did: for pleasure and personal cultivation. Typically, men could do so much more easily than women, not least because women could not obtain the necessary travel passes without the permission of their husbands.[94]

The idea that women were best suited to domestic pursuits—reading about others' travels rather than undertaking them themselves—was not new in the eighteenth century, but the reasons mustered to bolster such claims were. Unlike previous justifications, which relied on scripture, superstition, or simply the weight of tradition, many eighteenth-century discourses on gender roles marshaled evidence from newly valorized medical sciences to support the notion that a woman's place was in the home. Her anatomy and physiology—not only reproductive, but even skeletal and neurologic—were often posited as fundamentally different from those of men, not only

---

[91] Lady Elizabeth Craven, *A Journey through the Crimea to Constantinople. In a Series of Letters from the Right Honourable Elizabeth Lady Craven to His Serene Highness the Margrave of Brandebourg, Anspach, and Bareith. Written in the Year MDCCLXXXVI* (London: Printed for G. G. J. and J. Robinson, 1789), as quoted in Wolff, *Inventing Eastern Europe*, 121.

[92] Craven, *A Journey*, as quoted in Wolff, "Travel Literature," 190.

[93] Montagu, *Turkish Embassy Letters*, "Letter XXI, Vienna, 16 January 1717," 43.

[94] On women traveling in the eighteenth century, see Andrea Geselle, "Reisende Frauen," in *Grenze und Staat*, 410–14. For a survey of recent scholarship on eighteenth-century women's travel writing published in English, see the special issue "Journeys to Authority: Reassessing Women's Travel Writing, 1763–1863" of *Women's Writing* (24, no. 2 [2017]), esp. the introductory article by Carl Thompson.

rendering her uniquely able to bear and nurture children, but determining her existence, physically, emotionally, and socially. Intellectual pursuits were incompatible with anatomical studies revealing women's brains to be smaller than men's.[95]

These new ideas may have been less consequential if they had not arisen in the context of—perhaps indeed because of—the emergence of an Enlightened public sphere, a discursive realm in which private individuals generated, shared, and debated ideas, many of which pertained to issues of state authority. In Jürgen Habermas's classic formulation, the rise of the public sphere in the late seventeenth and eighteenth centuries was fostered by the gradual consolidation of administrative, fiscal, military, and judicial powers in the hands of modern nation-states (rather than ecclesiastical or feudal authorities) and by the advent of capitalism and the increased access to goods and information that attended it. Both of these developments encouraged the separation of state authority and civil society, but they also led to a fundamental reconceptualization of the household as a space of intimacy, nurturing, and affection rather than as a site of administration or of economic production and trade, functions taken over by the state and the capitalist marketplace, respectively.[96] Medical evidence of essential differences between the sexes supported the notion that in its new formulation, the private sphere of the home was the natural domain of women. Appealing to scientific grounds to legitimize women's limited participation in the emerging public sphere eased anxieties about their marginalization in an age that supported, at least in theory, the notion that all humans were equally endowed with reason, but that simultaneously perceived women's full participation in the public sphere as a threat to its independence, for women

---

[95] On eighteenth-century attempts to define fundamental differences between men and women, see Outram, *The Enlightenment*, chap. 7; Thomas Laqueur, *Making Sex: Body and Gender from the Greeks to Freud* (Cambridge, MA: Harvard University Press, 1990); and Ludmilla Jordanova, *Sexual Visions: Images of Gender in Science and Medicine between the Eighteenth and Twentieth Centuries* (Milwaukee: University of Wisconsin Press, 1989). Matthew Head has questioned the influence of medical discourses on broader eighteenth-century views of women, particularly in Germany; see Matthew Head, *Sovereign Feminine: Music and Gender in Eighteenth-Century Germany* (Berkeley: University of California Press, 2013), 8–9.

[96] On Habermas's public sphere as expounded in his *The Structural Transformation of the Public Sphere: An Inquiry into A Category of Bourgeois Society*, see Melton, "Introduction: What Is the Public Sphere?" in *The Rise of the Public*, 1–15; and Joan B. Landes, "The Public and the Private Sphere: A Feminist Reconsideration," in *Feminists Read Habermas: Gendering the Subject of Discourse*, ed. with an introduction by Johanna Meehan (New York: Routledge, 1995), 91–116. For a sustained investigation of the relationship of women to the public sphere, see Joan B. Landes, *Women and the Public Sphere in the Age of the French Revolution* (Ithaca, NY: Cornell University Press, 1988).

themselves allegedly lacked autonomy, beholden to familial obligations and to the intrinsic emotionality ascribed to them.[97]

Although eighteenth-century women did participate in the public sphere of ideas and opinions, their position was an ambivalent one that was largely circumscribed by their perceived role as civil society's primary guardians of morality and virtue. Women were valued as civilizing forces and often facilitated and actively participated in dialogue in social settings—notably as *salonnières* or at parties—or contributed to public discourse within the constraints of prevailing ideals of femininity: as translators, as authors of didactic material in moral weeklies or other periodicals, or even as authors of novels, many of which were published anonymously or under pseudonyms. More commonly, relatively privileged women did not make their writing public; their literary endeavors were confined instead to private genres such as diaries and letters. As historian James Van Horn Melton has summarized, wealthy women who had the time and education necessary to write "risked social disapproval by becoming published authors. [...] By exposing [themselves] in print, [they] became 'public women' accessible to everyone, just as eighteenth-century streetwalkers were commonly known as 'public girls.'"[98] Even Lady Mary, the original editor of whose *Turkish Embassy Letters* referred to her as "an ornament and model to [her] sex,"[99] was the author of private correspondence, which was published only after her death, and even then against the wishes of her family. Unlike men, whose reputations were built on publicity, a woman's virtue and modesty depended on shunning it.[100]

Although living within these boundaries safeguarded a woman's respectability, it simultaneously limited her authority, for as Melton has argued, "to the extent that the ideal of the public sphere rested on the assumption that print was the medium best suited for the effective and rational articulation of

---

[97] On women as a threat to the independence of the public sphere, see Outram, *The Enlightenment*, 19–20.

[98] Melton, *The Rise of the Public*, 148. For an in-depth examination of women's agency through their activities as musical *salonnières*, see Rebecca Cypess, *Women and Musical Salons in the Enlightenment* (Chicago: University of Chicago Press, 2022).

[99] "Advertisement of the Editor," *Letters of the Right Honourable Lady M- -y W- - -y M- - - -e*. The *Turkish Embassy Letters* are based on the letters Lady Mary wrote to her friends and family while abroad as well as on her private journal; see Montagu, *Turkish Embassy Letters*, 168n1. As Head has noted, in the eighteenth century, such editorial "framing devices" were good for marketing, "tend[ing] to render the publication more enticing and meaningful [...]." See Head, *Sovereign Feminine*, 6.

[100] On writing and reputation, see Dena Goodman, "Suzanne Necker's *Mélanges*: Gender, Writing, and Publicity," in *Going Public: Women and Publishing in Early Modern France*, ed. Elizabeth C. Goldsmith and Dena Goodman (Ithaca, NY: Cornell University Press, 1995), 210–23.

public opinion, the function of authors became central."[101] Notwithstanding the importance of the visual and performing arts in the transmission of ideas in the eighteenth-century public sphere, Habermas and others have pointed to the centrality of text as a vehicle of Enlightenment.[102] Individuals laid claim to authority by writing and by making their writing public. Not only were socioeconomically privileged women much less likely than men to have had the kind of firsthand encounters critical to Enlightenment anthropological aspirations, they were also much less likely openly to publish accounts of such experiences if they did have them.[103] Both circumstances limited their authority as well as the prestige and influence it conferred in the public sphere, whose power increasingly rivaled and challenged that of organized government.

***

Like Nicolai, whose "primary purpose" in traveling through the German-speaking lands in 1781 was "to observe people," Georg Forster, who accompanied Cook on his second voyage in the Pacific, declared in his subsequent essay "Cook the Discoverer" (1787) that "the most important object of our researches [is] our own species."[104] As the capital of a multinational monarchy, Vienna offered the possibility of encountering a variety of cultures without leaving the city, let alone traveling to the other side of the globe. The music of Hungarian Romani performers was one among a range of vernacular offerings in Vienna's inns, taverns, beerhouses, and wine cellars, sites of sociability officially open to the public but unofficially off-limits to the city's socioeconomically privileged women. Despite the proximity of such music, Vienna's elite women experienced it in the same secondhand way as their counterparts in much less ethnically and culturally diverse cities, who had access to much of the same reading material they did. In this respect, at least,

---

[101] Melton, *The Rise of the Public*, 124.

[102] See Outram, *The Enlightenment*, chap. 2; and Landes, "The Public and the Private Sphere."

[103] Of roughly 1,400 travelogues published in Britain and Ireland between 1690 and 1800, for instance, only approximately forty, or less than 3 percent, were by women. See Carl Thompson, "Journeys to Authority: Reassessing Women's Early Travel Writing, 1763–1862," *Women's Writing* 24, no. 2 (2017): 147n14. See also *Women's Travel Writing, 1780–1840: A Bio-Bibliographical Database*, https://btw.wlv.ac.uk (accessed 22 October 2021).

[104] Nicolai, *Beschreibung einer Reise*, vol. 1 (Berlin and Stettin: n.p., 1783), "Aufenthalt in Koburg," 87: "Mein Hauptzweck war: Menschen zu beobachten." The quotation from Forster is given in Outram, *The Enlightenment*, 63. Under the original title "Cook der Entdecker," Forster's essay served as a preface to his German translation of the published account of Cook's third Pacific voyage. See M. E. Hoare, "'Cook the Discoverer': An Essay by Georg Forster, 1787," *Records of the Australian Academy of Science* 1, no. 4 (November 1969): 7–16.

they were less privileged not only than men, but also than their own personal attendants. As Pezzl commented about Viennese ladies' maids, "altogether they are generally better educated and bred than most of the young Fräuleins because their freer life-style allows them more experience of people and situations, leading to greater refinement."[105] Indeed, for "young Fräuleins," socioeconomic privilege clearly intersected with gender-based oppression.

The extent to which media and institutions of Enlightenment transcended social divisions of class, gender, and urbanization remains historiographically contested terrain. Given the limited evidence of the experiences of the socioeconomically disadvantaged, it remains difficult to determine the degree to which cultural reference points were shared across social strata; whether such commonality was a goal of the Enlightenment, if it is appropriate to think in such definite terms, is itself questionable.[106] Experiences of Hungarian Romani music-making in Vienna suggest that vernacular music could be construed as a point of cultural contact—between elite and masses, men and women—albeit an ambivalent one. Class and gender were critical determinants of an individual's exposure to this music—in person vs. in print—and discursive authority over it, ultimately bolstering and validating social and gender hierarchies.

---

[105] Pezzl as translated in Landon, *Mozart and Vienna*, 147–48.
[106] On these points see, for instance, the summary of disagreements between historians Roger Muchembled, Roland Chartier, and Robert Darnton on the extent to which the late eighteenth century was a period of "great cultural convergence" in Outram, *The Enlightenment*, 22–25.

3
Playing Hungarian Dances at the Keyboard

Descriptions of Hungarian music and music-making were part of a large literature about music throughout Europe and beyond its borders during the eighteenth century, a century defined by cross-cultural encounters. Musicologist Estelle Joubert has investigated how in German-language periodicals alone, readers could learn about "musical communities around the world, including those in North America (Iroquois), China, Egypt, India, Indonesia (Javanese), West Africa, South Africa, New Zealand, Japan, Tahiti, and Turkey."[1] Like much of the literature I have discussed in the two preceding chapters, this corpus of articles, along with more voluminous writings like travelogues and histories of music throughout the world, bears witness to the Enlightenment's anthropological bent and to music's frequent use as a measure of civilization. However, despite the wealth of information—about melody, harmony, and rhythm; instruments and tunings; and ritual uses of music and dance, among other topics—disseminated about global music in the eighteenth century, much of this information was consumed in the absence of copious notated examples of the musics in question. Only a small minority of periodical articles, for instance, which Joubert notes were much more readily accessible and widely read than larger writings, included notated music in-text or as a textual supplement. To be sure, collections of world musics adapted for European consumption were in circulation—"Hindostannie airs" in William H. Bird's *Oriental Miscellany* (1789) and a veritable smorgasbord of global music in William Crotch's *Specimens of Various Styles of Music* (1808–1815), to give but two examples from Britain[2]—but it is often unclear whether and how these relatively small,

---

[1] Estelle Joubert, "Analytical Encounters: Global Music Criticism and Enlightenment Ethnomusicology," in *Studies on a Global History of Music: A Balzan Musicology Project*, ed. Reinhard Strohm (London: Routledge, 2018), 43. I thank Professor Joubert for kindly sharing with me her "List of Reviews of Non-European Music in German Periodicals, ca. 1750–1800," an unpublished appendix to her chapter.

[2] Ian Woodfield, "Collecting Indian Songs in Late 18th-Century Lucknow: Problems of Transcription," *British Journal of Ethnomusicology* 3 (1994): 73, notes that "Hindostannie airs" was the most common eighteenth-century nomenclature and spelling for "short pieces derived from original Indian tunes and arranged in a European idiom."

independent repertoires may have interfaced with descriptive literature about the musics they represented.

Accounts of Hungarian music and music-making, in contrast, were consumed within the context of a large repertoire of notated music purportedly adapted from the performances of Romani musicians for amateurs' domestic enjoyment. In the decades around 1800, hundreds of pieces of such music were distributed by Viennese publishers, in print and manuscript, in collections typically including between six and twelve but in some cases as many as twenty-eight individual pieces. Most of these were dances to be played at the keyboard or, somewhat less frequently, in small chamber ensembles usually consisting of two violins and *basso*. The popularity and commercial success of this music are evident not only from its quantity, but also from the frequency with which it was reissued, either by the original publisher or by a new one. Individual pieces of music, or passages from them, furthermore, often appeared in more or less varied versions in multiple publications. The wide circulation of much of this music thus clearly reveals its currency within Viennese musical culture over many years.[3] One of the earliest collections of Hungarian dances published in Vienna—Joseph Bengraf's set of *XII. Magyar Tántzok Klávicembalomra Valók/XII. Danses Hongroises pour le Clavecin ou Piano-Forte*—serves as a case in point. Johann Traeg initially advertised the set for sale in manuscript copy in the *Wiener Zeitung* in August 1784. In May 1790, Artaria advertised its availability in print, and the publisher's plates were subsequently taken over by Giovanni Cappi, who reissued the set between 1802 and 1807.[4] Meanwhile, in the *Wiener Zeitung* in February 1791, Ferdinand Kauer advertised a set of *12 Ungarische Tänze mit 2 Violin und Baß nach Bengrafs Idee*; musicologist Géza Papp has suggested that this arrangement for string trio of Bengraf's dances for keyboard was distributed in manuscript, but unfortunately no copy of it is extant.[5]

---

[3] Extensive information about the publication of Hungarian dances in Vienna around 1800 is given in Géza Papp, ed., *Hungarian Dances 1784–1810*, Musicalia Danubiana 7 (Budapest: Magyar Tudományos Akadémia, Zenetudományi Intézet, 1986), 345–62; and Géza Papp, "Die Quellen der 'Verbunkos-Musik': Ein bibliographischer Versuch. A) Gedruckte Werke I. 1784–1823," *Studia Musicologica* 21, nos. 2–4 (1979): 151–217.

[4] "Musikalien," WZ, 18 August 1784, 1900 col. 2. Information about Artaria's and Cappi's publications is in Papp, *Hungarian Dances*, 346–47; Papp, "Die Quellen," 153; and Ferenc Bónis, ed., *Ungarische Tänze für Klavier/Hungarian Dances for Piano*, Diletto Musicale 662 (Vienna: Doblinger, 1993), "Revisionsbericht und Quellennachweis."

[5] "Neue Musikalien," WZ, 5 February 1791, 300 col. 1; 9 February 1791, 332 col. 2; 12 February 1791, 366 col. 1; and Papp, *Hungarian Dances*, 347.

Newspapers and periodicals not only advertised the availability of Hungarian dances to the purchasing public, but they also reviewed this music; despite its commercial success, reviews were not necessarily favorable. In August 1791, for instance, the *Musikalische Korrespondenz der teutschen Filarmonischen Gesellschaft* notified readers that Bengraf's set of twelve Hungarian dances for keyboard was available for purchase in Speyer, where the periodical was published.[6] Three months later, as part of a "Catalogue raisonné," the journal offered the following caustic opinion of the dances and their composer: "Mr. Bengraf's muse is so impoverished in charm and novelty of thought and has such a commonplace and monotonous bass as accompaniment that the musical public would have lost nothing if the infant had been suffocated in birth."[7] Years later, the *Allgemeine musikalische Zeitung* advertised Johann Nepomuk Hummel's *Balli ongaresi*, op. 23, recently published by the Kunst- und Industrie-Comptoir in Vienna, as part of a substantial article on Hungarian dances. Prefacing his comments with the disclaimer that this "little work [...] admittedly has nothing outstanding [about it] for the artist," the anonymous reviewer went on to praise Hummel for the character of his dances, but chastised him for often writing uncomfortable bass lines, noting that "such little things come first for dilettantes who have little ability."[8] Musicologist László Dobszay's assessment that the value of this repertoire "is not primarily aesthetic" thus clearly echoes contemporary criticism of it.[9]

Why then did amateurs purchase and play these dances so avidly? The *Allgemeine musikalische Zeitung*'s review of Hummel's *Balli ongaresi*, which includes information about the repertoire and performance practices of the

---

[6] "Musikalien," *Musikalische Korrespondenz der teutschen Filarmonischen Gesellschaft*, 17 August 1791, 264.

[7] "Catalogue raisonné," *Musikalische Korrespondenz der teutschen Filarmonischen Gesellschaft*, 30 November 1791, 378: "Die Muse des Hrn. Bengrafs ist so arm an Reiz und Neuheit an Gedanken, und hat einen so alltäglich und einförmigen Bass zur Begleitung, daß in der That das musikalische Publikum nicht das mindeste würde verloren haben, wenn das Kindlein in der Geburt wäre erstikt worden."

[8] "Ungarische Tänze," *Allgemeine musikalische Zeitung* 9, no. 25 (18 March 1807): cols. 404–5: "ein Werkchen, das freylich für den Künstler, als solchen, nichts Ausgezeichnetes hat [...] Hr. H. hat den Charakter überall ziemlich, und einigemal, z. B. in No. 1.[,] in No. 7., sehr gut getroffen; nur hätte er dem Basse an mehrern Stellen, z. B. S. 3. oftmals, eine bequemere Lage geben sollen, da dergleichen Sächelchen doch zunächst für Dilettanten und Dilettantinnen kommen, die nur wenig vermögen, aber hier, wo sie für die Sache gewonnen werden sollen, besondere Rücksicht verdienen." The text of the entire article is given in the appendix (as text D). Hummel's dances were advertised in the *Wiener Zeitung* on 29 October 1806—see Alexander Weinmann, "Vollständiges Verlagsverzeichnis der Musikalien des Kunst- und Industrie Comptoirs in Wien 1801–1819. Ein bibliographischer Beitrag," *Studien zur Musikwissenschaft* 22 (1955): 239.

[9] László Dobszay, unpaginated foreword to Papp, *Hungarian Dances*.

Romani musicians upon which the composer's set was ostensibly based, provides some clues. The author advised readers inclined to play Hummel's dances themselves that through improvisation and altered trills, they could approximate the performance of Romani musicians, "those children of nature."[10] Certainly, such an approach could counteract the lack of "charm" and "novelty" that critics underscored in this repertoire. Such advice also betrays a certain striving for authenticity, here imputed to amateur keyboard players but also evident in composers' comments about the relationship of their dances to those played by Romani musicians. Especially when such comments appeared as prefaces to collections of Hungarian dances, they provided an explicit context within which amateurs were invited not only to appreciate and to understand the music in their hands but also to play it. In so doing, their performances carried out cultural work, much like the texts that led literary scholar Jane Tompkins to develop the concept. As Tompkins has explained, "cultural work" is "the notion of literary texts [...] doing work, expressing and shaping the social context that produced them," a productive interpretive substitute for or complement to "the critical perspective that sees [literary texts] as attempts to achieve a timeless, universal idea of truth and formal coherence."[11]

In this chapter, I explore the complex cultural work that could have been accomplished by the domestic performance of Hungarian dances in the eighteenth century, especially given that most amateur keyboard players were women and girls. When they played these dances, adapted by composers to suit prevailing tastes and abilities, amateur keyboardists could not only imagine but physically enact community with professional male Romani musicians, adopting performance practices they read about.[12] As musicologist and cellist Elisabeth Le Guin has virtuosically explored, such identification on the part of performers with the composers

---

[10] "Ungarische Tänze," 406: um jenen musikal. "Naturkindern näher zukommen [...]."

[11] Jane Tompkins, *Sensational Designs: The Cultural Work of American Fiction, 1790–1860* (Oxford: Oxford University Press, 1985), 200. The idea of "cultural work" has been productively applied to music performance by musicologists including Ruth Solie, Suzanne G. Cusick, and Rebecca Cypess. See Ruth Solie, "Whose Life? The Gendered Self in Schumann's *Frauenliebe* Songs," in *Music and Text: Critical Inquiries*, ed. Steven P. Scher (Cambridge: Cambridge University Press, 1992), 219–40; Suzanne G. Cusick, "Gender and the Cultural Work of a Classical Music Performance," *repercussions* 3, no. 1 (Spring 1994): 77–110; and Rebecca Cypess, *Women and Musical Salons in the Enlightenment* (Chicago: University of Chicago Press, 2022), esp. chap. 5, where she also cites Solie's and Cusick's work. I am especially indebted to Cusick's ideas of the "cultural obedience" and "cultural resistance" of music performance.

[12] I borrow the idea of "imagined community" from political scientist Benedict Anderson's seminal book *Imagined Communities: Reflections on the Origin and Spread of Nationalism* (London: Verso, 1983).

whose music they played was real and encouraged in the eighteenth century, and it should therefore inform scholarship today. It extended, furthermore, beyond music to discursive treatments of embodiment more generally in the Enlightenment. In the preface to his *Traité des sensations* (1754), for instance, Abbé Étienne Bonnot de Condillac instructed his reader explicitly "to put yourself exactly in the place of the statue which we are going to observe."[13] I argue that the unique intersection of Hungarian dances in the music market with textual descriptions of Romani performances of them invited a similar identification. The stark differences of gender, ethnicity, class, and professional status between keyboard players and Romani musicians, moreover, opened up a range of potential and sometimes contradictory subject positions for relatively privileged women, from the culturally obedient and affirming to the more resistive and transgressive: expressing hegemony, fostering sympathy, defying containment.

Reading and Playing Diverging Texts

On Christmas Day 1784, Joseph Stahel advertised Bengraf's *Trois Divertissemens pour le Clavecin Seul, avec un Ballet Hongrois* for sale in the *Wiener Zeitung*.[14] Bengraf himself included a note on his "Hungarian ballet" explaining that he had composed the music originally for a masked ball of Szekler hussars and then adapted it to the harpsichord as best he could, although he admitted that "this kind of national dance has so much that is unique, in its execution and accompaniment as well as in its inventiveness, that one must hear it in order to grasp its genius and energy."[15] Bengraf's disclaimer notwithstanding, written descriptions of the defining characteristics of Hungarian dances appeared with some frequency in conjunction with published versions of them around 1800: as notes or brief forewords to sets of dances and in periodical articles

---

[13] As given in Elisabeth Le Guin, *Boccherini's Body: An Essay in Carnal Musicology* (Berkeley: University of California Press, 2006), 258. See also pp. 7 and 14.

[14] *WZ*, 25 December 1784, 2943 col. 1.

[15] As given just above the music of the "Ballet Hongrois" in A-Wgm, VII 3445, as well as in Papp, *Hungarian Dances*, 25: "J'avois composé le ballet suivant pour une masquerade d'Houssarts dits Szeklers, et je le donne maintenant au jour, accommodé au Clavecin autant qu'il etoit possible, cette sorte de danse nationale ayant tant de Singulier aussi bien dans l'execution et dans l'accompagnement, que dans l'invention, qu'il faut l'ecouter pour en saisir le genie et l'energie. Les notes marquées d'un / demandent un accent plus fort."

that either reviewed such sets or included music from them to illustrate points made in the descriptions (see appendix).

Despite their varying lengths and amounts of detail, these accounts all present quite similar information to readers. Hungarian dances—or national music as a more general category—reflect the unique character of the nation and its inhabitants: Hungarians and their dance music tend to be proud and heroic but also mournful and sometimes pathetic. At the same time, much Hungarian music is artless, simple, cheerful, and even gentle; one of the descriptions (appendix text A) ties these qualities explicitly to melody. The same idea is implicit in two other accounts (texts B and D), which emphasize that simple music or melodic figures are constantly varied in performance by Romani musicians—"bare nature lacking in art and science," "the crudest class of people," "the children of nature" (texts A, B, and D, respectively)— who are repeatedly identified as Hungary's national musicians. "Almost all the pieces played in Hungarian national circles," readers are told, "are the products of the moment's imagination." They are "neither the product of proper musicians, nor are they set down in notation." (Both quotations are from text B.) Perhaps incongruously, given the reported improvisatory abandon of the musicians, the author of text C underscores the metrical regularity of Hungarian dances, which, he explains, emphasize downbeats; according to two other accounts (texts A and B), phrase divisions often occur on weak beats.[16] Authors also praise the "expressive harmony" of Hungarian dances (quotation from text B), which is manifest through modulations, often to distant keys, and through a preference for the minor mode, or at least brief digressions to it when the home key is major. Finally, two descriptions (texts B and D) relate how dances themselves, which may be slow or fast, are performed. These same two accounts refer with more or less detail to the instruments used to play Hungarian dances: violins, *basso*, and hammered dulcimer. Text D, furthermore, describes how players of the dulcimer often let their mallets tremble on long notes, producing one of the most iconic sounds of Hungarian national music. The "favorite trills in thirds, fourths, fifths, and sometimes also in sixths" mentioned in text C may be a reference

---

[16] "die Einschnitte und Absätze auf kurze Tacttheile [spelled 'Takttheile' in text B] fallen." As Stephanie Vial has noted, terms such as "Einschnitt" and "Absatz," which she explains "are used to describe the interior divisions of the musical period," are difficult to translate and are used variably by eighteenth-century writers. See Stephanie D. Vial, *The Art of Musical Phrasing in the Eighteenth Century: Punctuating the Classical "Period,"* Eastman Studies in Music 55 (Rochester, NY: University of Rochester Press, 2008), xvi. I thank Professor Vial for her additional help in translating and understanding this passage.

to this same performance practice, as may be the *Bebung* markings on the final notes of some phrases in Franz Paul Rigler's *12 Ungarische Tänze fürs Forte Piano* (before 1796; Rigler's prefatory note to this collection is given as text A, and four dances from his set were included as a supplement to text B).[17]

In an article in the *Allgemeine musikalische Zeitung* in March 1810, the Pest correspondent to the journal captured much of this information in a very poetic description of Hungarian music:

> Every nation that is still really a nation has its own national music, or at least something national in its music [...]. [...] The Hungarian dances much and often: his national music is therefore first and foremost dance music. It is gloomy, plaintive, enraptured, but also raging and inspiring to war. Hungarians love minor keys most of all, like the Russians, and if a dance begins in a major key, it soon turns to the minor, and its transitions meander wonderfully through nothing but semitones. [...] In his dances, the Hungarian can just as wildly rejoice as cry, depending how the chord of his feelings is struck. [...] The harmony itself unfolds without [following] any rules of music, because the so-called Hungarian lyre players, namely the Gypsies, understand nothing of them and are merely artists of nature.[18]

Despite their lack of formal musical training, the author admitted that the Romani musicians' "brilliance," "talent," and "their method, their precision in their own expressions and transitions, which they perform purely by ear and according to their very own feeling, cannot easily be imitated by any other

---

[17] The *Bebung* markings in the original undated manuscript that Papp used to prepare his edition of *Hungarian Dances* were not retained in the dances included in the supplement to the 28 May 1800 issue of the *Allgemeine musikalische Zeitung*. Rigler died in 1796.

[18] "Nachrichten: Pest in Ungarn, d. 6ten Febr.," *Allgemeine musikalische Zeitung* 12, no. 24 (14 March 1810): cols. 369–71: "Jede Nation, die wirklich noch eine Nation ist, hat ihre Nationalmusik, oder wenigstens etwas Nationales in ihrer Musik [...]. [...] Der Ungar tanzt sehr viel und sehr gern: seine Nationalmusik ist also zunächst Tanzmusik. Diese ist finster, klagend, schwärmerisch, aber dann auch stürmend und zum Kriege begeisternd. Die Ungarn lieben die Moll-Tonarten vorzüglich, gleich den Russen; und wenn auch ein Tanz in Dur anfängt, so fällt er doch bald wieder in Moll, und ihre Uebergänge schlängeln sich in lauter halben Tönen wunderbar in einander. [...] Der Ungar kann bey seinem Tanze eben sowol wild jauchzen, als weinen, je nachdem die Saite seines Gefühls berührt wird. [...] Der Zusammenklang der Musik selbst geschieht ohne alle Gesetze der Tonkunst, denn die eigentlichen sogenannten ungarischen Lyranten, nämlich die Zigeuner, verstehen nichts von alle dem und sind blos Naturalisten." The article also includes substantial information about vocal and theatrical music in Hungary.

practitioner of music, even if he were really a virtuoso."[19] The sentiment of the correspondent's comment clearly echoes Bengraf's note about his *Ballet Hongrois* over two decades earlier; it perhaps explains, furthermore, why the journal's correspondent did not offer his readers any notated examples of Hungarian dances in-text or as a supplement to his report. Indeed, unlike the accounts included in the appendix, the Pest correspondent's description is not linked to any published sets of Hungarian dances, yet his assessment that Romani performance practices cannot readily be reproduced—or at least captured in notation—is clearly borne out by such collections.

The descriptions in the appendix make a direct connection between the repertoire and performance practices of Hungarian Romani musicians, on the one hand, and the keyboard dances for amateur consumption to which the accounts are linked, on the other, yet the stylistic characteristics of the two corpora diverge quite drastically. In most cases, authors note or imply the care composers have taken to imitate the original music (texts A, B, and D). In a more drastic move, the author of the preface to (and the composer of) the four volumes of *Originelle Ungarische Nationaltänze* consciously and explicitly effaced his agency, signing his preamble simply "The Collector" ("Der Sammler"; text C). But even in this multivolume collection of ninety-three dances, the predominance of the major mode coupled with simplistic harmonic frameworks and repetitive formal structures stand in stark contrast to the wild improvisation, striking tonal organization, and extreme virtuosity reported in descriptions of the original repertoire and its performance.

Musicologist Géza Papp has compiled extensive bibliographies of Hungarian dances published in Vienna in the late eighteenth and early nineteenth centuries—and edited hundreds of these dances—greatly facilitating access to and analysis of this repertoire, much of which I have examined in detail.[20] Hungarian dances were overwhelmingly published in sets, including anywhere from six, eight, or twelve dances to as many as twenty-two, twenty-four, or twenty-eight. The collections are invariably of the *Folge*, or series, type, meaning that they contain dances all of one kind (here, Hungarian

---

[19] "Nachrichten: Pest in Ungarn," col. 371: "Diese Leute besitzen aber wirklich oftmals etwas Genialisches, und kein geringes, ganz eigenthümlich modificirtes Musiktalent; und ihre Methode, ihre Präcision in den ihnen eigenen Ausdrücken und Transitionen, die sie blos nach dem Gehör und nach dem ihnen ganz eigenen Gefühl ausführen, sind von jedem andern Musikübenden, sey er auch wirklich ein Virtuos, nicht leicht nachzuahmen."

[20] See, for instance, Papp, "Die Quellen der 'Verbunkos-Musik'"; and Papp, *Hungarian Dances*. My analytical comments in this section are adapted, with permission of the publisher, from my article "Reconsidering an Early Exoticism: Viennese Adaptations of Hungarian-Gypsy Music around 1800," *Eighteenth-Century Music* 6, no. 2 (September 2009): 161–81.

dances as opposed to waltzes or Ländler, for instance) and that they do not betray a particular overall tonal organization; keys change from one dance to the next without a discernible pattern.[21] From the 1780s until about 1810, furthermore, the stylistic characteristics of published Hungarian dances remained in many respects quite constant, despite a modest trend toward increasing complexity after the turn of the century, as may be noted in contemporary music for domestic consumption more generally. In summarizing the features of this repertoire, I have not restricted myself only to dances that were directly connected to descriptions of Hungarian national music, because their style does not differ meaningfully from that of dances which circulated without being explicitly linked to such accounts.

Despite contemporary assertions of the Hungarian preference for the minor mode, published dances are overwhelmingly in major keys, with individual collections including anywhere from one and a half to eleven times more major- than minor-mode dances. Neither mode, furthermore, is correlated with particular tempi, where these are explicitly given, and slow and fast tempi occur with approximately the same frequency. With fewer than a handful of exceptions, the favored keys in both modes are those with signatures containing no more than three sharps or flats. Tonally, published dances are devoid of the strange, rampant, and expressive modulations described in coeval accounts of Romani performances. When tonicizations or brief modulations are present at all, they are limited almost exclusively to diatonically related keys. The harmony of many published dances, especially from the 1780s and 1790s, consists entirely of alternations between tonic and dominant chords, and even in cases where the chordal vocabulary is enriched with predominant functioning chords, chromatic chords are very rare.

Parallel to the lack of "transitions meander[ing] wonderfully through nothing but semitones," the impression that the melodies of published dances "are the products of the moment's imagination" is typically completely absent. Four-measure phrases are ubiquitous, and they are combined into eight-measure periods, or less commonly sentences or hybrid forms, framed by repeat signs. Many dances do not extend beyond sixteen notated

---

[21] On organizational strategies in dance sets, see Walburga Litschauer and Walter Deutsch, *Schubert und das Tanzvergnügen* (Vienna: Verlag Holzhausen, 1997), 109–24; on the *Folge* specifically, see 123–24. In the *Kette*, or chain, type of set, dances of a single kind are all in the same key; in a *Zyklus*, or cycle, of dances, successive pieces reveal a clear key scheme and are meant to be performed as a unit.

measures, though additional eight-measure units, sometimes labeled as trios or codas, are more common after about 1800. Regardless, however, of the total length of a given dance, its construction is repetitive and modular. A similar structure is mirrored at the measure level, where short figures typically contained within a single beat and constructed of eighth and/or sixteenth notes are combined in succession or repeated sequentially. Figures proceeding by skip (chordal arpeggiations or wide, usually chordal, leaps) or by step (scalar or turn motives) are both very common. Anticipations, appoggiaturas, and figures employing lower neighbor notes, both diatonic and chromatic, are also prevalent. Especially at cadential points, lower-neighbor figures recall the distinctive melodic and rhythmic profiles of the Hungarian *bokázó* ("heel-clicking" or, literally translated, "ankling") figure, one of the few stylistic elements of published dances suggesting their putative origin.[22]

The simple melodies of published dances from the 1780s and 1790s were ornamented typically with only occasional grace notes. After the turn of the century, however, embellishments proliferated in many dances to include not only grace notes but mordents and trills along with triplet and thirty-second-note figurations, whether in an effort toward greater stylistic imitation of Romani ornamentation practices or simply as a reflection of a more general trend toward increased decoration in keyboard music. Along with dotted rhythms, especially when deployed in chains, these figurations enliven later dances and lend them greater color and character, despite the persistent simplicity of harmonies and accompaniment patterns. Similarly, although published Hungarian dances are invariably in 2/4 time, syncopated figures often disrupt their metrical regularity. Especially in dances published after about 1800, the effect of syncopation is often created or reinforced through notated dynamic accents, though Bengraf included these in his *Ballet Hongrois* (as he explained in the note he appended to it) as early as 1784.

Given the size of the published repertoire, selecting representative examples of it is daunting. Nonetheless, examples 3.1 and 3.2 may serve to illustrate common stylistic features of earlier and later dances, respectively. The brief third dance of Bengraf's *XII. Magyar Tántzok Klávicembalomra*

---

[22] For a meticulous analysis of the *bokázó* and other melodic figures ubiquitous in published Hungarian dances, see Csilla Pethő, "*Style Hongrois*: Hungarian Elements in the Works of Haydn, Beethoven, Weber and Schubert," *Studia Musicologica* 41, nos. 1–3 (2000): 199–284.

Example 3.1. Joseph Bengraf, *XII. Magyar Tántzok Klávicembalomra Valók/ XII. Danses Hongroises pour le Clavecin ou Piano-Forte*, no. 3 (Vienna: Artaria, 1790). Transcribed with permission of the HUN-REN Research Centre for the Humanities, Institute for Musicology, from the critical edition prepared by Géza Papp, *Hungarian Dances 1784–1810*, Musicalia Danubiana 7 (Budapest: Magyar Tudományos Akadémia, Zenetudományi Intézet, 1986), 67–68.

Valók/XII. Danses Hongroises pour le Clavecin ou Piano-Forte of 1790 (ex. 3.1; no copy of the version advertised by Traeg in 1784 is extant) consists of two eight-measure periods, each of which is repeated. The first period remains in the home key of A major, with tonic and dominant chords alternating to support a melody that descends from the fifth to the first scale degree, embellished with neighbor-note and *échappée* figures. The second period opens in the relative minor, the tonic chord of which eventually functions as a predominant to facilitate a cadence in the home key. This period is governed by tonic chords and features scalar melodic motion with

Example 3.2. *22 Originelle Ungarische Nationaltänze für das Clavier*, vol. 1, no. 1 (Vienna: Chemische Druckerey, 1806/1807). Transcribed with permission of the HUN-REN Research Centre for the Humanities, Institute for Musicology, from Géza Papp, ed., *Hungarian Dances 1784–1810*, Musicalia Danubiana 7 (Budapest: Magyar Tudományos Akadémia, Zenetudományi Intézet, 1986), 208–9.

(*continued*)

Example 3.2. Continued.

expressive leaps closing each four-measure phrase. Syncopation throughout this short, graceful dance coupled with a slow tempo lend it a somewhat wistful character, and the left-hand accompaniment pattern may evoke the *esztam* figure typical of many Hungarian national dances, in which the second violin and *basso* support the first violin with an "oompah" effect by playing alternating eighth notes.[23]

This same accompaniment pattern—the "commonplace and monotonous bass" derided in the *Musikalische Korrespondenz der teutschen Filarmonischen Gesellschaft*'s review of Bengraf's dances—is featured throughout the first dance of the first volume of *Originelle Ungarische Nationaltänze* of 1806 or 1807 (ex. 3.2). Indeed, despite its much greater

---

[23] On traditional accompaniment patterns, see David E. Schneider, *Bartók, Hungary, and the Renewal of Tradition: Case Studies in the Intersection of Modernity and Nationality* (Berkeley: University of California Press, 2006), 21–24.

length and variety of melodic material, this keyboard piece shares many characteristics with Bengraf's earlier dance: modular form consisting of a succession of eight-measure units, each of which is repeated; major mode with two brief digressions to the relative minor; and harmonization exclusively with tonic and dominant chords. The duple meter, however, is much more downbeat-oriented; along with the "maestoso" marking and opening dotted rhythms marked *forte*, the character overall is proud and heroic. Although some of the scalar and turn figures in the melody resemble those in Bengraf's dance, they are embellished with occasional grace notes, and the triplet figuration in measures 13–15 is particularly expressive, leading beautifully into the dotted rhythms and melodic augmented second at the direct modulation to C minor in measure 17. The decoration of the cadences, in particular, renders them much more interesting than Bengraf's culminating bare spondees. Cadential *bokázó* figures (mm. 8, 16, 24, and 36) alternate with trills (mm. 12, 20, and 28, as indicated by the asterisks and cross-hatching, discussed in more detail below), and the final cadence features a scalar flourish in thirty-second notes (m. 40).

Despite their appeal, published Hungarian dances were clearly far removed from the strikingly exotic music and virtuosic, improvisatory performances of Romani musicians described in contemporary accounts. Perhaps, as Bengraf opined, the "genius" and "energy" of the original performances simply could not be captured in notation. Or, as Papp has suggested, perhaps composers writing Hungarian dances for publication in Vienna—those he refers to as "educated musicians"—were simply not well acquainted with the original repertoire, which was not notated.[24] Moreover, much as musicologist Ian Woodfield has observed about the popular "Hindostannie airs" that I mentioned in the introduction to this chapter, "striving for authenticity was inherently problematic. The tension between the desire to remain faithful to the [. . .] originals and the need to present something that was acceptable as being in good taste in European terms threw up musical dilemmas that were impossible to resolve."[25] The world of Hungarian Romani music described in eighteenth-century accounts undoubtedly fascinated readers at least in part because it was so different from their own. But while one can easily understand the thrill of reading about "artists of nature" playing pieces that are "the

---

[24] Papp, *Hungarian Dances*, 29.
[25] Ian Woodfield, *Music of the Raj: A Social and Economic History of Music in Late Eighteenth-Century Anglo-Indian Society* (Oxford: Oxford University Press, 2000), 177.

product of the moment's imagination," unbound by "the rules of music," it is harder to imagine a close imitation of such music in a Viennese home.

The stylistic characteristics of the published repertoire, in contrast, made it extremely marketable, catering to the tastes and abilities of amateurs in a way that more faithful imitations of the original music could not have. Although we lack specific information about the individuals who acquired collections of Hungarian dances, it is reasonable to assume that they were primarily the same ones who played other keyboard music of similar difficulty and function: women and girls. As numerous scholars have documented, women were the principal consumers of keyboard music in the eighteenth and early nineteenth centuries, regardless of whether a given publication was overtly marketed to them. In this sense, as musicologist Matthew Head has observed, explicit dedications to women on the title pages of music scores were redundant.[26] Rather, the stylistic simplicity of keyboard music was the primary indicator that women were its intended market, for "easiness," with its associations to beauty, charm, and naturalness, was synonymous with femininity itself. Many of the markers of "easiness" that Head has identified— "keys without many sharps and flats, melody-centered styles, and avoidance of both figuration (however easily it might fall under the hands) and thick, reinforced textures"[27]—are in evidence in collections of Hungarian dances published for the pleasure of amateurs. Perhaps surprisingly, given their at least ostensible origins in the practices of professional male musicians, published Hungarian dances were thus coded female.

The cultivation of simplicity in keyboard music for domestic enjoyment was symptomatic of the broader construction of privileged femininity in the eighteenth century, which prized modesty and disdained overt labor, even at music. Beyond reflecting women's musical containment,[28] however, the easiness of the repertoire also reflected the very real limitations of the typical

---

[26] Matthew Head, "'If the Pretty Little Hand Won't Stretch': Music for the Fair Sex in Eighteenth-Century Germany," *Journal of the American Musicological Society* 52, no. 2 (Summer 1999): 208. Head's chapter is reprinted with slight revision in his monograph *Sovereign Feminine: Music and Gender in Eighteenth-Century Germany* (Berkeley: University of California Press, 2013), 48–83. I have also drawn attention to women and girls as the primary performers of Hungarian dances for keyboard in my chapter "In Vienna 'Only Waltzes Get Printed': The Decline and Transformation of the *Contredanse Hongroise* in the Early Nineteenth Century," in *Consuming Music: Individuals, Institutions, Communities, 1730–1830*, ed. Emily H. Green and Catherine Mayes, Eastman Studies in Music 138 (Rochester, NY: University of Rochester Press, 2017), 166. I thank the publisher for allowing me to reproduce a very small portion of that text here.

[27] Head, "'If the Pretty Little Hand Won't Stretch,'" 214.

[28] I borrow the term and notion of female "containment" from Richard Leppert, *Music and Image: Domesticity, Ideology and Socio-Cultural Formation in Eighteenth-Century England* (Cambridge: Cambridge University Press, 1988); and Head, "'If the Pretty Little Hand Won't Stretch.'"

amateur's skills, in Vienna as elsewhere. In May 1808, in the first month of its publication, the Viennese *Vaterländische Blätter für den österreichischen Kaiserstaat* offered an "overview of the current state of music in Vienna," about which the periodical raved: "Nowhere is this divine art so widely pursued, so beloved, and so enthusiastically practiced as here; nowhere will one find among music-lovers (*Dilettanten*) so many consummately accomplished performers on all instruments, some of whom could sit alongside professors of this art, indeed some even surpass them."[29] Yet only a few years earlier, the *Allgemeine musikalische Zeitung* had offered a more measured—and undoubtedly more realistic—portrayal of amateur music-making in the capital city. Like the article in the *Vaterländische Blätter*, which noted that "it really is a rarity to see a boy or girl from an educated middle-class household to whom this art [music] has remained a stranger,"[30] the article in the *AMZ* declared that "there are few cities where the love of music [*Liebhaberey zur Musik*] is so universal as here. Everyone plays, everyone learns music." Yet according to the unsigned report's author, "really good amateurs [*brave Dilettanten*]" were "no longer as common. One sees music as something easy that can be learned in passing, one thinks one can do everything right away, and then one excuses oneself at the end with the word *Dilettant* and views the whole thing as a matter of style and good manners. [...] Every girl, whether she has talent or not, must learn to play the keyboard or to sing" in order to make an advantageous matrimonial match.[31]

Amateurs' reported perception of music as merely a fashionable pastime and their attendant lack of industry were not wholly to blame for their limited abilities, which also reflected the low level of much music instruction. In October 1792, for instance, "a young man with the best recommendations"

---

[29] "Uebersicht des gegenwärtigen Zustandes der Tonkunst in Wien," *Vaterländische Blätter für den österreichischen Kaiserstaat*, 27 May 1808, 39: "nirgends wird diese göttliche Kunst so ausgebreitet betrieben, so sehr geliebt, und so eifrig ausgeübt, wie hier; nirgends wird man unter den Liebhabern (Dilettanten) auf fast allen Instrumenten so viele vollendete Ausübende finden, deren manche sich den Professoren dieser Kunst an die Seite setzen dürfen, ja wohl einige sie sogar noch übertreffen." David Wyn Jones, *Music in Vienna 1700, 1800, 1900* (Woodbridge: Boydell Press, 2016), 117, has suggested that this article was likely penned by Ignaz von Mosel.

[30] "Uebersicht des gegenwärtigen Zustandes der Tonkunst," 39: "wirklich ist es eine Art von Seltenheit geworden, einen Jüngling oder ein Mädchen aus einem Hause des gebildeten Mittelstandes zu sehen, welchem diese Kunst fremd geblieben wäre."

[31] "Nachrichten: Kurze Uebersicht des Bedeutendsten aus dem gesammten jetzigen Musikwesen in Wien," *Allgemeine musikalische Zeitung* 3, no. 4 (22 October 1800): cols. 65–66: "Es wird wenig Städte geben, wo die Liebhaberey zur Musik so allgemein ist, als hier. Alles spielt, alles lernt Musik. Natürlich, dass es unter der grossen Menge auch sehr brave Dilettanten giebt: doch sind sie nicht mehr so häufig als sonst. Man sieht die Musik für zu leicht an, als wenn sie so im Vorübergehn zu erlernen wäre, glaubt gleich alles zu können, entschuldigt sich am Ende mit dem Worte *Dilettant*, und nimmt das Ganze mehr als Sache der Galanterie und des guten Tons. [...] Jedes feine Mädchen, habe sie Talent oder nicht, muss Klavierspielen oder singen lernen [...]."

took out an advertisement in the *Wiener Zeitung* in hope of securing a position in which he could put his talents to good use; he could, he specified, "play the keyboard and violin well, such that he can give music lessons," but he was additionally well versed in "arithmetic and writing, hair dressing and barbering [...], as well as in surgery."[32] Similarly, in two successive issues of the same newspaper in March 1798, a "single, thirty-year-old man" with experience as a tutor and a secretary, "equally knowledgeable in Latin, German, and French and able to give music lessons as well," sought a position where he could apply his skills.[33] Such advertisements suggest that music was often taught by jacks-of-all-trades rather than by professional specialists, not least because a conservatory was not established in Vienna until 1817. Despite the relative abundance of evidence about highly skilled teachers—Mozart, Wagenseil, Porpora, and Beethoven, for instance—and the accomplishments of their outstanding pupils, they were clearly the exception rather than the rule. An "overview of the state of music in Königsberg" in the *Allgemeine musikalische Zeitung* in 1809 confirms, furthermore, that this circumstance was not unique to Vienna. The author of the article did not hesitate to lay blame for the poor state of music in the city at the feet of bad teachers, bemoaning that "people who cannot even properly write an *Angloise* give music lessons, often cheaply enough. I recently attended a music lesson. The teacher explained to the student the difference between major and minor: 'Where crosses are drawn, that's major, where Bs, that's minor.' (!) This man was paid three *Groschen* for the hour."[34]

---

[32] *WZ*, 3 October 1792, 2695 col. 2: "Dienstsuchender. Ein junger Mensch mit den besten Empfehlungen, welcher gut Clavier und Violin spielt, so daß er in der Musik Unterricht geben kann, im Rechnen und Schreiben geübt, frisiren und barbieren kann, wie auch in der Chyrurgie erfahren ist, wünscht als Hausoffizier, oder seinen Talenten nach angestellet zu werden. Es ist im Bischofhof beym Portier zu erfragen."

[33] *WZ*, 3 March 1798, 619 col. 1; and 7 March 1798, 652 col. 2–653 col. 1: "Anstellung Suchender. Ein unverheiratheter 30jähriger Mann, der bereits mehrere Jahre theils als Erzieher, theils als Secretair in herrschaftlichen Häusern gestanden, der lateinisch- deutsch- und französischen Sprachen gleich kundig, wie auch in der Musik Unterricht zu geben fähig ist; wünschet entweder in der Stadt, oder allenfalls auf dem Lande auf gleiche, oder sonst einer seiner Fähigkeit angemessene Art angestellt zu werden. Zu welchem Ende er mit den besten Zeugnissen sowohl seines Wohlverhaltens, als seiner Kenntnisse von Seiten mehrerer hohen und ansehnlichen Personen versehen, in jedem Erforderungsfalle sich ausweisen wird. Ist sich darüber in der Löwelstrasse Nr. 16 bey Hrn. Fritsch anzufragen."

[34] M. † Z., "Uebersicht des Zustandes der Musik in Königsberg," *Allgemeine musikalische Zeitung* 11, no. 40 (5 July 1809): col. 633: "An dem schlechten Zustande der Tonkunst, trotz aller Liebe, die im Ganzen dafür herrscht, sind sicher die vielen schlechten Lehrer hauptsächlich Schuld. Man sollte diese, wie schon die liebenswürdige Nina von Engelbrunner meynt, wie die tollen Hunde todtschlagen. Menschen, die nicht eine Angloise richtig auf Noten setzen können, geben Unterricht in der Musik, oft wohlfeil genug." The footnote appended to this sentence has the hapless teacher misnaming and misinterpreting the meaning of sharps and flats: "Ich wohnte vor kurzem einem Musik-Unterricht bey. Der Lehrer erklärte dem Schüler den Unterschied zwischen dur und moll. 'Wo Kreutze vorgezeichnet sind, das ist dur, wo Been, das ist moll.' (!) Dieser Mann erhielt für die Stunde 3 Groschen."

As musicologist Katalin Komlós has reminded us, in the eighteenth century, Mozart's keyboard and chamber music were widely regarded as beyond the reach of the average amateur. Even Koželuch, whom the Viennese *Journal des Luxus und der Moden* praised in 1788 as the composer who "for the lady dilettantes [...] counts the most on the pianoforte," had been criticized only two years earlier in another Viennese magazine for the demands his music placed on amateurs. Although "his compositions bespeak an excellent mind, [...] no other fault is to be found with them than that they are too difficult."[35] Given the context within which amateurs typically cultivated keyboard music—as a primarily feminine adornment taught by instructors who must often have been barely more skilled than their students—it is easy to understand why. Much like Mozart's sets of variations, several of which Komlós notes were published in simplified and truncated versions to accommodate the needs of amateur keyboardists,[36] Hungarian dances circulated as mere shadows of the music played by Romani performers, placing them within the grasp of amateurs and, as I explore below, enabling a range of subject positions and cultural work through their domestic performance.

Hegemony, Sympathy, Defiance

Matthew Head has observed that musical "easiness" may be understood as a reflection of a generalized eighteenth-century aesthetic, one that was neither necessarily gendered nor negative. For instance, as Head has written:

> Johann Mattheson's remarks on the foundations of melody in *Der vollkommene Capellmeister* (1739) furnish a close to comprehensive inventory of what was musically at stake in "easiness" in music for the fair sex: the avoidance of excessive melodic embellishment and of rapid changes in meter, tempo, and register; restriction to diatonic harmony; uniformity

---

[35] *Journal des Luxus und der Moden*, 1788, 230: "In der Liebhaberei der Damen gilt auf dem Pianoforte vor allen Koželuch." *Pfeffer und Salz*, 1786: "Seine Compositionen verrathen indessen einen vortreflichen Kopf, und man kann ihnen keine andre Fehler ausstellen, als dass sie zu schwer sind." Both passages are given and translated in Katalin Komlós, *Fortepianos and Their Music: Germany, Austria, and England, 1760–1800* (Oxford: Clarendon Press, 1995), 110. Her comments on the difficulty of Mozart's music are on pp. 112–13.

[36] Komlós, *Fortepianos and Their Music*, 113–14; and Katalin Komlós, "'Ich Praeludirte und Spielte Variazionen': Mozart the Fortepianist," in *Perspectives on Mozart Performance*, ed. R. Larry Todd and Peter Williams (Cambridge: Cambridge University Press, 1991), 42–43.

rather than diversity; and cultivation of "noble simplicity." A rejection of conspicuous compositional artifice underwrites these elements.[37]

Indeed, as musicologists Ruth Katz and Carl Dahlhaus have summarized, the notion "that a 'genuine emotion' manifests itself simply, and that simplicity guarantees the 'genuineness' of an emotion was the central thesis of the aesthetics of the Enlightenment."[38] Nonetheless, as Head has argued, the "gender-specific deployment" of markers of easiness in music composed for the largely female amateur keyboard market "summoned a rhetoric of deprofessionalization of female music-making that was in place even prior to the emergence of the repertory."[39] Similarly, the straightforwardness of published Hungarian dances, especially in contrast to the dazzling virtuosity of Romani musicians, may be read as part of a broader propensity to minimize the complexity of non–Western European music "in keeping," as historian Vanessa Agnew has explained, "with prevailing racial and anthropological theories."[40] That is, the harmonic and melodic simplicity, repetitiveness, and lack of development typical of published Hungarian dances may reflect a fundamental conceptualization not only of Hungarian national music but of the peoples and cultures of Eastern Europe more generally as less cultivated than their Western counterparts.

Stylistically, published Hungarian dances evince a kinship to the eighteenth-century pastorella—a type of Christmas church music for vocal and instrumental forces common throughout Central Europe—as well as to pieces in the *Volkston*. In the context of his work on the pastorella, musicologist Geoffrey Chew coined the term *stylus rusticanus* to describe a topic typical of this genre, which "include[s] fast 2/4 time, unison passages, melodies with broken-chord figuration, 'Lydian' sharpened fourths, and other unusual chromaticism [... and] extended pedal points."[41] Musicologist Steven

---

[37] Head, "'If the Pretty Little Hand Won't Stretch,'" 214.

[38] Ruth Katz and Carl Dahlhaus, eds., *Contemplating Music: Source Readings in the Aesthetics of Music*, vol. 2, *Import* (Stuyvesant, NY: Pendragon Press, 1989), 114, as quoted in Erin Helyard, *Clementi and the Woman at the Piano: Virtuosity and the Marketing of Music in Eighteenth-Century London*, Oxford University Studies in the Enlightenment (Liverpool: Liverpool University Press, 2022), 145.

[39] Head, "'If the Pretty Little Hand Won't Stretch,'" 214.

[40] Vanessa Agnew, "Encounter Music in Oceania: Cross-Cultural Musical Exchange in Eighteenth- and Early Nineteenth-Century Voyage Accounts," in *The Cambridge History of World Music*, ed. Philip V. Bohlman (Cambridge: Cambridge University Press, 2013), 192.

[41] Geoffrey Chew, "The Austrian Pastorella and the *Stylus Rusticanus*: Comic and Pastoral Elements in Austrian Music, 1750–1800," in *Music in Eighteenth-Century Austria*, ed. David Wyn Jones (Cambridge: Cambridge University Press, 1996), 140–41. See also Geoffrey Chew, "Pastorella," in *Grove Music Online*, www.oxfordmusiconline.com (accessed 7 December 2022).

Zohn has noted that Telemann's Polish style (what he calls the *style polonais*), which shares many similarities with music *alla turca* and with published Hungarian dances from the eighteenth century, could well be subsumed into Chew's *stylus rusticanus*.[42] This topic, furthermore, resonates strongly with J. A. P. Schulz's description of the *Volkston* in the preface to his own three-volume anthology of *Lieder im Volkston*, which he explained prized the unaffected ("ungesucht") and artless ("kunstlos"), qualities that were reflected in "melodies of the utmost simplicity and comprehensibility."[43] As musicologist David Gramit has argued, the simplicity and artlessness of the *Volkston* as a style or topic functioned not merely as an imitation of the music of the folk but as a translation of their perceived lack of cultivation,[44] in Schulz's case underscoring differences of status and power between the composer and the consumers of his music, on the one hand, and those whose idioms they ostensibly reproduced, on the other. The overlap of topics used to represent Eastern European national musics as well as pastoral and folk ones more generally similarly emphasizes, to use historian Larry Wolff's term, Western Europe's "invention" of Eastern Europe during the Enlightenment as its rustic and unrefined social, cultural, political, and economic complement, a vast expanse of land where time stood still and progress was scant.[45] Wolff's description of the perception of Eastern Europe as a preeminent "folkloric domain of song and dance" was one important aspect of its larger definition, for where better could folk musics and dances, widely considered the most ancient arts, flourish than in lands and among peoples who were themselves rooted in the past?[46]

---

[42] Steven Zohn, *Music for a Mixed Taste: Style, Genre, and Meaning in Telemann's Instrumental Works* (Oxford: Oxford University Press, 2008), chap. 9. Erika Buurman has also identified similar "rustic" stylistic features in Beethoven's Ländler; see Erika Buurman, *The Viennese Ballroom in the Age of Beethoven* (Cambridge: Cambridge University Press, 2022), 50–51.

[43] J[ohann] A[braham] P[eter] Schulz, preface to *Lieder im Volkston, bey dem Claviere zu singen*, vol. 2 (Berlin: George Jakob Decker, 1785): "Zu dem Ende habe ich [...] mich in den Melodien selbst der höchsten Simplicität und Faßlichkeit beflissen [...]."

[44] David Gramit, *Cultivating Music: The Aspirations, Interests, and Limits of German Musical Culture, 1770–1848* (Berkeley: University of California Press, 2002), 65. Gramit's argument resonates strongly with Mary Hunter's approach in "The *Alla Turca* Style in the Late Eighteenth Century: Race and Gender in the Symphony and the Seraglio," in *The Exotic in Western Music*, ed. Jonathan Bellman (Boston: Northeastern University Press, 1998), 43–73, from which I borrow the ideas and terminology of "imitation" and "translation."

[45] Larry Wolff, *Inventing Eastern Europe: The Map of Civilization on the Mind of the Enlightenment* (Stanford, CA: Stanford University Press, 1994).

[46] The quotation is from Wolff, *Inventing Eastern Europe*, 331. I discuss the translation into music of the Western European perception of Eastern Europe in detail in my article "Eastern European National Music as Concept and Commodity at the Turn of the Nineteenth Century," *Music & Letters* 95, no. 1 (2014): 70–91. Some of the material here is taken from this article, with permission of the publisher.

In his introduction to the *Allgemeine musikalische Zeitung*'s article on Hungarian national dances in 1800 (given—without the introduction—in the appendix as text B), the journal's editor Friedrich Rochlitz distinguished between national dances and their music "as they are among the people [*Volk*] themselves" and "how our high society now sets to music and dances this and that," concluding perspicaciously that "one nation takes this and that from the other, but always combines what is its own with it, and thereby (as happens with true amalgamation) brings its own more clearly to light."[47] Several decades later, in an article on national literature, poetry, and music, the composer, conductor, and writer Eduard von Lannoy astutely underscored the power dynamics at play in such "amalgamation":

> In most modern pieces of music one finds polonaises, boleros, Scottish and other melodies, and important collections, for example in the archive of the Gesellschaft der Musikfreunde in Vienna, have already been organized; nevertheless more remains unknown, and the real character of these folk melodies was mostly obliterated by those who collected them, because they wanted to improve and supposedly refine [them] instead of writing down the notes exactly and unchanged as the wandering musician played them or the farm girl sang them.[48]

The result of such "improvement" and "refinement" was the assimilation of Hungarian dances into what musicologist Peter van der Merwe has described as the "polka family," a "family of musically similar dances in lively 2/4 time," which predated the advent of the polka itself in the 1830s. Like

---

[47] Friedrich Rochlitz, introduction to "Ueber die Nationaltänze der Ungarn," *Allgemeine musikalische Zeitung* 2, no. 35 (28 May 1800): col. 610: "wie sie unter dem Volke selbst sind, und nicht, wie unsre feine Welt diese und jene heut'ges Tages in Musik sezt und tanzt! [...] wie die eine Nation von der andern wohl das und jenes annimmt, aber überall ihr Eigenes damit amalgamiert, und nun gerade dadurch (wie es beym eigentlichen Amalgamieren geschiehet) ihr Eigenes desto sicherer zu Tage legt."

[48] Eduard von Lannoy, "Nationalliteratur, Nationaldichter, Nationalmusik," in *Aesthetisches Lexikon: Ein alphabetisches Handbuch zur Theorie der Philosophie des Schönen und der schönen Künste. Nebst Erklärung der Kunstausdrücke aller ästhetischen Zweige, als: Poesie, Poetik, Rhetorik, Musik, Plastik, Graphik, Architektur, Malerei, Theater, &c.*, ed. Ignaz Jeitteles, vol. 2 (Vienna: Carl Gerold, 1837), 119: "In den meisten modernen Musikstücken findet man Polonaisen, Bolleros, schottische und andere Melodien, und bedeutende Sammlungen, z. B. im Archive der Gesellschaft der Musikfreunde zu Wien, sind schon veranstaltet worden; dennoch ist noch Mehres unbekannt, und der eigentliche Charakter dieser Volksmelodien wurde meistens von jenen, die sie sammelten, verwischt, weil sie bessern und angeblich veredlen wollten, statt die Töne, wie sie der wandernde Musikant spielte oder die Bauerndirne sang, genau und unverändert niederzuschreiben." Lannoy's authorship of the *Lexikon*'s articles on music is revealed in the preface to its first volume (1835).

published Hungarian dances, the enormously popular dances of the polka family, including the contredanse, écossaise, and galop, typically feature simple major-mode melodies parsed into four- and eight-measure units and supported by tonic and dominant harmony.[49] Such an assimilative process, furthermore, was not unique to the Viennese music market; in describing the British repertoire of "Hindostannie airs," for example, musicologist Nicholas Cook has observed that in many instances, "the assimilation of Indian music within the English glee tradition—and, of course, within the metropolitan economy—[is] so complete" that titles and generic designations alone betray the airs' origins. Perhaps most strikingly, in his review of Carl Goldmark's second symphony in 1888, the notable Viennese critic Ludwig Speidel reflected not only on the composer's evocation of Hungarian Romani music, but on his Viennese predecessors' imperialistic approach to it:

> National music is to the composer what nature is to the painter. Thus Haydn, Beethoven, and Schubert have taken up Gipsy music and attached it as an interesting province to the empire of German music. It is therefore no longer something foreign or is so only insofar as everything Romantic is foreign, but in its foreignness is felt at the same time to be attractive and pleasing.[50]

The cultural appropriation underscored by Speidel, whereby the music of a socially, culturally, and economically disadvantaged group (Hungarian Romani musicians) was rendered "attractive and pleasing" by and for dominant ones (Viennese composers, publishers, and consumers), reflected and contributed to the latter's power and authority. Yet simplification and assimilation to prevailing taste, style, and musical abilities need not be construed only as instruments of control; they were also necessary preconditions to the cultivation of sympathy—the fellow-feeling that we would today call empathy—a cornerstone of Enlightenment morality. As many

---

[49] Peter van der Merwe, *Roots of the Classical: The Popular Origins of Western Music* (Oxford: Oxford University Press, 2004), 231–38. I discuss the stylistic assimilation of Hungarian dances to Viennese dance music in detail in my article "Reconsidering an Early Exoticism."

[50] Ludwig Speidel, "Konzerte," *Fremden-Blatt*, 2 March 1888, 4 col. 2: "Dem Tonkünstler ist die Nationalmusik, was dem Maler die Natur ist. So haben Haydn, Beethoven und Schubert die Zigeunermusik aufgefaßt und mit ihr dem Kaiserreich der deutschen Musik eine interessante Provinz angegliedert. So ist sie kein Fremdling mehr oder doch nur insofern, als alles Romantische als fremdartig, aber in seiner Fremdartigkeit zugleich als anziehend und gefallend empfunden wird." I thank Professor David Brodbeck for kindly bringing this review to my attention.

eighteenth-century philosophers argued, engagement with the arts was critical to experiencing, if only imaginatively, the subjectivity of others. Adam Smith, David Hume, Moses Mendelssohn, and Gotthold Ephraim Lessing all articulated the important role of the arts in eliciting emotional responses through sensual engagement, which in turn fostered the sympathy that allows individuals and societies to act morally.[51] Johann Gottfried Herder perhaps articulated these ideas most clearly and directly. For Herder, "true cognition [*Erkennen*] is loving, is feeling in a human way." Understanding arises only when we place ourselves imaginatively in the shoes of another, "feeling our way into" their experiences. As Herder explained, "the sensing [*empfindende*] human being feels his way into everything [*fühlt sich in Alles*], feels everything out of himself, and imprints it with his image, his impress. [...] It is only through ourselves that we can, so to speak, feel into others [*hinein fühlen*]."[52] In other words, as philosopher and political scientist Michael L. Frazer has summarized, sympathetic feeling is "a matter of imaginative projection of the self into the position of the other."[53]

Reading was one of the most important ways to "feel into" the experiences of others in the eighteenth century. As characters came alive in the minds of readers, they shared imaginatively in their lives and feelings regardless of differences of gender, class, or ethnicity, for instance. Herder valued a variety of literature, from fiction to travel accounts, as important means of cultivating sympathetic understanding of other individuals and societies. Much like works of fiction, which eschewed direct instruction in moral precepts, travel literature could foster "the recognition of the humanity in the human being [...], expand[ing] our horizon and multiply[ing] our sensitivity for every situation of our brothers."[54] As Frazer has observed, however, Herder's recognition of humanity did not preclude judgment of others or erase differences between individuals and cultures. It provided, rather, the "absolute standard" against which they could be measured, without "prejudice or presumption."[55] The sympathetic feelings engendered by reading, moreover, ideally not only enabled a more just comparison of difference but could also foster recognition and communal feeling. The "imagined

---

[51] Cypess, *Women and Musical Salons*, chap. 2.
[52] As given and translated in Michael L. Frazer, *The Enlightenment of Sympathy: Justice and the Moral Sentiments in the Eighteenth Century and Today* (Oxford: Oxford University Press, 2010), 149 and 154–55.
[53] Frazer, *The Enlightenment of Sympathy*, 154.
[54] As given and translated in Frazer, *The Enlightenment of Sympathy*, 159.
[55] Frazer, *The Enlightenment of Sympathy*, 161.

community" essential to the advent of nationalism as expounded by political scientist Benedict Anderson was made possible by reading—and especially by reading newspapers—which encouraged identification with others one had no expectation of ever meeting.[56]

As literary and cultural historian Simon During has explored, reading was a particularly accessible form of "self-othering"—"constructing or finding a self as another or by identification with others"—for women because it was an activity that could be enjoyed in private,[57] much like music-making. While reading about the feelings and experiences of others might cultivate a sense of imagined community with them, playing representations of their music had the potential to foster an even stronger sense of sympathetic identification—not only imagining, but enacting community in a bodily way.[58] Most interesting in this regard are two texts (given in the appendix) that provide specific performance directions to readers, inviting them to execute more faithfully the published Hungarian dances to which they are linked. In his foreword to the four-volume collection of *Originelle Ungarische Nationaltänze* (text C), their "collector" asserted that the Hungarian's "favorite trills are in thirds, fourths, fifths, and sometimes also in sixths." To indicate the notes on which such trills should be performed, the "collector" explained that he had "adopted a sign of [his] own for their proper performance; it is as follows * and the notes above which it is located (they are half or quarter notes) are cross-hatched three times." In the first dance of the first volume of the collection (transcribed as ex. 3.2), indications to perform these trills occur five times (in mm. 2, 6, 12, 20, and 28). Playing such trills—either as double trills or by trilling on the upper note while sustaining the lower one—was undoubtedly beyond the abilities of many amateurs, presenting a technical challenge that exceeded the typical demands of published Hungarian dances or of music composed with amateurs in mind more generally.

---

[56] Anderson, *Imagined Communities*.

[57] Simon During, "Rousseau's Patrimony: Primitivism, Romance and Becoming Other," in *Colonial Discourse/Postcolonial Theory*, ed. Francis Baker, Peter Hulme, and Margaret Iversen (Manchester: Manchester University Press, 1994), 47–71 (quotation at p. 47).

[58] Joubert, "Analytical Encounters," 56, has similarly questioned "the potential impact of circulating three [transcriptions of Iroquois] songs, with instructions on pronunciation and a description of the dances and costumes. Would French and German readers have tried to sing the songs, potentially placing themselves in an imaginary ritual performance, even identifying with some of the participants?" She concludes (p. 57) that "the indigenous ritual itself is communal, but the act of reprinting the music, along with descriptions of dance and rituals, extends the boundaries of community to French and German readers."

126　HUNGARIAN DANCES AND MUSICAL LIFE

The author of the article on Hungarian dances in the *Allgemeine musikalische Zeitung* (text D) that appeared at approximately the same time as the first two volumes of *Originelle Ungarische Nationaltänze*, however, suggested an interpretation of similarly marked trills in Hummel's contemporaneous *Balli ongaresi* that would have made them easier to perform. (Nonetheless, Hummel's *Balli* are overall more demanding to play than most published Hungarian dances.) He advised keyboardists to play the trills indicated on the half notes in measures 4 and 12 of the first dance (ex. 3.3) as rapid alternations between the two notes a third apart, thus imitating "the player of the dulcimer, one of the main Hungarian instruments, which is always present." This musician "lets the mallets tremble on these longer notes, which one cannot do on the pianoforte with the actual trill, but which one

Example 3.3. Johann Nepomuk Hummel, *Balli ongaresi per Pianoforte composti e dedicati A. S. A. S. la Principessa Leopoldina di Liechtenstein nata Principessa d'Esterhazy*, op. 23, no. 1, "Ballo patetico" (Vienna: Contor delle arti e d'industria, [1806]). Transcribed from A-Wn, L18.Kaldeck MS40603-qu.4° MUS MAG (Department of Music, Austrian National Library).

Example 3.4. Execution of trills in Hummel's *Balli ongaresi*, op. 23, no. 1, as given in the unsigned article "Ungarische Tänze," *Allgemeine musikalische Zeitung* 9, no. 25 (18 March 1807): col. 406.

can imitate through a very rapid, as it were, buzzing, alternation of these tones." An in-text music example showed readers how to execute this ornament (ex. 3.4), which also recurs in the fifth dance of the set. Adopting this performance practice would have made the published music more accessible to amateurs, while also allowing them to approximate more nearly Romani playing styles. (A keyboard instrument equipped with a pantalon stop could have provided a different opportunity to simulate the sound of the dulcimer, further helping to bridge the gap between a player's real and imagined experiences.[59]) Similarly, the reviewer observed that the "buzzing, lively figure[s]" that make up the rest of Hummel's first *Ballo* (mm. 17–24) would be "extemporized by the national musicians, or at least varied again and again according to their own imagination—which one may also do here and which is even better than writing down and playing back such figure[s]."

Improvising short melodic figures in the manner of Romani musicians may have rendered Hummel's dances more appealing to proficient players, but such a practice—applied to Hummel's set or to other published Hungarian dances, in which such figures are widespread—also hints at this repertoire's subversive potential. As musicologist Erin Helyard has documented, improvisation, along with extensive ornamentation and "difficult" keyboard music, was the purview of professional, male musicians in the eighteenth century. As he writes, "in many examples in literature and letters of the time we read of inappropriate musical acts for which a transgressive performer was to be censured. Probably the most inappropriate act was of overstepping one's bounds and playing and practicing music that was a professional's domain."[60] The ability to improvise was a primary yardstick by which professional male performers were judged, but it was "a decidedly

---

[59] On the pantalon, see Sarah E. Hanks, "Pantaleon's Pantalon: An 18th-Century Musical Fashion," *Musical Quarterly* 55, no. 2 (April 1969): 215–27. I thank Professor Mark Ferraguto for kindly bringing this technology and this article to my attention.

[60] Helyard, *Clementi and the Woman at the Piano*, 80.

unusual musical act for a female amateur."[61] The kind of improvisation encouraged by the reviewer of Hummel's *Balli ongaresi* in the *AMZ* would therefore most likely have been indulged in private, away from the ears of family and friends, where the keyboard player had more liberty to experiment and make mistakes, and where an act of autonomous self-expression also carried less risk of disapproval.

Reading as a similarly private activity that could enable and encourage female resistance to social norms and expectations has been well documented and was indeed much discussed in the eighteenth century. A woman who (over)indulged in reading—and especially in reading novels—risked succumbing to dangers as varied (and often contradictory) as laziness, apathy, neglect of domestic duties, politicization, and sexual licentiousness, along with a host of medical disorders.[62] Likewise, the transgressive potential of vocal music has received considerable attention; as musicologist Richard Leppert has commented, "the connection between song texts and female morality was rather old hat by the eighteenth century. It was not a new issue but an old one hanging on."[63] Perhaps because it was considered intrinsically meaningless, instrumental music was generally less of a concern, except when it exceeded the bounds of technical acceptability, as Helyard has explored, or when it simply took up too much of a woman's time. But even in the absence of improvisatory flourishes or high technical demands, the self-othering inherent when amateur women played Hungarian dances at the keyboard carried the potential of defiant subversion of social norms; the option of improvisation, however limited, simply heightened this potential. The dances' capacity, especially when consumed in conjunction with the informative descriptions that were often issued in connection with them, to foster keyboard players' identification with and embodiment of musicians of a different gender, ethnicity, class, and professional status from their own points to their potential as tools of sociocultural disobedience. The stylistic demureness of the music as notated, furthermore, masked this potential, perhaps increasing its transgressive power through secrecy. Indeed, although the published dances were closely aligned stylistically with

---

[61] Helyard, *Clementi and the Woman at the Piano*, 175; see also 181.

[62] For a brief discussion of the controversial status of reading in the eighteenth century, see James Van Horn Melton, *The Rise of the Public in Enlightenment Europe* (Cambridge: Cambridge University Press, 2001), esp. 110–13.

[63] Leppert, *Music and Image*, 30. Head, "'If the Pretty Little Hand Won't Stretch,'" includes insightful discussion of selected song texts.

other eighteenth-century keyboard music marketed to female amateurs, descriptions of Romani musicians and music-making were far removed from feminized genres such as the moral weekly or even the controversial sentimental novel, with their preoccupation with the domestic realm and private experiences.

The subject position women were invited to take on as they played the music and possibly replicated some of the practices of foreign, discursively highly Othered, professional male musicians, moreover, was not mitigated by the strategies that could attenuate qualms about potentially suspicious literature. Samuel Richardson's *Pamela* (first published in 1740), one of the most widely read, frequently translated, and influential novels of the eighteenth century, may serve as a case in point. To be sure, much like the anonymous composers or self-styled "collectors" of Hungarian dances for the keyboard, Richardson portrayed himself merely as the editor of the eponymous heroine's letters that make up the epistolary novel—not as their author—thereby both increasing the work's authenticity and deflecting criticism for any impropriety from himself. Moreover, he prefaced the novel with the following declaration:

> If to *divert* and *entertain*, and at the same time to *instruct* and *improve* the minds of the YOUTH of *both sexes*:
>
> If to inculcate *religion* and *morality* in so easy and agreeable a manner, as shall render them equally *delightful* and *profitable*:
>
> If to set forth in the most exemplary lights, the *parental*, the *filial*, and the *social* duties:
>
> If to paint VICE in its proper colours, to make it *deservedly odious*; and to set VIRTUE in its own amiable light, to make it look *lovely*...
>
> If these be laudable or worthy recommendations, the *Editor* of the following letters, which have their foundation both in *Truth* and *Nature*, ventures to assert, that all these ends are obtained here, together.[64]

---

[64] As given in T. C. W. Blanning, *The Culture of Power and the Power of Culture: Old Regime Europe 1660–1789* (Oxford: Oxford University Press, 2003), 148.

Critics decried Richardson's preface as no more than a "specious pretence" for spreading "the most artful and alluring amorous ideas."[65] Yet, despite the transgressive appeal of the numerous sexual advances recounted in the novel—not to mention the original edition's implicit questioning of class barriers and structures of power—there was no doubt, at least officially, that the reader was expected to identify with and to emulate the virtuous Pamela rather than to give in to the improper advances of a Mr. B. Pamela's letters provided a glimpse into her soul, allowing readers to "feel into" her experiences and reactions to them; just as Mr. B. is converted to virtue by reading her letters, so too should be the reader who shares sympathetically in the heroine's subjectivity and is improved by her morality.

The sympathetic fellow-feeling that could be elicited by playing Hungarian dances at the keyboard, in contrast, could promote individual agency and expression that defied female containment, unmitigated by the frame of a moralizing preface or of a narrative of redemption. Ultimately, however, its resistive potential was surely limited by the privacy of domestic music-making. It posed no more of a real and direct threat to the social order than carnivalesque masquerade—a parallel kind of "self-spectacularisation," to use During's phrase, typically associated with public display rather than private indulgence—or than reading about the marriage of a maidservant to an aristocrat in *Pamela*.[66] Published Hungarian dances and their enjoyment at the keyboard are emblematic of the Enlightenment's approach to the exotic, characterized by historians George Rousseau and Roy Porter as "that realm of the excluded which is not absolutely prohibited, but merely signposted by danger lights. [...] It is marked by frisson more than fear."[67] In that sense, the thrill of the exotic overlapped significantly with that of the pastoral, a space in which ordinary social constraints did not apply: enjoyment of either was temporary and exciting because it suggested the forbidden without being truly threatening. Indeed, as socially sanctioned modes of self-othering, exotic and pastoral fantasies may even be understood as disciplinary strategies that reinscribed the very norms from which they briefly freed participants.

***

[65] The quotation is from the subtitle of the anonymous *Pamela Censured* (London: Printed for J. Roberts, 1741), as given in Melton, *The Rise of the Public*, 111.

[66] During, "Rousseau's Patrimony," esp. 62–64. Matthew Head has discussed masquerade and the carnivalesque extensively in connection to eighteenth-century music in his book *Orientalism, Masquerade and Mozart's Turkish Music* (London: Royal Musical Association, 2000).

[67] G. S. Rousseau and Roy Porter, "Introduction: Approaching Enlightenment Exoticism," in *Exoticism in the Enlightenment*, ed. G. S. Rousseau and Roy Porter (Manchester: Manchester University Press, 1990), 4.

The vast eighteenth-century repertoire of Hungarian dances for the amateur market may be likened to the copious quantities of reading material churned out by contemporary writers of Europe's many Grub Streets to satisfy the appetites of an often less-than-discerning public.[68] While these media fed the Enlightenment's music and reading revolutions, they are easily—and perhaps understandably—dismissed or entirely forgotten today. As Géza Papp has commented about published collections of Hungarian dances, the "aim—to be simple at all costs—deprives many sets of dances of the quality of being representative [of actual Hungarian Romani music], and of their possibly being enjoyed today in their original form," though he holds out hope that at least some dances could find new life through pedagogical application.[69] As I've suggested in this chapter, however, by delving beneath the surface of the music, interrogating and interpreting the cultural work that could have been accomplished by the domestic enjoyment of this large repertoire, we may better understand it on the terms of its own time. Playing Hungarian dances at the keyboard did not enable a single subject position but many, suggesting both the ambivalence and the richness that characterized cross-cultural encounters in the eighteenth century, as now. Such encounters offered opportunities simultaneously to express and reinforce hegemony, cultivate sympathy, and voice resistance to social norms and expectations. If we ourselves can imaginatively "feel into" the experiences of amateur female keyboardists of the eighteenth century, attempting sympathetically to understand what may have made Hungarian dances valuable and enjoyable to them, we may be better able to recognize and to appreciate these dances' significance and the cultural work they enabled in their own time.

---

[68] For a bibliography including some of the most important literature on the concept of Grub Street, see Melton, *The Rise of the Public*, 157–59.

[69] Papp, *Hungarian Dances*, 31–32 (quotation at p. 31).

4

Dancing the *Ungarischer*

On 31 January 1788, Archduke Franz and his new bride, Archduchess Elisabeth, attended a masquerade ball in the imperial Redoutensäle in Hungarian dress.[1] The couple had married only weeks earlier, on 6 January, and perhaps for that reason, a masked reveler took advantage of their appearance at the ball to bestow a gift on the archduchess: a set of twelve *Contredanses Hongraises* for the harpsichord. Two years later, in the index of *Hadi és Más Nevezetes Történetek* (War Stories and Other Remarkable Tales), the Viennese Hungarian-language periodical the gift-giver himself edited, he disclosed his identity publicly: Demeter Görög (1760–1833), a polymath and notable patron of Hungarian arts and sciences who was tutor to the Kollonich and Esterházy families before becoming head imperial educator at the Habsburg court in 1802.[2] A manuscript copy of the *Contredanses Hongraises* survives in the "Kaisersammlung" of the Austrian National Library, with a title page commemorating the collection's presentation to the archduchess (see fig. 4.1),[3] which Görög also briefly related in the pages of his periodical.[4]

Görög included one of the most charming of the *Contredanses Hongraises* (the fifth dance of the extant manuscript; see ex. 4.1) as a supplement to the

---

[1] The archduke (1768–1835) was the nephew of Joseph II; he reigned as Franz II, the last Holy Roman Emperor, from 1792 to 1806 and assumed the title of Emperor Franz I of Austria in 1804. The archduchess (1767–1790) was born Elisabeth of Württemberg, a sister of Sophia Dorothea, whom I discussed in chapter 1.

[2] For a detailed biography of Görög, see Edina Zvara, *Egy tudós hazafi Bécsben: Görög Demeter és könyvtára* (Budapest: Országos Széchényi Könyvtár—Gondolat Kiadó, 2016).

[3] A-Wn, Mus.Hs.13010 MUS MAG. The twelve dances are divided into two groups, numbered 1–3 and 1–9, respectively, in the manuscript. The dances are transcribed in Géza Papp, ed., *Hungarian Dances 1784–1810*, Musicalia Danubiana 7 (Budapest: Magyar Tudományos Akadémia, Zenetudományi Intézet, 1986), 121–33, from the manuscript in A-Wn.

[4] *Hadi és Más Nevezetes Történetek*, 12 February 1790, 208. I am aware of no evidence supporting Gerhard Croll's assertions that the *Contredanses Hongraises* were played at the masked ball at which Görög gave them to Archduchess Elisabeth and that she danced them there. See Gerhard Croll, "'Fremdländische' Redouten-Tänze zur Zeit Mozarts," in *Telemanniana et alia musicologica: Festschrift für Günter Fleischhauer zum 65. Geburtstag*, ed. Dieter Gutknecht, Hartmut Krones, and Frieder Zschoch, Michaelsteiner Forschungsbeiträge 17 (Oschersleben: Ziethen Verlag, 1995), 190.

Figure 4.1. *Contredanses Hongraises pour le Clavecin presentées à Son Altesse Royal Made L'Archiduchesse Elisabeth à l'occasion, qu'Elle parut avec S. A. R^{le} Msg^r l'ArchiDuc François en habit Hongrais à la Redoute. ce 31. Janv. 1788. par un Masque hongrais*, title page. Reproduced from A-Wn, Mus.Hs.13010 MUS MAG (Department of Music, Austrian National Library; https://onb.digital/result/131ACA15).

Example 4.1. *Contredanses Hongraises pour le Clavecin*, no. 5 (1788). Transcribed with permission of the HUN-REN Research Centre for the Humanities, Institute for Musicology, from Géza Papp, ed., *Hungarian Dances 1784–1810*, Musicalia Danubiana 7 (Budapest: Magyar Tudományos Akadémia, Zenetudományi Intézet, 1986), 125–27. Papp prepared his critical edition from the manuscript preserved in the Austrian National Library (A-Wn, Mus.Hs.13010 MUS MAG; https://onb.digital/result/131ACA15). The only editorial alteration is the "Fine" marking.

Example 4.1. Continued.

journal, inviting readers to enjoy the music in much the same way as the archduchess, whom he noted "very much liked the tunes, and often amused herself with them at the keyboard."[5] Elisabeth's reported esteem for the music was undoubtedly a point of national pride for Görög and his readers, while it simultaneously revealed and encouraged shared tastes and practices of

---

[5] *Hadi és Más Nevezetes Történetek*, 208: "igen meg tettzettek a' Nóták, és gyakorta is múlatta magát vélek a' Klavikordiumán." My translation of this passage is based on that given in Papp, *Hungarian Dances*, 26. One other Hungarian dance was included in the same supplement in 1790 and two further ones in 1791—see Géza Papp, "Die Quellen der 'Verbunkos-Musik': Ein bibliographischer Versuch. A) Gedruckte Werke I. 1784–1823," *Studia Musicologica* 21, nos. 2–4 (1979): 154–55 (entries 3 and 4).

music-making across social classes. Middle-class amateur musicians reading the periodical and playing the music therein must have felt a sense of kinship and shared experience with the archduchess as they did so, in spite of the physical and socioeconomic distance that separated them from the future empress.

Görög did not suggest that Elisabeth used the *Contredanses Hongraises* as anything other than simple keyboard repertoire for her personal enjoyment, but the reference in the collection's title to the contredanse, one of the most popular social dances of the eighteenth century, raises the possibility that this set, and potentially many others like it, was used as functional dance music. The portion of the Kaisersammlung—Franz's library, incorporating Elisabeth's collection as well as Franz's second wife Marie Therese's[6]—now housed in the Austrian National Library alone contains ten sets of Hungarian dances. As musicologist John A. Rice has meticulously documented, much of the dance music in the Kaisersammlung belonged to Marie Therese, empress from 1792 until her death in 1807.[7] One of the sets, Ferdinand Kauer's *XII. Neue Ungarische Tänze für das Forte piano gewiedmet Ihro Königlichen Majestet Maria Theresia*, which is extant in the Kaisersammlung in a keyboard version as well as in one for two violins and *basso*,[8] was dedicated to the empress by the composer on the occasion of her husband's coronation in Hungary in June 1792. But Kauer also advertised this same set, in both versions, for sale to the public in the *Wiener Zeitung* three times that spring.[9] Indeed, especially in the early 1790s, Vienna's newspapers included numerous advertisements for collections of *Ungarische*, and as I demonstrate in this chapter, many of these advertisements strongly suggest this music's functional use in social dancing.

Recent research has established that despite imperial decrees officially allowing for the mixing of socioeconomic classes in late eighteenth-century Vienna's ballrooms, spaces for social dancing remained largely segregated by class (much like the sites of sociability that I explored in chapter 2); when individuals of different classes did share the same spaces, they rarely danced

---

[6] Maria Theresa of Naples and Sicily (1772–1807).
[7] John A. Rice, *Empress Marie Therese and Music at the Viennese Court, 1792–1807* (Cambridge: Cambridge University Press, 2003), esp. chap. 1.
[8] A-Wn, Mus.Hs.13003 MUS MAG and Mus.Hs.11351 MUS MAG, respectively.
[9] *WZ*, 26 May 1792, 1479 col. 2; 30 May 1792, 1519 cols. 1–2; 2 June 1792, 1551 col. 2.

together.[10] The extent to which dance *practices* were also socioeconomically contingent, especially beyond the imperial ballrooms, however, has received much less attention, and for good reason, as evidence is scarce, fragmentary, and most often indirect. In this chapter, I explore where, how, and by whom *Ungarische* were likely used as social dances in Enlightenment Vienna. Contemporary sources—including newspaper advertisements and articles; extant dance music; and writings about dance, music, and aesthetics—suggest that these dances lent themselves to enjoyment as relatively simple contredanses in private, domestic gatherings among those who could afford a keyboard instrument.[11] These social dances, furthermore, differed tremendously from the elaborate presentational contredanses staged by the aristocracy. I argue that somatic experiences of Hungarian dances thus reinforced the physical and sociocultural distance that separated Vienna's socioeconomic classes, undermining the sense of cross-class community and shared taste suggested by extant sheet music alone. At the same time, accounts of social dancing in Hungary published together with Hungarian dances for keyboard may well have informed the dance practices of Vienna's middle classes, suggesting manners and movements that they too could adopt and fostering kinship with their fellow dancers across the border. Hungarian music and dance practices thus had the power both to reaffirm and to transcend boundaries of class and culture in eighteenth-century Vienna.

Advertisements for *Ungarische* in the Viennese Press

The 14 January 1792 issue of the *Wiener Zeitung* included advertisements from four different music dealers for Hungarian music: *12 Ungarische* "mit allen Stimmen" for two florins and the same set "fürs Klavier" for fifty kreutzers from Joseph Haydenreich; *Original Ungarische a 3 Violini und*

---

[10] See, for instance, Joonas Korhonen, *Social Choreography of the Viennese Waltz: The Transfer and Reception of the Dance in Vienna and Europe, 1780–1825* (Helsinki: Academia Scientiarum Fennica, 2014), chap. 2; Joseph Giovanni Fort, "Incorporating Haydn's Minuets: Towards a Somatic Theory of Music" (PhD diss., Harvard University, 2015), chap. 1; and Erica Buurman, *The Viennese Ballroom in the Age of Beethoven* (Cambridge: Cambridge University Press, 2022), chap. 1.

[11] I have explored the connection between *Ungarische* and contredanses in "In Vienna 'Only Waltzes Get Printed': The Decline and Transformation of the *Contredanse Hongroise* in the Early Nineteenth Century," in *Consuming Music: Individuals, Institutions, Communities, 1730–1830*, ed. Emily H. Green and Catherine Mayes, Eastman Studies in Music 138 (Rochester, NY: University of Rochester Press, 2017), 154–75. I have included small portions of my essay in this chapter, with permission of the publisher.

Basso for two florins from Johann Traeg; *6 Ungarische a due Violini e Basso* identified as being by "Hr. Ossowsky" for forty kreuzers and the same set of six "im Clavierauszug" for twenty-four kreutzers from the Musikalisches Magazin; and the same music by Stanislaus Ossowski in the same two instrumentations for the same prices from Franz Anton Hoffmeister.[12] The high concentration of announcements for *Ungarische* in this one issue may simply have been happenstance, although the appearance of the advertisements during the carnival season, which began after Epiphany and lasted until the beginning of Lent, when dance music was particularly heavily advertised in the Viennese press, suggests that the sets may have been offered at least in part because they could be used to accompany social dancing. Indeed, in an advertisement taken out the previous year in the *Wiener Zeitung*, Hoffmeister specified that the music he had available for the current carnival season—including a set of *Ungarische* by Ossowski, a renowned dance-music specialist—consisted of "completely new, different minuets and German dances as well as other national dances, so often requested, dedicated to the lovers of dance."[13]

The headings and contents of the advertisements in the 14 January 1792 issue, which are consistent with numerous other announcements for *Ungarische* in the years around 1790, further support the functional use of this music in social dancing. Hoffmeister's and the Musikalisches Magazin's advertisements are specifically for "Tanzmusikalien," and they include only dance music: German dances, minuets, contredanses, polonaises, Cossack dances ("Kosakische"), and Ländler, along with the *Ungarische*. Hoffmeister's listing of Ossowski's set for keyboard is qualified, furthermore, specifically as *6 Ungarische Tänze für das Klavier* (the emphasis is mine). Haydenreich's and Traeg's advertisements, on the other hand, are simply for "Neue Musikalien," but their organization of a large variety of music by genre clearly situates the Hungarian sets within the category of dance music.

---

[12] The advertisements appear on pp. 121–23. In its advertisement, the Musikalisches Magazin also informed readers of Ossowski's change of publisher: "Zugleich wird einen verehrungswürdigen Publikum zur Nachricht ertheilt, daß Hr. Ossowsky den bisherigen Verlagsort seiner Musikalien verändert habe, und in der Zukunft nicht allein die in der ersten und zwoten Hoffmeisterischen Anzeige enthaltene Musikalien, sondern alle seine übrige bisher erschienene Aufsätze einzig und allein in der obgedachten Handlung, und zwar alle mit (S. O.) gestempelt zu haben seyn werden."

[13] *WZ*, 9 February 1791, 332 col. 2: "In meiner Handlung, sind für gegenwärtige Faschingszeit zu haben, des Herrn Ossowsky ganz neue, verschiedene, Menuets und Deutsche, wie auch andere einer so oft Anfrage wegen, verfertigte, und den Tanzliebhabern gewidmete Nationaltänze [...]." On Ossowski as a dance-music composer, see Buurman, *The Viennese Ballroom*, 101; and Erich Schenk, "Der Langaus," *Studia Musicologica* 3, nos. 1–4 (1962): 301–16.

Haydenreich's advertisement first lists dances (minuets and *Ungarische*) followed by an assortment of vocal music arranged for keyboard and for various small ensembles ranging from eight-part *Harmoniemusik* to string quartets and flute duos. Traeg's listing is more extensive and more tightly organized, proceeding from chamber music to symphonies to dances, a category that includes German dances, contredanses, and minuets along with the set of *Ungarische*. Perhaps to entice buyers further, Traeg indicated the provenance of some of this dance music (German dances from the "Prager- und Brünner Freyball" of 11 October 1791 and the *Redoutenmenuetten und Deutsche von 1791, sowohl vom grossen als kleinen Saal*) and the composers (Mozart and Wranitzky) of yet other sets. Mozart's *7 neue Kontratänze mit einer Ouverture*, furthermore, were offered "nebst Figuren," the very figures to which the contredanses would be danced. This evidence makes clear that the advertised sets, including the *Ungarische*, were conceived and marketed as functional dance music, in addition to being enjoyable simply to play or to listen to. The variability of the headings under which this music was advertised—"Tanzmusikalien" as well as simply "Musikalien"—reflects both of these functions.

The instrumentations in which publishers made the *Ungarische* available suggest, furthermore, that they would most often have accompanied social dancing in private, domestic settings. Announcements for Hungarian dances in full orchestral parts ("mit allen Stimmen" or "vollstimmig"), like Haydenreich's, are rare. In contrast, throughout the 1790s, minuets and German dances were routinely marketed in the press in orchestral parts as well as in keyboard and in string trio versions. Advertisements for contredanses and Ländler in full parts were somewhat less frequent, but they still surpass by far those for Hungarian dances, polonaises, quadrilles, gallopades, and Cossack dances, which with few exceptions were available only for keyboard and/or for small string ensemble, most often consisting of two violins and *basso*.[14] As musicologist Erica Buurman has observed, when orchestral parts were offered for sale, they were presumably aimed mainly at dance hall orchestras.[15] In other cases, the parts may have been used in large house balls. An advertisement in the *Wiener Zeitung* in February 1790, for instance, offered contredanses "from a respectable house ball" in a version

---

[14] Keyword searches "mit allen Stimmen" and "vollstimmig" on the Austrian National Library's indispensable ANNO (AustriaN Newspapers Online) website (https://anno.onb.ac.at).
[15] Buurman, *The Viennese Ballroom*, 22–23.

for keyboard and in one for orchestra; a different advertisement in January 1788 for "Neue Redoute Tänze" lists minuets and German dances in full parts as well as in piano reduction, and advises readers that the music dealer also rents out musicians for house balls and concerts, presumably with an eye to playing the very music he was selling.[16] (One can also well imagine situations in which only some of the instrumental parts were played if fewer musicians were on hand.) The notable paucity of *Ungarische* offered in orchestral parts, especially as compared to the frequency with which minuets and German dances were advertised in full parts, suggests that Hungarian dances were generally not performed in Vienna's public dance halls or in larger private gatherings in the late eighteenth century. Rather, the routine availability of *Ungarische* for keyboard and for string trio signals that they would typically have been enjoyed at smaller house balls, where these two instrumentations were the ones that most commonly accompanied dancing. As many Viennese, especially among the more privileged classes, favored smaller gatherings over the city's crowded ballrooms as the eighteenth century drew to a close, collections of dances that could easily be played by soloists or small ensembles in the home held great consumer appeal.[17]

Dancing the *Ungarischer*

Social dancing was a beloved activity across classes in eighteenth-century Vienna, and contemporary writers attested that instruction in it was not a privilege reserved only for the wealthy. In his description of the city, the Austrian statistician Ignaz de Luca declared that "the most common people

---

[16] *WZ*, 24 February 1790, 482 col. 2: *12 neue Contratänze aus einem ansehnlichen Hausball*; and 19 January 1788, 155 col. 2. Another option would have been to go to the Hoher Markt at nine o'clock in the morning to hire the dance musicians who routinely gathered there—see Ignaz de Luca, *Wiens gegenwärtiger Zustand unter Josephs Regierung* (Vienna: Wucherer, 1787), 200; and Ignaz de Luca, *Topographie von Wien*, vol. 1 (Vienna: In Kommission bey Thad. Edlen v. Schmidbauer und Komp. am Graben zur blauen Krone, 1794), "Die Tanzmusik," 386.

[17] For more on domestic dance gatherings, see Herbert Lager and Hilde Seidl, *Kontratanz in Wien: Geschichtliches und Nachvollziehbares aus der theresianisch-josephinischen Zeit* (Vienna: Österreichischer Bundesverlag, 1983), 44; Walter Salmen, "Tanzinstrumente und -ensembles," in *Mozart in der Tanzkultur seiner Zeit*, ed. Walter Salmen (Innsbruck: Helbling, 1990), 58; Reingard Witzmann, *Der Ländler in Wien: Ein Beitrag zur Entwicklungsgeschichte des Wiener Walzers bis in die Zeit des Wiener Kongresses* (Vienna: Arbeitsstelle für den Volkskundeatlas in Österreich, 1976), 13 and 54–55; and Monika Fink, *Der Ball: Eine Kulturgeschichte des Gesellschaftstanzes im 18. und 19. Jahrhundert* (Lucca: Libreria musicale italiana, 1996), 89–91 and 169.

of both sexes take dance lessons. There are dance schools in which chiefly housemaids practice their dancing."[18] The Viennese satirist Joseph Richter concurred, noting that dancing masters taught "the kitchen staff early in the day and the lad[ies] in the afternoon."[19] Directories of businesses and services in the city listed the names and addresses of dancing masters alongside those of a host of other professionals, from apothecaries and architects to music and language instructors.[20] Dance teachers also put out signs advertising their services: as de Luca explained, "many dance schools offer instruction in all kinds of dances to the public for a fee. In front of the houses in which such teaching takes place, a placard is usually tacked up, on which one sees persons practicing dancing."[21] Some details about the instruction offered in these schools may be gleaned from the newspaper advertisements dancing masters took out. Beyond promising good results at low (but unspecified) prices, they listed the dances that they taught: minuets, German dances, *Strassburger*, contredanses (and specifically the English longways contredanse, in eighteenth-century Vienna referred to simply as "Englischer," "englischer Tanz," "anglaise," or "angloise"), and Cossack dances.[22]

Absent from these advertisements, however, are many dances frequently referenced in contemporary sources, raising questions about how they would have been learned and performed. In the *Wiener Zeitung* in January 1796, for instance, the music dealer Schmidtbauer advertised what he called a "quodlibet" consisting of a minuet, German dance, Ländler, polonaise, English contredanse, Masurian dance, gallopade, Cossack dance, Hungarian dance, and *Strassburger*. He specified that these newly composed dances, from the pen of "Pechatschek" (Franz Martin Pecháček [1763–1816], the

---

[18] De Luca, *Topographie von Wien*, vol. 1, "Die Tanzmusik," 383: "Das Tanzen ist eine Hauptleidenschaft meiner Landsleute; die gemeinsten Personen beyderley Geschlechts nehmen Unterricht im Tanzen. Man hat eigene Tanzschulen, in welchen vorzüglich die Dienstmädchen im Tanzen sich üben […]."

[19] [Joseph Richter], *Das alte und neue Wien, oder Es ist nicht mehr, wie eh. Ein satyrisches Gemählde entworfen von einem alten Laternputzer* (Vienna: Christoph Peter Rehm, 1800), as quoted in Fort, "Incorporating Haydn's Minuets," 25: "in der Früh den Kuchelmenschern und am Nachmittag der gnädigen Frau Unterricht gibt." Fort, p. 25, quotes de Luca as well.

[20] See, for instance, the multiple issues of the *Wienerisches Kommerzialschema oder Auskunfts- und Geschäftsbuch für Inländer und Fremde* (Vienna: Gerold, 1782–1798); Fort, "Incorporating Haydn's Minuets," 25, cites the 1798 issue.

[21] De Luca, *Wiens gegenwärtiger Zustand*, "Tanzschulen," 358: "Tanzschulen in welchen man in allen Arten von Tänzen gegen ein bestimmtes Honorarium öffentlichen Unterricht ertheilt, sind viele. Vor den Häusern, in welchen eine dergleichen Schule gehalten wird, ist gewöhnlich eine Tafel angeheftet, auf welcher man Personen sieht, die sich im Tanzen üben."

[22] See, for instance, the *WZ*, 27 April 1785, 988 col. 1; 31 October 1792, 2955 col. 2; and 7 November 1792, 3016 col. 1.

father of Franz Xaver Pecháček [1793–1840]), were "essential for balls." Pecháček, he explained, had written them for performance in "the casino" (Philipp Otto's casino in the Spiegelgasse?), which explains why they were offered in full orchestral parts; these could presumably have been adapted to more modest settings by paring down the instrumentation as needed.[23] A similarly large variety of dances is referenced in the ninth scene of the first act of the popular Viennese playwright Joseph Ferdinand Kringsteiner's farce *Der Tanzmeister* (1807), in which the chorus of guests at a ball hosted by the eponymous dancing master declare that "carnival is a merry time devoted to dancing." They then go on to list and to demonstrate the dances one could enjoy: minuets, German dances, and Ländler; English, Turkish, Cossack, and Hungarian dances; and finally the *Kehraus*. The text indicates that as each dance was named, it was also performed, to the accompaniment of a few measures of its music.[24]

Many of these dances, like many of those in Schmidtbauer's advertisement, overlap with the ones that Viennese dancing masters are known to have taught their pupils or were variants of them—the Ländler, for instance, was a choreographic variant of the German dance.[25] Direct evidence about how Masurian, Turkish, or Hungarian dances would have been executed in eighteenth-century Vienna, however, is scarce; the issue is all the more vexing when one considers, for example, the bewildering variety of dances included

---

[23] *WZ*, 2 January 1796, 17 col. 1: "Neue Tanz-Musikalien, von der Composition des Hrn. Pechatschek, welche für den Fasching 1796 sind gemacht worden, und in dem Casino allein producirt worden, sind am Graben in der Buchhandlung des Edl. V. Schmidtbauer und Comp., dem Elephanten gegenüber zu haben, als: [...] ein Quodlibet, in welchem ein Menuett, Deutscher, Landler, Pohlnischer, Englischer, Mazur, Gallopad, Kosakischer, Ungarischer und Straßburger Tanz vorkommen, und für die Bälle sehr nothwendig sind, vollstimmig 4 fl. 30 kr."

[24] [Joseph Ferdinand Kringsteiner], *Der Tanzmeister: Eine Posse mit Gesang in drey Aufzügen vom Verfaßer des Zwirnhändlers* (Vienna: bey Matthias Andreas Schmidt, Universitäts-Buchdrucker, 1807), 22: "Chor. Der Fasching, das ist halt 'n lustige Zeit, / Die g'hört nur zum Tanzen, die g'hört nur zur Freud; / Der Teufel möchte immer im Bette kampirn, / Wir wolln heut auf d'Nacht auch 'n Tanzel probirn. / (Der Musik wechselt, und spielt jene Tänze, welche genennt werden). / Der Anfang, so ists Etikett, / Der g'schieht mit einem Menuet. (tanzen einige Takt Menuet). / Dann wirbeln gleich die Pauken drein, / Und 's fallen halt die Deutschen ein; (wie oben) / Dann geht's erst, so ists der Brauch, / Uiber d'Landlerischen auch. (wie oben) / Ist das vorbey, so weiß man eh, / Da kömmt sodann das englische. (wie vor) / Dann wechseln wir mit türkischen, (wie vor). / Bald wieder mit Kosakischen; (wie vor) / Damit man endlich alls probirt, / Wird Ungarisch auch produzirt; (wie vor) / Und habn wir g'nug tanzt, dann erst gehn wir nach Haus, / Doch vorher, versteht sich, kömmt noch der Kehraus." The chorus is given in Witzmann, *Der Ländler in Wien*, 83; and in Walburga Litschauer and Walter Deutsch, *Schubert und das Tanzvergnügen* (Vienna: Verlag Holzhausen, 1997), 12–13.

[25] On the Ländler, see Buurman, *The Viennese Ballroom*, esp. 43–47. The *Kehraus*, or last dance of the ball, is described in the *Neuestes Sittengemählde von Wien*, vol. 1 (Vienna: bey Anton Pichler, 1801), "Achter Brief," 113–16.

only a few years later in a collection by Michael Pamer for the 1818 carnival season, which contains items such as the "Monimasque," "Madratura," and "böhmischer Konfusionstanz."[26] Perhaps dances such as these were indeed taught to the masses; dancing master Weninger, after all, promised to teach "all kinds of dances," not just the minuets, German dances, *Strassburger*, and English contredanses that he itemized in his 1785 advertisement.[27] An advertisement in the *Wiener Zeitung* on 24 February 1808, for instance, for "new German dances, minuets, Ländler, écossaises, contredanses, and Hungarian dances for keyboard as well as for violin" available from Artaria suggests that these dances could have been used in instructional settings, in which the accompaniment of a solo violin was common.[28] At balls, furthermore, a dancing master or lead couple could have demonstrated steps and choreographies, but as Buurman has noted, there is little evidence that these were common practices in eighteenth-century Vienna.[29]

More likely, many dances, including many national dances, would have been performed in much the same way as the dances specifically listed by dancing masters or as choreographic variants of them. The fact that national dances were sometimes treated not as distinct genres in their own right but as offshoots of others such as the German dance supports this contention. The Kaisersammlung, for instance, includes an undated eighteenth-century manuscript of a set of *6 Deutsche Tänze nach Türkischen geschmack für's Clavier* by an unidentified composer.[30] Similarly, the dance music advertised in the 14 January 1792 issue of the *Wiener Zeitung*, discussed in the preceding section of this chapter, includes a set of *6 Kosaky Deutsche* from Hoffmeister and a set of *12 Deutsche nach ungarischen Geschmack* from the Musikalisches Magazin, the latter of which is also preserved in the Kaisersammlung with an

---

[26] Cited in Witzmann, *Der Ländler in Wien*, 83.
[27] WZ, 27 April 1785, 988 col. 1: "Tanzmeister. Herr Weninger, Tanzmeister in Wien, der dermal anfangs Man seine Reise Wienisch-Neustadt nehmen wird, macht sowohl daselbst, als auch in allen umliegenden, nahe und weit entfernten Orten bekannt, daß bey ihm jeder alle Gattungen Tänze, sowohl der Menuetten, als auch Deutschen, Straßburger, Englischen und dergleichen mehr um die billigsten Preise erlernen kann; auch bietet er sich an Lektionen zu geben in Gegenden, die auch von dort 4–5 Stund entfernet sind. Er schmeichelt sich einen allgemeinen Zuspruch, und versichert, daß niemand weiter über seine Lehrart, auch hohe Preise zu klagen haben wird."
[28] WZ, 24 February 1808, 954: "Musikalische Anzeige. Bey Artaria und Compag., k. k. priv. Kunsthändlern am Kohlmarkt Nr. 1919, sind ganz neu erschienen: Neue Tanz-Musik. Hummel XII Neueste Redout-Deutsche fürs Klavier. Preis 1 fl. 30 kr. Dann andere neue Deutsche, Menuetten, Ländler-Tänze, Ecossoisses, Contredances, und ungarische Tänze, sowohl fürs Klavier, als für die Violine, sind ebenfalls in Menge zu haben."
[29] Buurman, *The Viennese Ballroom*, 36–38 and 80.
[30] A-Wn, Mus.Hs.12919 MUS MAG.

attribution to Ossowski.[31] As the titles of these collections reveal, German dances of varying flavors seem to have been particularly popular in Vienna, and the sets of Cossack- and Hungarian-inflected German dances listed in the 14 January newspaper appeared alongside *Schäfer Deutsche, Jagddeutsche, Ueberraschungsdeutsche,* and *Deutsche nach ländlichem Geschmack.* Despite Viennese dancing master Andreas Lindner's assertion that he had "invented such easy steps for the popular *Deutschtanzen à la Mongolfiere* that everyone can master this art in a short time,"[32] most German dances were undoubtedly all danced in much the same way, regardless of the specific flavor promised by their titles (though rarely borne out in their music, which is generally not strongly marked).

Ossowski's *12 Deutsche nach ungarischen Geschmack,* advertised six times by the Musikalisches Magazin in the *Wiener Zeitung* in January and February 1792, is the only set of Hungarian-inflected German dances from late eighteenth-century Vienna of which I am aware. Although overt titular associations with the contredanse were hardly more common—the set of *Contredanses Hongraises* from 1788 discussed at the beginning of this chapter and a "Contradanza all'ungarese" published twenty years later in the *Musikalisches Wochenblatt* (15 July 1809 issue) are the only two exemplars known to me—versions of or passages from at least seven of the twelve *Contredanses Hongraises* appeared in other collections of Hungarian dances for keyboard and/or for two violins and *basso* published over the next two decades. These include Ossowski's *VI Danses Hongroises* (Hoffmeister, 1791; Musikalisches Magazin, 1792), "Haydn's" *Zingarese* (Johann Traeg, 1792, erroneously attributed by the publisher), the *Ausgesuchte Ungarische*

---

[31] A-Wn, Mus.Hs.12864 MUS MAG. Hoffmeister's advertisement also appeared in the 4 January 1792 issue of the *Wiener Zeitung* (19 cols. 1–2), and he had advertised "Kosaky Deutsche" the previous year as well, in the 7 December 1791 issue of the *Wiener Zeitung* (3134 col. 2).

[32] *WZ,* 31 October 1792, 2955 col. 2: "Nachricht. Schon seit einigen Jahren geniesse ich das schmeichelhafte Glück, durch meinen Unterricht im Menuet- English- Kontra- Kosackisch- und Straßburgerisch, besonders aber im Deutsch-tanzen die allgemeine Zufriedenheit, und den ungetheilten Beyfall der edlen Bewohner Wiens zu erhalten. Aufgemuntert durch diese Güte, habe ich allen Fleis, und Mühe angewendet, den Unterricht in dieser Kunst so satzlich als möglich zu machen, und zu diesem Ende für das so beliebte Deutschtanzen à la Mongolfiere so leichte Schritte erfunden, daß jedermann diese Kunst in kurzer Zeit erlernen kann. Ich unterziehe mich hierüber der strengsten Prüfung mit jedem. Wer sich hievon durch den Augenschein überzeugen will, beehre mich mit seiner Gegenwart in meiner Wohnung, allwo sich auch die Liebhaber alle Woche dreymal—nemlich Sonntag, Dienstag, und Donnerstag mit Kontra, Quadrillen, und andern Tänzen beliebigst unterhalten können. Ich verspreche mir daher zur Belohnung meiner Erfindung von den verehrungswürdigen Bewohnern Wiens einen zahlreichen Zuspruch, und werde keinen Fleiß und Mühe sparen, Ihren Beyfall noch ferner zu verdienen. Andreas Lindner, Tanzmeister, wohnt im Stoß im Himmel nächst Maria Stiegen Nr. 415."

Nationaltänze im Clavierauszug von verschiedenen Zigeunern aus Galantha (Ignaz Sauer, 1803), a "new" set of *Ungarische Tänze* "composed by the best authors" (Artaria, 1808), and the third volume of *Originelle Ungarische Nationaltänze* (Chemische Druckerei, 1810/1811).[33] None of these collections was issued with a title indicating that it included contredanses—or recycled music.

Visitors to Hungary, furthermore, made connections between contredanses and Hungarian dances that predate these eighteenth-century sets. When the Silesian composer and music theorist Daniel Speer (1636–1707) traveled there, he observed that "Hungarian dances [a]re similar to Western dances but more orderly and charming." More specifically, Louis XIV's ambassador to Hungary, Abbé Révérend, described in his memoirs the dances he encountered there as "similar to French branles and contredanses," and the English naturalist Robert Townson called the recruiting dances he witnessed in Buda in 1793 "a kind of hornpipe," suggesting a perceived similarity to English country dances.[34] In the hands of Viennese composers, *Ungarische* became stylistically so similar to contredanses that Franz Paul Rigler, a prominent musician and teacher in Pressburg (Pozsony in Hungarian, now Bratislava, the capital of Slovakia) complained in the prefatory note to his own collection of *12 Ungarische Tänze* (composed before 1796) that "now some composers in Pest and Vienna have ventured to write

---

[33] Papp, *Hungarian Dances*, 352–53, has identified the correspondences; his English-language notes (pp. 346–62) give publication information about each of the collections. Two of the *Contredanses Hongraises* also appear in the Kaisersammlung's undated manuscript copy of *6 Hongroisses Pour le Clavecin Composes Pour* [!] *Mr Stanislaus d'ossowsci* (A-Wn, Mus.Hs.13004 MUS MAG), which is in turn a (possibly earlier) version of Ossowski's *VI Danses Hongroises* printed by Hoffmeister in 1791 (see Papp, p. 361). It thus seems likely that Ossowski composed the *Contredanses Hongraises*.

[34] The quotations from Speer and Abbé Révérend are given in László Kürti, "Hungary," in *International Encyclopedia of Dance*, ed. Selma Jeanne Cohen, vol. 3 (Oxford: Oxford University Press, 1998), 409. Kürti is referring to the *Mémoires historiques du Comte Betlem-Niklos, Contenant l'Histoire des derniers Troubles de Transilvanie*, vol. 1 (Amsterdam: Jean Swart, 1736), 23: "Toutes nos danses ne consistent qu'en ce que vous apellez en France les branles ou contredanses, chacun se tient par la main, le premier méne toute la chaîne, & commence d'abord d'un pas assez sérieux, puis un peu plus gai, & ensuite il finit par une espece de gavotte où l'on tourne plusieurs fois, l'homme embrassant des deux bras la Dame qui le suit, sans sortir néanmoins en tournant du demi-cercle que l'on forme [...]." (The preface of these memoirs explains their relationship to Abbé Révérend's.) The branle was a group dance performed either in a line or a circle and characterized by a sideways stepping motion; it was popular from at least the fifteenth through the late seventeenth or early eighteenth centuries, and the examples that survive in Beauchamp-Feuillet notation are similar to contredanses. See Daniel Heartz and Patricia Rader, "Branle," in *Grove Music Online*, www.oxfordmusiconline.com (accessed 10 August 2022).

The quotation from Townson is from Robert Townson, *Travels in Hungary, with a Short Account of Vienna in the Year 1793* (London: Printed for G. G. and J. Robinson, 1797), 88. On the hornpipe and its relation to country dances, see Margaret Dean-Smith, "Hornpipe (ii)," in *Grove Music Online*, www.oxfordmusiconline.com (accessed 11 April 2023).

Ungarische; in doing so they all over-hastily erased the truly characteristic [elements from these dances], and in the end one didn't know whether they had meant [to write] a Cossack dance or a contredanse."[35] (Rigler himself, however, noted similarities in phrasing between Hungarian dances and the English longways contredanse.[36]) Yet despite the availability of instruction in Cossack dancing advertised by Viennese dancing masters and the large number of *Kosakische* published in the late eighteenth-century capital, to my knowledge none were billed as "Hungarian." That is, unlike the extant *Deutsche nach Ungarischen Geschmack* and *Contredanses Hongraises*, I know of no "Kosakische nach ungarischem Geschmack" or "Cosaques hongroises."

As Rigler noted, the stylistic characteristics of *Ungarische* published in Vienna in the late eighteenth century clearly map onto those of the contredanse, and specifically of the *contredanse allemande*. Whereas the city's popular German dances and minuets were in triple meter, Viennese contredanses were typically in a lively duple meter. Further, contredanses were usually characterized by major keys, melodies unfolding across a narrow range supported by a simple harmonic framework, and clear four-measure phrases combined to form eight- or occasionally sixteen-measure periods. These were often enclosed within repeat signs and followed one another in an additive, chain-like fashion, much like the individual contredanses themselves, which were published in sets. In addition, specific attributes distinguish the three main types of contredanses: the *contredanse anglaise*, *contredanse française*, and *contredanse allemande*.[37] Although all were figure dances, dancers in *contredanses anglaises* were arranged in two columns, with men and women facing each other, while in both *contredanses françaises* and *contredanses allemandes*, couples were arranged in a square formation. Perhaps because of their similarity of execution, both the *française* and the *allemande* versions were referred to simply

---

[35] As given in Papp, *Hungarian Dances*, 349: "Nun haben es einige in Pest und Wienn gewagt Ungarische zu schreiben; allem ihnen abwischte dabey das wahre karakteristische zu geschwinde, und man wuste am Ende nicht, ob sie einen Kosakischen oder Contretanz gemeint hatten." The entire prefatory note is given as text A in the appendix. Several decades later, Franz Liszt, in *Des Bohémiens et de leur musique en Hongrie* (Paris: Librairie Nouvelle, 1859), 269, also noted the resemblance of Hungarian dances to Cossack dances.

[36] See appendix, text A: "in den meisten, so wie beym Englischen, die Einschnitte und Absätze auf kurze Tacttheile fallen." The same assertion is also made in the unsigned article "Ueber die Nationaltänze der Ungarn," *Allgemeine musikalische Zeitung* 2, no. 35 (28 May 1800): cols. 611–16 (given in the appendix as text B).

[37] As Buurman has explained, the contredanse family also included several other dances closely related to these types, especially in the early decades of the nineteenth century: the cotillon, the quadrille, the écossaise, and the tempête. See Buurman, *The Viennese Ballroom*, 77–79.

as "contredanses" or "Kontratänze" in eighteenth-century Vienna, while the longways English version was variously called "anglaise," "angloise," "Englischer," or "englischer Tanz." Musically, *contredanses françaises* had rondo-like structures and, like *contredanses anglaises*, phrases that typically began on an upbeat. *Contredanses allemandes*, in contrast, were characterized by phrases beginning on the downbeat, a turn figure or cadential ornament concluding phrases, and a formal structure following the pattern AA BB CC XX.[38]

The dance from the *Contredanses Hongraises* transcribed here as example 4.1 has all the features of a *contredanse allemande*: 2/4 meter; simple melodies rarely exceeding the range of an octave; symmetrical four-measure phrases combined to form eight-measure periods and one eight-measure sentence, each of which is repeated; major home key with only a brief excursion to the key of the subdominant; virtually exclusive use of tonic and dominant chords within each key area; phrases beginning on downbeats; turn figures ornamenting the melody typically every fourth measure; and a formal structure that can be represented as AA BB CC DD AA BB. Indeed, most Hungarian dances published in Vienna around 1800 exhibit the music-stylistic features of the *contredanse allemande*, one of the most audible attributes of which is its characteristic turn figures. The choreography of the *contredanse allemande*, furthermore, was itself defined by turning figures, which dancers performed with interlocked arms, rather than by specific steps.[39] Given the prominent turns and ornaments in the melodies of *Ungarische*, it is easy to imagine these turning, twining figures and movements, or perhaps mildly exotic variants of them, gracing these dances as well.

Unfortunately, we have little concrete evidence on which to draw in reconstructing them. Historical dance treatises are the primary basis for dance reconstructions, but as Buurman has observed, until 1830, very few dance manuals were published in Vienna, despite the large quantity of dance

---

[38] Eric McKee, "Ballroom Dances of the Late Eighteenth Century," in *The Oxford Handbook of Topic Theory*, ed. Danuta Mirka (Oxford: Oxford University Press, 2014), 166–68; Richard Semmens, "Branles, Gavottes and Contredanses in the Later Seventeenth and Early Eighteenth Centuries," *Dance Research: The Journal of the Society for Dance Research* 15, no. 2 (Winter 1997): 35–62; Buurman, *The Viennese Ballroom*, 77–78; Sarah Reichart, "The Thuillier Contredanses," *Proceedings of the Society of Dance History Scholars* 8 (1985): 103; and Sarah Reichart, "The Influence of Eighteenth-Century Social Dance on the Viennese Classical Style" (PhD diss., City University of New York, 1984), 302–9.

[39] Reichart, "The Influence of Eighteenth-Century Social Dance," 302–9; Reichart, "The Thuillier Contredanses," 102–3; and Buurman, *The Viennese Ballroom*, 34–43.

music available in the city. Furthermore, in Vienna, contredanses were rarely published together with the figures to which they were executed, as was common in other European centers; rather, social dancing was largely shaped by the ephemeral practices of dancing masters and dance venues. The extent to which descriptions of social dancing in Hungary (such as those included in texts B and D in the appendix) may have influenced these practices is difficult to evaluate, but it is reasonable to assume that these accounts could have informed the dancing of the amateur musicians who read them. While they offer few specifics with respect to steps and figures, they do describe manners and movements typical of Hungarian social dancing. From text B, for instance, the reader learns that the path of movement in Hungarian dances is circular. In social dancing, the woman faces her male partner

> with one or both hands at her side, directing her gaze at her partner's feet. He guides their path [*Gang*], their positions, and their turns through his own figures. Sometimes both dancers approach one another, the man holding his partner's waist while she places her hands on his shoulders, and so they turn around for a while. At other times, the female dancer makes a signal with her hand and turns alone; this position [*Stellung*] is one of the most beautiful in the dance.

The modesty of this dance, and especially of the female dancer, with her downturned gaze, is consonant with expectations regarding the performance of gender among relatively privileged Viennese women of the late eighteenth century. The description of the female dancer's attire—a dress with long skirt and fitted bodice embroidered in golden thread—further invited these same Viennese dancers to identify with her; while her dress was clearly seductive to the author of the account, it was also refined, elegant, and proper. Similarly, the male dancer's gentle guidance suggests qualities of leadership, self-discipline, and partnership consistent with eighteenth-century notions of masculinity beyond the Kingdom of Hungary. Text D emphasizes the same virtues of decency and modesty in Hungarian social dancing; indeed, the author of the description similarly underscores the female dancer's downturned gaze and characterizes her as "graceful," "lovely," "agile," and "delicate." Social dancing as practiced by relatively privileged Hungarians is thus presented in these accounts as familiar and respectable—in spite of its foreign movements and manners—a far cry from the dancing of Hungary's peasants and lower classes (see the quotations in the introduction to chapter 1, for instance). Hungarian dance practices could thus forge connections between amateur Viennese dancers and those of the neighboring Kingdom, challenging geographical and cultural boundaries and hierarchies of East and West.

Dance treatises published elsewhere in Europe must be approached with a degree of caution, as the precepts they preserve may not reflect Viennese practices, but along with accounts such as those just discussed, these manuals comprise the only tangible evidence we have of historical steps and choreographies.[40] The only description of the *Ungarischer* as a social dance in Western Europe of which I am aware appears in a treatise by the dancing master Carl Joseph von Feldtenstein published in Braunschweig in 1772, and it therefore merits quoting at length. Significantly, like contemporary accounts of social dancing in Hungary (texts B and D), Feldtenstein's description references turns or spins ("Umdrehung oder *Tournées*") as an important component of the *Ungarischer*:

> The Hungarian dance has the same affects as the three previously introduced, namely the Hannakian, Masurian, and Cossack, and these go so well together that those who dance them [... do so] with feeling because they are carried away by the composition of the charming and comical music. The affects expressed through this dance are, as it were, divided, and each sex is allocated its role, so that the flirtatious affect is given to the female dancer, and the free, comical wildness is given to the male dancer.
>
> I would still need to have various copper engravings made of choreographic symbols if I wanted to work with the steps and figures of this dance, but because I am writing mostly for my own pupils so that they can remember the information they received, I will make do with a demonstration. I mention as a caveat that the female dancers must avail themselves of flirtatious manners and the steps associated with these [manners], as well as *solid* turns, just like the male dancers, higher, and with changing positions, mixing regular and irregular [false positions], which can be seen on the second copper plate (figures 9 through 18), whereby every trained dancer must adopt a comfortable wildness (if I may say so). However, he must also lead his female partner in a certain, *solid* manner and at the same time unite himself with her in the flirtatious affect, revealing the apparent

[40] Buurman, *The Viennese Ballroom*, 6.

wildness as a boisterous and somewhat exaggerated joy only when each partner dances figures alone. Thus will the beautiful be granted also to this nation in its dance.[41]

Unfortunately, Feldtenstein's explanation of the *Ungarischer*—apparently a mere reminder to his students of what he had taught them—provides too few details about steps and choreography to allow a reconstruction of the dance. The engravings that he mentions show only the male dancer's initial foot positions in Beauchamp-Feuillet notation (see the figures marked 9–18 in fig. 4.2), half of which are the "false" positions that he references in his description.[42] These undoubtedly contributed to the male dancer's "comical

---

[41] Carl Joseph von Feldtenstein, *Erweiterung der Kunst nach der Chorographie zu tanzen, Tänze zu erfinden, und aufzusetzen; wie auch Anweisung zu verschiedenen National-Tänzen; Als zu Englischen, Deutschen, Schwäbischen, Pohlnischen, Hannak- Masur- Kosak- und Hungarischen; mit Kupfern; nebst einer Anzahl Englischer Tänze* (Braunschweig: n.p., 1772; reprint ed. Kurt Petermann, Leipzig: Zentralantiquariat der deutschen demokratischen Republik, 1984), "Von dem ungarischen Tanze," 103–4: "Der Ungarische Tanz hat von den vorherangeführten dreyen, als den Hannakischen, Masurischen, und Kosakischen Tänzen die Affekten zugleich, und diese sind so angenehm zusammen gesetzt, daß die, so ihn tanzen (und wann sie auch auf Befehl tanzen müßten, welches allemal der matteste Tanz ist,) wegen der Einrichtung der reizenden und komischen Musik hingerissen werden, daß sie dennoch aus Affektion tanzen würden. Dann die Affekten in der Declamation dieses Tanzes sind gleichsam getheilet, und jeden Geschlecht seine Rolle angewiesen, so daß der tändelnde Affekt der Tänzerin, und der Freye, und in das komische Wilde fallende dem Tänzer zugeeignet ist.
Ich würde, wann ich nach chorographischen Zeichen von denen Schritten und Touren dieses Tanzes handeln wollte, noch verschiedene Kupfer müssen stechen lassen, und da ich größtentheils für meine Lernenden schreibe, damit sie sich an die erhaltene Information erinnern können: so will ich es diesmal bey einer Demonstration bewenden lassen. Ich sage also zur Nachricht, daß die Tänzerinnen sich in ihrem Tanz eines tändelnden Anstandes, und damit verknüpften Schritts, wie auch *solider* Umdrehung oder *Tournées* bedienen müssen, so wie die Tänzer höher, und mit verwechselnden Positionen, wobey sie reguläre, und irreguläre zusammen mischen, welche sie auf der zweyten Kupfertafel (T. 2. Fig. 9 bis 18.) zu sehen haben, wobey ein jeder gebildeter Tänzer doch ein angenehmes Wildes (wann ich so sagen kann und darf) anzunehmen hat, doch muß er auch seine Tänzerin im drehen mit einen gewissen *soliden* Anstand führen, und gleichsam sich mit ihr in dem tändelnden Affekt vereinigen, das anscheinende Wilde aber als eine ausgelassene, und in etwas übertriebene Freude nur zeigen, wann jedes allein figuriret. Dadurch wird auch dieser Nation in ihren Tanze das Schöne bestimmet." The emphasis is original. Five years earlier, in the volume that preceded his *Erweiterung der Kunst nach der Chorographie zu tanzen*, Feldtenstein made only the briefest mention of national dances "such as the German, Swabian, Hungarian, and Hannakian," all of which, he declared, had been "relegated to the commonest inns" outside the regions in which they originated. See Carl Joseph von Feldtenstein, *Die Kunst nach der Chorographie zu Tanzen und Tänze zu schreiben, nebst einer Abhandlung über die äusserliche Wohlanständigkeit im Tanzen* (Braunschweig: im Verlage der Schröderschen Buchhandlung, 1767), 19.

[42] Such positions were typically associated with theatrical rather than social dancing, lending further weight to Eva Campianu's assertion that many national dances became popular social dances only after first having been displayed in the theater. See Eva Campianu, "Langaus, Quadrille, Zingarese: Joseph Haydn und der Tanz," *Morgen* 6, no. 23 (June 1982): 174. Christian Friedrich Daniel Schubart, *Ideen zu einer Ästhetik der Tonkunst* (1806; reprint with index and preface by Fritz Kaiser and Margrit Kaiser, Hildesheim: Georg Olms Verlagsbuchhandlung, 1969), 352, also confirms the suitability of the Hungarian dance to the theater, writing that "dieser Tanz verdient sehr auf das Theater gebracht zu werden."

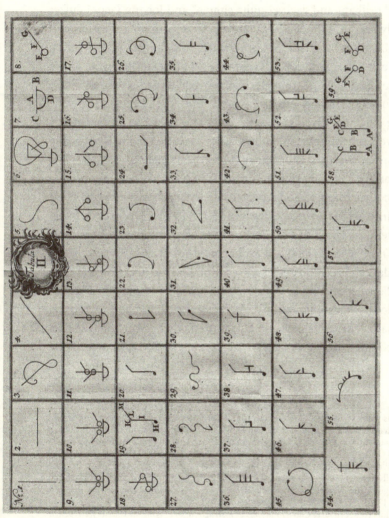

Figure 4.2. Carl Joseph von Feldtenstein, *Erweiterung der Kunst nach der Chorographie zu tanzen, Tänze zu erfinden, und aufzusetzen; wie auch Anweisung zu verschiedenen National-Tänzen; Als zu Englischen, Deutschen, Schwäbischen, Pohlnischen, Hannak- Masur- Kosak- und Hungarischen; mit Kupfern; nebst einer Anzahl Englischer Tänze* (Braunschweig: n.p., 1772), table 2. Reproduced from D-Dl, Dramat.566 (Sächsische Landesbibliothek—Staats- und Universitätsbibliothek Dresden; https://digital.slub-dresden.de/en/workview/dlf/7091/73). Figures 9–18 pertain to the Hungarian dance and, as indicated by the single semi-circle, show the male dancer's starting foot positions. Figures 9–13 show the male dancer standing in first through fifth positions (the closed circle represents the heel of the foot), while figures 14–18 show a variety of false positions, with toes pointing inward.

wildness" and "boisterous joy," which together with the female dancer's "flirtatiousness" and the music's "charm" seem for Feldtenstein to have largely defined the *Ungarischer*. Like his references to turns or spins, Feldtenstein's characterization of the *Ungarischer* is strongly consonant with eighteenth-century accounts of the contredanse, which Jean-Jacques Rousseau described as "brilliant and gay, yet quite simple" and Johann Georg Sulzer as "very lively and [...] moderately comical, thereby uniting pleasure and decorum."[43] Like Rousseau and Sulzer, Daniel Gottlob Türk and Heinrich Christoph Koch also emphasized liveliness, simplicity, artlessness, and a moderately comical character in their treatments of the contredanse.[44]

Feldtenstein's description on its own, in the absence of the specific directions he may have given his pupils, gives the impression that dancers' demeanors were more important to the proper execution of the *Ungarischer* than were particular steps and figures. Indeed, throughout Feldtenstein's treatise, exhortations to improvised or quasi-improvised performances of national dances are common and reflect the dancing master's support of naturalism in dance, which he believed was hindered by overly restrictive rules. For Feldtenstein, the *Hannakischer*, for instance, was not only similar in character to the *Ungarischer*, as he stated explicitly at the outset of his description of the latter dance, but it "possesses the ease of the *Schwäbischer*, that each couple can dance according to their own expression without it being necessary to follow [what] others [do]."[45] As musicologist and dance historian Kurt Petermann has explained, for Feldtenstein, "where national dances are concerned, the ability and taste of the dancers should take precedence

---

[43] Jean-Jacques Rousseau, *Dictionnaire de musique* (Paris: Chez la Veuve Duchesne, 1768; reprint Geneva: Editions Minkoff, 1998), "Contre-danse," 121: "Les Airs des Contre-Danses sont le plus souvent à deux tems; ils doivent être bien cadencés, brillans & gais, & avoir cependant beaucoup de simplicité; car comme on les reprend très-souvent, ils deviendroient insupportables, s'ils étoient chargés." Johann Georg Sulzer, *Allgemeine Theorie der schönen Künste*, vol. 2 (Leipzig: Weidmann, 1792; reprint Hildesheim: Georg Olms, 1967), "Englische Tänze," 66: "sie [sind] sehr lebhaft, und größtentheils etwas mäßig comisches haben, dadurch sie Vergnügen und Artigkeit mit einander vereinigen." The definition of the contredanse in Charles Compan, *Dictionnaire de danse* (Paris: Cailleau, 1787), is almost identical to Rousseau's.

[44] Daniel Gottlob Türk, *School of Clavier Playing, or Instructions in Playing the Clavier for Teachers and Students*, trans. with introduction and notes by Raymond H. Haggh (Lincoln: University of Nebraska Press, 1982; first published as *Klavierschule, oder Anweisung zum Klavierspielen für Lehrer und Lernende, mit kritischen Anmerkungen*, 1789), 393; and Heinrich Christoph Koch, *Musikalisches Lexikon* (Frankfurt am Main: August Hermann dem Jüngern, 1802; reprint Hildesheim: Bärenreiter, 1964), col. 536. Koch quotes Sulzer in his treatment of the contredanse in his *Versuch einer Anleitung zur Composition*, vol. 3 (Leipzig: bey Adam Friedrich Böhme, 1793), 47. McKee, "Ballroom Dances," also quotes Rousseau, Sulzer, Compan, Türk, and Koch on the contredanse.

[45] Feldtenstein, *Erweiterung der Kunst*, 101: "Er hat das bequeme von Schwäbischen an sich, daß jedes Paar nach ihren eigenen erfindenden Wendungen [...] tanzen kann, ohne genöthiget zu seyn, sich nach andern zu richten [...]."

over the structure and choreography of the dance."[46] This freedom helps to explain how certain dances rose to such prominence during Feldtenstein's lifetime (?–1785); as the dancing master noted, for instance, the incredibly popular German dance was essentially the same as the *Schwäbischer*, in which "the execution [...] remains free and unrestricted. Each male dancer can [...] guide his partner according to his own pleasure."[47]

This attitude reflects the broader democratization of dance in the second half of the eighteenth century, whereby previously exclusive venues such as Vienna's Redoutensäle were open to the public and previously elite dances like the minuet were danced by all classes. However, as I've already noted, dancers of different classes generally did not mix, and in spite of the widespread availability and popularity of dance instruction in the Habsburg capital, dance practices varied according to socioeconomic standing. One reads in the *Neuestes Sittengemählde von Wien* (1801), for instance, that in the suburban dance halls patronized by the middle classes ("die Mittelklasse des Volks"), "nothing is danced but minuets and German dances. It has often given me great pleasure to observe the strange twists and turns and graceful figures [*Krümmungen*] with which many a fleet-footed tailor winds his way through the solemn minuet."[48] Notwithstanding the avowed enjoyment this dancing provided him as a spectator, the author goes on to complain that while "minuets, when danced daintily and gracefully, are very beautiful," when they are danced "without decency, without the proper steps, without charm and dignity of movement, as they typically are in these dance halls, these dances are nothing but a boring, monotonous tripping about, tiring the eyes and the feet without fulfilling a single condition of the dance, cheerfulness or beauty of movement and dexterity of limbs."[49] Conversely, Ignaz de

---

[46] Feldtenstein, *Erweiterung der Kunst*, xx: "Bei den Nationaltänzen soll Geschicklichkeit und Geschmack der Tanzenden über die Struktur und den Verlauf des Tanzes entscheiden."

[47] Feldtenstein, *Erweiterung der Kunst*, 100: "Die Führung in diesem Tanze, bleibt frey und uneingeschränkt. Jeder Tänzer kann seine Tänzerin nach eigenen Gefallen, durch Zirkelwendungen, und Touren in Bewegung setzen [...]." Feldtenstein's comments about the similarity of German and Swabian dances are on p. 99. On Feldtenstein's birth and death dates, see Kurt Petermann's comments on pp. xii–xiii.

[48] *Neuestes Sittengemählde von Wien*, vol. 1, "Siebenter Brief," 106: "Hier wird nichts als Menuett und Deutsch getanzt, und es war mir oft eine rechte Lust, die seltsamen Wendungen und zierlichen Krümmungen zu beobachten, mit welchen sich mancher leichtfüßige Schneider durch den gravitätischen Menuet hindurch windet."

[49] *Neuestes Sittengemählde von Wien*, vol. 1, "Achter Brief," 108–9: "Die Menuets sind nun freylich, wenn sie zierlich und graziös getanzt werden, ein sehr schöner Tanz [...] aber so ohne Anstand, ohne gehörige Pas, ohne Reiz und Würde in den Bewegungen, wie sie auf den Tanzplätzen gewöhnlich herabgeschliffen werden, schienen diese Tänze nichts als ein langweiliges einförmiges Herumtrippeln, das Augen und Füße ermüdet, ohne eine einzige von den Bedingungen des Tanzes, Ausdruck der Fröhlichkeit oder Schönheit der Bewegungen und Gewandtheit der Glieder zu erfüllen."

Luca specified that "among distinguished persons, the minuet is danced very purely, with strict observance of the beat."[50] As I explore below, the execution of contredanses in late eighteenth-century Vienna was similarly highly contingent upon the socioeconomic status of the dancers. Contredanses, like other contemporary dances, were generally not social equalizers, despite their traditional democratic, anti-hierarchical associations.[51] Thus, while *Ungarische* lent themselves to enjoyment as one variety of these popular figure dances, they did not provide an unambiguous point of cultural contact across classes.

Contredanses and Class

Musicologist Curt Sachs has interpreted the ascendancy of the contredanse as a social dance in the second half of the eighteenth century as "analogous with the rise of bourgeois society and the decline of the aristocratic culture" so closely associated with the minuet.[52] Although by this time the minuet was no longer exclusively danced by the elite, Buurman has underscored that it retained its aristocratic connotation, especially in dance treatises and theatrical works, where "it continued to be understood as an expression of nobility."[53] In contrast, she explains, "the contredanse functioned as an effective metaphor for cross-class socializing [...]."[54] These persistent associations emphasize fundamental differences between these two iconic dances: while the minuet's steps, choreography, and etiquette required years of training to master, the contredanse was "essentially a walk or alternation of steps," as musicologist Wye Jamison Allanbrook has aptly described it, or in the nineteenth-century music critic and theorist Adolf Bernhard Marx's words, a "dancelike movement" performed by couples tracing a series of figures.[55] Simple walking and gliding steps ensured the accessibility of the contredanse

---

[50] De Luca, *Topographie von Wien*, vol. 1, "Die Tanzmusik," 384: "Unter den Personen von Unterscheidung wird Menuet sehr rein, mit genauester Beobachtung des Takts getanzt."

[51] For a survey of these associations in contemporary and more recent writings, see McKee, "Ballroom Dances," 168–74; and Buurman, *The Viennese Ballroom*, 75–77. I borrow the phrase "social equaliser" from Buurman, *The Viennese Ballroom*, 87.

[52] Curt Sachs, *World History of the Dance*, trans. Bessie Schönberg (New York: W. W. Norton, 1963), 398.

[53] Buurman, *The Viennese Ballroom*, 57.

[54] Buurman, *The Viennese Ballroom*, 91.

[55] Wye Jamison Allanbrook, *Rhythmic Gesture in Mozart: Le Nozze di Figaro and Don Giovanni* (Chicago: University of Chicago Press, 1983), 61; trans. from Adolf Bernhard Marx, *Die Lehre von der musikalischen Komposition*, vol. 2 (Leipzig: Breitkopf und Härtel, 1837–38), 57.

to dancers with little skill or experience; those with more training could import steps from other dances such as the gavotte, bourrée, and rigaudon. As dance historians Freda Burford and Anne Daye have explained, "figures were executed with any suitable steps familiar to the company or chosen by individual dancers," leaving ample room for improvisation and personal expression as well as current fashion.[56] Hungarian or other nationally themed contredanses could easily expand the "endless variety" of steps and figures that was, in musicologist Richard Leppert's formulation, "the most essential component of contredanses."[57]

The contredanse's versatility and adaptability led the eighteenth-century German writer and philosopher Friedrich Schiller to uphold it as a symbol of an ideal society in which "each seems only to be following his own inclination, yet without ever getting in the way of anybody else. It is the most perfectly appropriate symbol of the assertion of one's own freedom and regard for the freedom of others." Although Schiller celebrated the beautiful spectacle of a contredanse "composed of many complicated figures and perfectly executed," with "innumerable movements intersecting in the most chaotic fashion, changing direction swiftly and without rhyme or reason yet *never colliding*,"[58] in practice, in Vienna's crowded public ballrooms and dance halls, such coordination would have been next to impossible and collisions between dancers all but unavoidable. According to one contemporary author, "given the size of the *Redoute* and the number of people it attracts, performing contredanses there would be a Herculean, quite impossible undertaking" and, furthermore, "in a large company not accustomed to dancing with one another, [contredanses] require significant rehearsal to perform, whereby precious time [for dancing] is lost."[59] As a social dance,

---

[56] Freda Burford, revised by Anne Daye, "Contredanse," in *Grove Music Online*, www.oxfordmusiconline.com (accessed 19 August 2022).

[57] Richard Leppert, *Music and Image: Domesticity, Ideology, and Socio-Cultural Formation in Eighteenth-Century England* (Cambridge: Cambridge University Press, 1988), 96.

[58] Friedrich Schiller to Christian Gottfried Körner, 23 February 1793, as given in Friedrich Schiller, *On the Aesthetic Education of Man in a Series of Letters*, ed. and trans. with an introduction, commentary, and glossary of terms by Elizabeth M. Wilkinson and L. A. Willoughby (Oxford: Clarendon Press, 1982), 300. The emphasis is original.

[59] *Neuestes Sittengemählde von Wien*, vol. 1, "Achter Brief," 108: "auch wären Contretänze auf der Redoute wegen der Menge von Menschen und der Größe des Saals ein herkulisches, ja ganz unmögliches Unternehmen." *Neuestes Sittengemählde von Wien*, vol. 1, "Achter Brief," 111–12: "Die Angloisen besonders in doppelten Colonnen sind unstreitig der schönste gesellschaftliche Tanz, der aber nur die einzige Unbequemlichkeit hat, daß er in großer und nicht zussammen gewohnter Gesellschaft ohne langes probiren, wodurch die köstliche Zeit verloren geht, nicht aufgeführt werden kann [...]." Buurman, *The Viennese Ballroom*, 79–83, cites this source and provides further evidence of the marginal place of contredanses in Vienna's public ballrooms around 1800.

the contredanse was therefore largely enjoyed in smaller, private gatherings, where a degree of improvisatory freedom was both permitted and practicable, but through which, as Buurman has underscored, "social classes remained separate."[60] The dance's potential to foster cross-class contact therefore remained merely metaphorical; it did not translate into actual practice in eighteenth-century Vienna.

The same was true when contredanses were featured in "presentational dance performances," which musicologist Ralph P. Locke has defined as "occasions when aristocrats or professionals (or aristocrats and professionals performing together) executed carefully rehearsed numbers in front of a hand-chosen courtly audience"[61]—what I have referred to as "*divertissements*" in chapter 1. Buurman has drawn attention to this overlooked function of contredanses in eighteenth-century Vienna, and she has emphasized that in the role of presentational dances too, contredanses fostered segregation by social class, even though audiences were not necessarily only aristocratic.[62] She cites in particular the public ball held at Schönbrunn palace on the occasion of the visit by Grand Duke Paul of Russia (son of Catherine the Great and heir to the Russian throne) and his wife, Grand Duchess Maria Feodorovna, to the Habsburg court. Mozart was among thousands who took part in this grand event, and he related in a letter to his father that it included "two sets of contredanses—Romans and Tartars" performed by the nobility for the gathered onlookers, with the Austrian and Russian royalty physically closest to the dancers and everyone else watching from behind them.[63] Buurman comments that "the general public was kept at the bottom of the hierarchy, both through their non-participation in the dance and through a barrier of physical space separating them from the nobles. While the ball may have brought royalty and public together in the same ballroom, the contredanse performance enforced the social hierarchy amongst those who were present."[64]

Yet, as I discussed in chapter 1, Mozart's account of this ball is incomplete. As the contemporary press documented, the Roman and Tartar

---

[60] Buurman, *The Viennese Ballroom*, 77 and 80. Like Buurman, Leppert, *Music and Image*, 97, also notes that "in the eighteenth century [...], country dances were performed in class-specific groups, as was common to all social dancing [...]." On the contredanse in private settings, see also *Neuestes Sittengemählde von Wien*, vol. 1, "Achter Brief," 111; Lager and Seidl, *Kontratanz in Wien*, 26; and Witzmann, *Der Ländler in Wien*, 82. On improvisation as a feature of house balls, see Witzmann, *Der Ländler in Wien*, 13.

[61] Ralph P. Locke, *Music and the Exotic from the Renaissance to Mozart* (Cambridge: Cambridge University Press, 2015), 113.

[62] Buurman, *The Viennese Ballroom*, chap. 4, esp. 83–89.

[63] Mozart to his father, Vienna, 5 December 1781, in *The Letters of Mozart and His Family*, 781 (letter 435).

[64] Buurman, *The Viennese Ballroom*, 88.

contredanses were performed alongside dances from Hungary and Strasbourg as well as ones for sailors of unspecified origin. In the *Wiener Zeitung*'s article on the ball, the Roman dance is referred to as a "quadrille" and the Tartar ones as "contredanses," but when the newspaper reported on the reprise of the program at a smaller, private ball at the Hofburg the following week, all five varieties of dance were characterized as "quadrilles,"[65] a term that was used in Vienna around 1800 for contredanses performed in square formation (as opposed to longways).[66] Contemporary newspaper articles attest that the Hungarian nobility themselves performed Hungarian national dances, but these were apparently similar enough to contredanses to be qualified as such—and thereby rendered more familiar to readers.[67] The journalist's interpretation, furthermore, may have been colored by the fact that nationally themed contredanses were a common variety of presentational dance in late eighteenth-century Vienna, contributing local color and variety to entertainments that emphasized pastoral or more generally rustic topics. In early 1774, for example, the *Wienerisches Diarium* described to its readers festivities involving thirty-two aristocratic couples—including Maria Theresa and her husband—performing three contredanses dressed as English sailors. The report specified that the event was choreographed by Jean-Georges Noverre, the imperial ballet master, who was handsomely rewarded for his efforts on this occasion.[68] In his diary, the head of the court household Prince Johann Joseph Khevenhüller-Metsch, who witnessed the performance, described it as "a contredanse of thirty-two couples, half English and half French peasants *de la Provence*."[69] The following

---

[65] I cite the reports in the section titled "A Snapshot from 1781."
[66] Buurman, *The Viennese Ballroom*, 78.
[67] On dances of western Hungary that resembled the contredanse, see Kürti, "Hungary," 409.
[68] "Wien den 2. Hornung," *Wienerisches Diarium*, 2 February 1774, 4 cols. 1–2: "Bey dem am letztern Montage auf allerhöchsten Befehl angeordneten Kammerfeste sind von 32 Paar als engländische Matrosen verkleideten Herrschaften, drey vom Herrn Noverre angegebenen ausnehmend schöne Contratenze auf die prächtigst und ergötzlichste Art aufgeführt worden: 16 Paar, unter welchen sich Ihre königl. Hoheiten befanden, waren mit weißen Atlaß und rosenfarben Bändern, die andern 16 Paar aber mit weißen Atlaß und blauen Bändern geziert, angethan; diese letzteren öffneten das Kammerfest mit dem ersten Contretanz, die ersteren aber folgten mit dem zweyten, und endlich vereinigten sich alle und führten alsdenn den dritten Contretanz auf eine so bewunders- und sehenswürdige Art auf, daß beyde kais. Majestäten ein sehr großes Vergnügen und Zufriedenheit darob zu äußern geruhet haben. Der Herr Noverre und dessen zween Gehilfen wurde von Ihro Majest. ansehnlich beschenket."
[69] Maria Breunlich-Pawlik and Hans Wagner, eds., *Aus der Zeit Maria Theresias. Tagebuch des Fürsten Johann Joseph Khevenhüller-Metsch, kaiserlichen Obersthofmeisters 1742–1776*, vol. 8 (1774–1780) (Vienna: Adolf Holzhausen, 1972), 10: "Den 31. [January 1774] war das erste und einzige Cammerfest, bei welchen eine letzthin in der Redoute aufgeführte Contredanse von 32 Paaren, halb englisch-, halb französischer Baueren de la Provence reproduciret wurde, im solche der Kaiserin sehen zu machen." As Bruce Alan Brown has noted about the ballet *Un Port de mer dans la Provençe* (the synopsis of which I've included in chapter 1), "Provence" in this case as well is likely a misspelling of "province." See Bruce Alan Brown, "Magri in Vienna: The Apprenticeship of a Choreographer," in *The Grotesque Dancer on the Eighteenth-Century Stage: Gennaro Magri and His World*, ed. Rebecca Harris-Warrick and Bruce Alan Brown (Madison: University of Wisconsin Press, 2005), 86.

year, Khevenhüller-Metsch related a similar event at court, during which twenty-four pairs of dancers dressed as shepherds performed a contredanse choreographed by Noverre's replacement, Gasparo Angiolini.[70] Given their associations with naturalism and simplicity, contredanses contributed to the bucolic pretense of these occasions, although as Rice has observed, highly rehearsed and professionally choreographed presentational contredanses such as these were "closer to ballet[s] than social dance[s]."[71]

***

In 1807, Leipzig's *Allgemeine musikalische Zeitung* published a substantial article on Hungarian dances (given as text D in the appendix). Its anonymous author commented that in some German cities, these national dances, along with polonaises as well as Cossack and Masurian dances, were gaining in popularity and lending much needed variety to social dancing. The fast-tempo Hungarian dance, with which the article's author assumed some familiarity on his readers' part, was performed, he noted, with quick turns ("schnelle Dreher"), like those of contredanses ("anglaises") and quadrilles, the very dances that the author asserted had eclipsed national ones among Germany's high society for the last twenty or thirty years. Included in the article is a review of Johann Nepomuk Hummel's *Balli ongaresi*, op. 23, recently published by the Kunst- und Industrie-Comptoir in Vienna; this "little work," the author noted, "could help spread the reawakening of love for characteristic dance."[72] Such a reawakening was hardly necessary in Vienna itself, where advertisements in the press as well as extant sheet music confirm that *Ungarische* did not suffer the same fate in the last decades of the eighteenth century as the article's author declared they did elsewhere. *Ungarische* were widely distributed, in print and manuscript, and served not only as simple

---

[70] Breunlich-Pawlik and Wagner, eds., *Aus der Zeit Maria Theresias*, vol. 8, 100: "die von dem Signor Angiolini componirte Contre-Danse produciret worden. Diese bestunde in 24 Paar, die als Schäffer angekleidet waren [...]." The passages from Khevenhüller-Metsch's diaries are also cited in Witzmann, *Der Ländler in Wien*, 82; and Fink, *Der Ball*, 169.

[71] Rice, *Empress Marie Therese*, 127. Rice provides several examples of presentational dances (including contredanses) that were staged in Vienna in the early years of the nineteenth century on pp. 124–27.

[72] "Ungarische Tänze," *Allgemeine musikalische Zeitung* 9, no. 25 (18 March 1807): cols. 404–5: "ein Werkchen, das [...] gut genug gerathen ist, um, zur Verbreitung jener wiedererwachenden Liebhaberey am charakteris[tis]chen Tanze sein Scherflein beytragen zu können." In his review of the *Balli ongaresi*, the author lamented that Hummel composed only one slow-tempo dance for his collection of seven Hungarian dances. The first sixteen measures of this dance are included in the article, because the author acknowledged that this type of slow-tempo Hungarian dance was unfamiliar to his readers, implying that the fast-tempo type was known to them and required no introduction.

keyboard repertoire but as functional dance music, lending themselves especially to the accompaniment of contredanses in small, private gatherings. Descriptions of movements and manners common in social dancing in Hungary may well have informed these dances, fostering an imagined community of dancers across geographical and cultural divides.

Contredanses, however, were also commonly put to use as aristocratic presentational dances in the Habsburg capital, and in this role, they differed greatly from the contredanses enjoyed in social dancing. As presentational dances, contredanses were designed to entertain spectators while displaying wealth and power, and even when costumes and props cast dancers as rustic characters, their skilled execution of elaborate choreographies confirmed that they were anything but. As social dances, on the other hand, contredanses were danced primarily for the enjoyment of the participants themselves, and simple steps and figures that could be adapted to the skills of the dancers and that allowed for a measure of improvisatory license meant that in intimate house balls, contredanses were accessible to nearly everyone. In such domestic settings, it is easy to imagine the *Contredanses Hongraises* bestowed upon Archduchess Elisabeth shortly after her marriage in early 1788—or any of the host of other *Ungarische* that circulated as sheet music in eighteenth-century Vienna—accompanying convivial dancing among family and friends. To be sure, the archduchess herself may well have enjoyed the *Contredanses* in this same way, but those outside her immediate circle could have had no knowledge of such private amusements. The public's awareness of the aristocracy's performance of contredanses was limited to presentational dances that they had either witnessed personally or read about in the press. As presentational dances, the function of aristocratic contredanses overlapped significantly with that of the minuet as danced by Vienna's elite. According to contemporary newspapers, for instance, only weeks before Görög gave Archduchess Elisabeth the *Contredanses Hongraises*, she and her new husband had opened the ball held in the Redoutensäle in honor of their wedding by performing a minuet in front of over 4,000 assembled guests—a scene highly reminiscent of the one during which Mozart witnessed the performance of presentational contredanses on the occasion of the royal Russian visit in 1781.[73]

---

[73] The *Wiener Zeitung* reported that the ball held on the day after the marriage was for "4500 durch Billete gelade Personen." See "Inländische Begebenheiten. Wien," *WZ*, 9 January 1788, 62 col. 1. The opening minuet is mentioned in the *Journal des Luxus und der Moden*'s extensive description of Franz and Elisabeth's wedding festivities. See "Vermählungs-Feyer des Erzherzogs Franz mit ihrer Durchl. der Prinzessin Elisabeth von Würtemberg. Wien, den 12. Jan. 1788," *Journal des Luxus und der Moden* 3 (February 1788): 57.

The socioeconomic contingency of contredanse practices meant that while readers of Görög's journal, like the archduchess herself, may well have "very much liked" the *Contredanses Hongraises*, among many other *Ungarische*, and "often amused [themselves] with [them] at the keyboard," their experiences on the dance floor differed sharply. But much like the title page of the *Contredanses Hongraises*, which recalled their presentation to Elisabeth at the masked ball of 31 January 1788, Görög's mention of the occasion in his periodical allowed readers and keyboard players to feel part of the event even if they had not experienced it firsthand. Indeed, musicologist Nicholas Mathew has argued that the domestic enjoyment of great quantities of early nineteenth-century Viennese topical, celebratory, and patriotic music collapsed the divide between public and private, serving as mementos of ceremonial or theatrical performances.[74] More vividly than such souvenirs, commemorative dance music for the domestic market invited middle-class amateurs to imagine themselves as—even to become, at a distance—protagonists in performances in which they would never participate, conjuring images of aristocratic ballrooms and practices and offering them a transgressive, vicarious thrill. Whether amateur Viennese dancers pictured themselves in elaborate performances of Hungarian music and dance at the imperial court or adopted some of the manners and movements of more modest social dancing from the neighboring Kingdom, their dance practices thus had the power to transcend, if only imaginatively, boundaries of class, culture, and belonging.

---

[74] Nicholas Mathew, *Political Beethoven* (Cambridge: Cambridge University Press, 2013), 12.

Epilogue

In 2017, over two centuries after the appearance of the Viennese writer and civil servant Johann Pezzl's *Sketch of Vienna*, Sebastian Kurz, at the helm of the Austrian People's Party (Österreichische Volkspartei, or ÖVP), became the Federal Chancellor of Austria. Austria's major centrist-right political party since the end of World War II, the ÖVP swung much farther to the right under Kurz's leadership, adopting the anti-immigrant and Islamophobic stances and policies that Kurz had championed when he became Austria's State Secretary of the Interior Ministry for Social Integration in 2011 and during his subsequent tenure as Austria's Foreign Minister (2013–2017). Whereas Pezzl enjoyed the "pleasant feast for the eyes" provided by "the variety of national costumes from different countries" worn in late eighteenth-century Vienna,[1] Kurz repeatedly called for bans on veils and headscarves. Whereas Pezzl's contemporary, the German writer, editor, and book dealer Friedrich Nicolai, marveled at the number of languages he heard spoken during his stay in the Habsburg capital,[2] Kurz demanded that imams preach in German. Perhaps most disturbingly, the ÖVP and its ruling coalition partner from 2017 to 2019, the far-right Freedom Party of Austria (Freiheitliche Partei Österreichs, or FPÖ), consistently blamed rising anti-Semitism in Austria on the country's Muslim community, refusing to acknowledge their own members' involvement in anti-Semitic and radical right-wing groups.[3]

To be sure, the rosy picture painted by eighteenth-century commentators masked an often darker reality, one that included, among other things, demeaning representations and caricatures of numerous Others, often Muslim,

---

[1] Johann Pezzl, *Skizze von Wien* (1786–1790), as translated in H. C. Robbins Landon, *Mozart and Vienna* (New York: Schirmer, 1991), 65–66.

[2] Friedrich Nicolai, *Beschreibung einer Reise durch Deutschland und die Schweiz, im Jahre 1781. Nebst Bemerkungen über Gelehrsamkeit, Industrie, Religion und Sitten*, vol. 3 (Berlin and Stettin: n.p., 1784), "Ueber die Einwohner in Wien und ihre Anzahl," 170.

[3] The information on Sebastian Kurz is from "Factsheet: Sebastian Kurz" compiled by the Bridge Initiative Team, https://bridge.georgetown.edu/research/factsheet-sebastian-kurz/ (accessed 6 April 2023). Georgetown University's Bridge Initiative is an important multiyear project that aims in part "to inform the general public about Islamophobia" (https://bridge.georgetown.edu/about-us/).

in contemporary operatic and theatrical works. As a government official and staunch Josephinist, Pezzl, in particular, undoubtedly depicted Viennese life and values in the best light possible, yet by the same token his writings reflect what were at least in theory official Habsburg positions of Enlightened toleration, underscored by Joseph II's patents and edicts of religious tolerance and abolition of perpetual serfdom. Similarly, his imposition of German as the administrative language throughout the Habsburg lands was undertaken in the spirit of bureaucratic efficiency rather than out of fear of cultural difference. In Austrian schools today, in contrast, newly arrived children who have not attained the mandated level of proficiency in German are taught the language via a model of segregated education, whereby they attend separate classes, which many critics refer to as "ghetto classes."[4] One recent study reported more negative than positive effects of this system because it fosters social exclusion and stigmatization; children's language learning, furthermore, is impoverished when it cannot take place through play with native German-speaking peers.[5] According to Austria's Federal Ministry of Education, Science, and Research, music—along with theater and creative writing—plays an important role in these language classes because, in addition to lending much-needed pedagogical variety, it "promotes attention, perception, cooperation, and self-esteem in addition to verbal expression." Indeed, given music's critical role in forging identity and belonging, it is an apt tool to develop the "social competence and intercultural empowerment" emphasized in the curriculum—essentially, the cultural assimilation of the child, reminiscent of Maria Theresa's approach to Hungary's Roma.[6]

Austria's recent illiberalism mirrors that of many of its neighboring countries (and beyond), where immigration and multiculturalism are seen as both security and cultural threats. In historian Holly Case's words, Hungary's prime minister, Viktor Orbán, for instance, "portrays the future of Europe as

---

[4] See, for instance, Agence France-Presse's article "Austria's 'Ghetto' Language Classes Stir Segregation Fears," https://www.france24.com/en/20200118-austria-s-ghetto-language-classes-stir-segregation-fears (accessed 6 February 2024).

[5] Katharina Resch, Marie Gitschthaler, and Susanne Schwab, "Teacher's [sic] Perceptions of Separate Language Learning Models for Students with Immigrant Background in Austrian Schools," *Intercultural Education* 34, no. 3 (2023): 288–304.

[6] As given in the "Bundesgesetzblatt für die Republik Österreich, 230. Verordnung (31 August 2018)," https://www.ris.bka.gv.at/Dokumente/BgblAuth/BGBLA_2018_II_230/BGBLA_2018_II_230.pdfsig (accessed 6 February 2024): "Auch kreative Lese- und Schreibaufgaben, Musik und theaterpädagogische Elemente ermöglichen einen abwechslungsreichen Zugang zur deutschen Sprache und fördern neben dem Ausdruck die Aufmerksamkeit, die Wahrnehmung, die Kooperation und den Selbstwert. [...] Lernbereich 4: Selbstkompetenz, soziale Kompetenz, interkulturelle Handlungsfähigkeit."

a dystopia, where migrants have overrun the continent and white Europeans are on a sure path to extinction." On a trip to Vienna in March 2018, as Case has recounted, Orbán's cabinet minister János Lázár videotaped himself walking through one of the city's neighborhoods, where he decried the lack of "white, German-speaking residents."[7] In response to the refugee crisis of 2015 and attendant fears of what they consider a dire future of ethnic and cultural diversity, Hungary's leaders ordered the construction of border barriers, effectively cutting off entry to Europe through the Balkan route, a move supported by Kurz, who called for closing off the Mediterranean route as well.

Such nationalist, xenophobic responses to migration—including the very definition of what constitutes a migrant—are not only deeply inhumane but fundamentally ahistorical. Hungary's Romani citizens are no more "migrants," as Orbán has characterized them,[8] than Vienna has ever been a city inhabited only by white German speakers. The editors of the International Musicological Society's journal *Acta Musicologica*, noting parallels to the plight of refugees fleeing Nazism and fascism in the twentieth century, have urged scholars not to remain professionally aloof from these pressing matters, but to respond to them by embracing a "musicology of borders" that "could reformulate the increasing centrality of marginal musics and marginalized peoples."[9] With no intention of downplaying the severity and immediacy of twenty-first-century political and humanitarian crises or of mischaracterizing the eighteenth century as an era of universal tolerance, an essential premise of this book is that the importance of historiographically marginalized musics in Vienna is not new. As I outlined in the introduction to this study, a long-standing scholarly focus on Haydn, Mozart, and Beethoven has painted a distinctly Austro-German picture of Viennese musical life in the later eighteenth century. In so doing, musicologists have overlooked the significant contributions and influences of the city's "Hungarians, Poles, Armenians, Wallachians, Moldavians, Serbians, Greeks, Muslims, Jews, Bohemians, Transylvanians, and Croats" to whom Pezzl drew attention, thereby tacitly endorsing a narrow conception of Viennese culture.

---

[7] Holly Case, "Goulash Democracy. Hungary: A Nation in Fear of the Future," *Times Literary Supplement*, 20 June 2018, 14.
[8] Case, "Goulash Democracy."
[9] Philip V. Bohlman and Federico Celestini, "Editorial: Musicians at the Borders," *Acta Musicologica* 88, no. 1 (2016): 3.

In this book, I have aimed to establish the integral, unique place of Hungarian dances and their music in the lives of the eighteenth-century capital's women and men, privileged and disadvantaged, and to underscore how their experiences were fundamentally mediated by gender and class, contributing to their identities, perceptions of themselves and others, and places in society. At court and in its theaters, in public sites of sociability, at the keyboard, and in social dancing, encounters with Hungarian dances both allowed the imaginative exploration of new identities and affinities and marked existing boundaries of social and cultural belonging. Yet Pezzl's kaleidoscopic list of the many peoples of Enlightenment Vienna reminds us that, as with our world's many other zones of cross-cultural contact, much work remains to be done in bringing to light the vitally important histories of musical diversity in that city, histories that would reveal difference and exchange as elements that have always been fundamentally constitutive of the fabric of Viennese life rather than as motives for fear, oppression, and exclusion.

APPENDIX

Descriptions of Hungarian Dances Issued in Connection with Dances for Keyboard

Text A) Franz Paul Rigler, prefatory note to *12 Ungarische Tänze fürs Forte Piano oder 2 Violinen und einem Basse der Ungarischen Nation gewidmet und komponirt von H: Musikprofessor Rigler zu Pressburg*. Undated manuscript containing twelve dances for keyboard, composed before 1796, the year of Rigler's death (D-HR, III 4 1/2 4° 703). The version for string trio referenced in the title remains unknown. Transcribed from Géza Papp, ed., *Hungarian Dances 1784–1810*, Musicalia Danubiana 7 (Budapest: Magyar Tudományos Akadémia, Zenetudományi Intézet, 1986), 348–49.

"Anmerkung. § 1. Unter den Nationaltanzen zeichnen sich die Minuetten, Englische Contretänze—Teütschen, Polnischen und Kosakischen besonders aus; vermuthlich darum, weil sich mancher geschikte Mann um ihre Berichtigung und Erfindung befließe. Der Ungarische Nationaltanz unterscheidet sich von allen andern durch seinen ihm ganz eignen karakteristischen Gange, deßen weßentliches in kunstloßen herzlichen und fröhlichen Ausdrücken der Melodie besteht, wo in den meisten, so wie beym Englischen, die Einschnitte und Absätze auf kurze Tacttheile fallen, obwohl man auch bei einigen dieser im Niederschlage verzögern kann wenn im Aufschlage angefangen wird.

§ 2. Schade ist es daß bisher noch für die Ausbildung und Verbesserung dieses gewis muntern Tanzes so wenig gesorgt worden ist.—Aber der Ungar schreibt oder komponirt selbst nicht und wollte man den Zigeüner als National Spielmann für die Quelle nehmen, bei der zu schopfen ist, so würden nur blos seine beßern Melodien und deren Modulationen, zu benüzen seyn; weil bey ihm Vortrag und Harmonie so schlecht bestellt sind, daß der Kenner gleich bemerkt, wo es der nakten Natur an Kunst und Wissenschaft mangelt.

§ 3. Nun haben es einige in Pest und Wienn gewagt Ungarische zu schreiben; allem ihnen abwischte dabey das wahre karakteristische zu geschwinde, und man wuste am Ende nicht, ob sie einen Kosakischen oder Contretanz gemeint hatten. Ob ich mit meinen Versuche glüklicher bin wird der Kenner an Melodie und Harmonie leicht entscheiden können; beyde haben ihre Schwürigkeiten, ich habe sie darum mit möglichster Genauheit und Sorge bearbeitet; weil sie so wohl zum Muster der Orthographie und Melodie, als auch zur Nachahmung in beiden dienen sollen."

Text B) "Ueber die Nationaltänze der Ungarn," *Allgemeine musikalische Zeitung* 2, no. 35 (28 May 1800): cols. 611–16. In his preface to the article (cols. 609–11), the journal's editor, Friedrich Rochlitz, qualified its author as "ein sehr bedeutender Mann aus Presburg." In notes to his edition of *Ungarische Tänze für Klavier/Hungarian Dances for Piano*, Diletto Musicale 662 (Vienna: Doblinger, 1993), Ferenc Bónis has indicated that the unsigned article was penned by the composer and teacher Heinrich Klein. The four dances included in the journal as a supplement to the article are adapted from Franz Paul Rigler's collection of *12 Ungarische Tänze fürs Forte Piano* (before 1796), and correspondences of wording in some passages suggest that Klein referred to Rigler's prefatory note to his own collection (text A) in writing this article.

"Der Ungar ist ein enthusiastischer Liebhaber der Musik. Er kann sich nicht entschliessen ruhig zu bleiben, sobald er eines von seinen National-Stücken spielen hört, sondern er ist sogleich in voller Bewegung, indem er entweder ein Lied nachtrillert, oder mit seinen Sporen und Händen den Takt schlägt. Soll ihm aber die Musik gefallen, so muss sie entweder heroisch-rauschend, oder mit schmelzenden Klagetönen erfüllt seyn, (ein Zug, der jeder ursprünglich asiatischen Nation eigen zu seyn scheint).

Die Instrumente bey der ungarischen N. Musik sind gewöhnlich eine oder mehrere Violinen, eine Bassgeige und ein so genanntes Hackbrett (Zimbal). Andere Instrumente, Fagott, Oboe, Waldhorn u. a. findet man bey derselben nie. Selten findet sich eine geringere als drey Mann, und noch seltner eine grössere als 8 oder 10 Mann starke Truppe Musiker beysammen, von welchen immer der Eine, oder ein Paar erste Violin, ein Anderer den Bass, und die Uebrigen, den Zimbalisten ausgenommen, zweyte Violin spielen. Ist aber die Gesellschaft mehr als fünf Glieder stark, so spielt eines derselben die Variation des Textes nach Angabe seiner eigenen Phantasie, und bringt dadurch einige Mannigfaltigkeit in die sonst sehr einfachen Töne. Ich sage: in die einfachen Töne; denn kein Sätzchen aus den Anfangsgründen für Lehrlinge kann man sich so einfach denken, als es die Musik zu den ung. Nat. T. ist. Den Grund hiervon suche ich darinnen, weil sie weder das Produkt eigentlicher Tonkünstler sind, noch in Noten gesezt werden. Fast alle Stücke, die in den Zirkeln der N. Ungarn gespielt werden, sind das augenblickliche Produkt der Phantasie. Da stellt sich nicht selten ein Mann, wenn ihm die Stücke der Musik nicht gefallen, vor die Musiker hin und trillert ihnen die Töne, die ihm gerade einfallen, oder die er von andern Musikern hörte, so lange vor, und lässt sie sich einzeln so lange nachfiedeln, bis die Virtuosen aus denselben ein Ganzes heraus zu fiedeln vermögen. Hieraus kann man sich auch das Einförmige erklären, welches allen ung. Tänzen eigen ist. Man sieht daraus aber auch, woher es komme, dass ein und dasselbe Stück von verschiedenen Gesellschaften gespielt, sehr verschiedenartige Modulationen hat. Bey so bewandten Umständen könnte nun freylich die National-Musik der Ungarn zu keiner Festigkeit gelangen, wenn nicht gute Tonkünstler sich Muhe gäben, dieselbe den Händen der rohesten Klasse von Menschen, der Zigeuner, zu entreissen. Wir können uns aber jezt doch schon einiger Männer rühmen, die sich um die Verbesserung und Vervollkommnung der Nat. Musik Verdienste erwerben, und ein von solchen Männern komponirtes Stück, gut gespielt, ist so empfindungsreich, und so hinreissend schön, dass ich wenig andere N. Stücke damit vergleichen kann. Ich lege ein Paar solcher Stücke bey,[1] zum Theil um das eben Gesagte zu bestätigen, zum Theil aber auch um dadurch dasjenige zu erläutern, was ich für diesesmal über die N. Musik der Ungarn sagen will.

Es ist für den Tonkünstler, der Nationaltänze richtig beurtheilen will, ein vorzügliches Erforderniss, dass er vorerst die Hauptzüge in dem Charakter der Nation wohl kenne, deren Musik er vor sich hat.[2]

Der Ungar ist wie der Spanier, stolz, und dünkt sich zur ersten Nation auf dem Erdboden zu gehören. Vorzüglich aber äussert er diesen Stolz durch seine majestätische Stellung, und durch seinen gesezten, festen Schritt—zwey Eigenthümlichkeiten, welche

---

[1] Siehe die musikalische Beylage.
[2] So wie es für den Menschenbeobachter ein bedeutendes Hülfsmittel ist, um den Charakter der Nation kennen zu lernen, wenn er ihre Nationaltänze und Nationalmusik vor sich hat.

man auch dem Viehhirten, der nie eine Stadt sieht, nicht absprechen kann, die man aber vorzüglich an dem schönen Gardisten, an dem fast durchgehends gut gewachsenen Edelmann, und an dem Soldaten nicht verkennt.

Seine Kleider, die den schlanken Körperbau genau bezeichnen und den vortheilhaften Eindruck desselben erheben, nähren seinen Stolz, und sind so national, dass er in der Kleidung eines Deutschen (seltner in der eines Engländers) eine elende Rolle spielt. Ferner ist der Ungar von Natur sehr feurig und zum Helden geschaffen; aber dabey dennoch so ganz Gefühl, dass es sehr leicht ist, seinen Willen, auch für die grössten Aufopferungen, zu stimmen. Die Geschichte der Maria Theresia und auch unsers Franz liefern Belege genug zur Bestätigung des hier Gesagten. Diesem Zuge aus seinem Charakter sind nun alle Volkslieder und Volkstänze angemessen. Alle nähren seinen Stolz, indem ihre Rhythmen Stellungen und Schritte erlauben, ihre Melodien sie verlangen—Stellungen und Schritte, welche ganz der Abdruck jenes Stolzes sind. Alle diese Melodien sind, bey Gravität, doch auch so schmelzend, dass der National-Ungar ohnmöglich gleichgültig bleiben kann, wenn eines seiner Volkslieder gesungen oder einer seiner N. Tänze gespielt wird. Und eben in der Verbindung jener beyden Eigenschaften unterscheiden sich unsere N. Tänze von jedem andern Tanz; und ich glaube behaupten zu können, keine Menuett, kein deutscher, kein Contretanz u. s. w. ist so ausdrucksvoll, so heroisch und zugleich zart, bey aller Einfachheit, als der ungarische N. Tanz.

Seine Melodie gehet grösstentheils in der weichen (Moll-) Tonart einher. Wenn N. Stücke auch wirklich in der harten (Dur-) Tonart ihren Anfang nehmen, so weichen sie doch sehr bald, und zwar in die entferntesten weichen Tonarten aus, und ihre Wirkung ist dann die der ausdruckvollsten Harmonie.[3] Der Gang der Melodie hat darin meistentheils einige Aehnlichkeit mit den englischen Tänzen, dass die Einschnitte und Absätze auf kurze Takttheile fallen. Nur in einigen Fällen geht es an, dass man im Niederschlage verzögern kann, wenn im Aufschlage angefangen wird. Uebrigens sind alle ung.

---

[3] Es liegt überhaupt etwas Bemerkenswerthes, Seltsames und Tiefes darin, dass die Nationalmusik (zu Tänzen und Gesang) der meisten Völker aus Moll-Tonarten gehet; ja dass das Volk, wie auch oben der Verf. von den Ungarn bemerkt, und ich z. B. von dem Cur- und Liefländischen Bauer weiss, die Melodien aus Dur-Tönen, wenn sie ihm auch ganz, wie sie sind, beygebracht werden, nach und nach beym Gebrauch stellenweiss in Moll umschaft. Es ist das nicht ein Ueberbleibsel der, durch unsere allein aufgenommenen zwey, verdrängten andern, Tonarten wie es z. B. in verschiedenen Choralmelodien der Fall seyn mag, wo der gemeine Mann an manchen Orten noch bey der veralteten Tonart bleibt (wie z. B. in seinem "Es woll uns Gott genädig seyn;" "O wie seelig seyd ihr doch, ihr Frommen," u. a.); es ist auch nicht das bey dem durch Musik gar nicht Gebildeten hin und wieder Zurückkehrende der natürlichen Tonleiter, welche durch unsere künstliche abgeschaft ist, aber wie bekannt, in manchen unsrer Blasinstrumente, (wie in der Trompete) noch gehört wird: sondern es ist ein wirkliches, rührendes, oft hinreissendes Vermischen unsers Dur und Moll, oder vielmehr, wie gesagt, ein charakteristisches, wehmüthiges Abstimmen unsers Dur hin und wieder in Moll. Ich will es durch ein Beyspiel anschaulich machen. Vor mehrern Jahren hatten sich verschiedene wackere Männer in Curland verbunden, eine Sammlung der besten volksmässigen deutschen Lieder von Göthe, Bürger, Jacobi, Hölty u. a. in die zwar arme, aber zum Bewundern natürlich- poetische, lettische Sprache zu übersetzen und mit ihren Melodien bekannt zu machen. Dies geschahe, und die Lieder verbreiteten sich weit—erst vornehmlich unter dem Landadel, dann unter Aufsehern und Pächtern, endlich hin und wieder unter den Landleuten selbst. Man kann sich kaum etwas für einen Deutschen Ueberraschenderes denken, als vielleicht ein kleines Chor wasserschöpfender oder Vieh tränkender ganz ärmlicher Mädchen, die bey ihrer Arbeit gemeiniglich mit recht guten Stimmen ein vaterländisches "Rosen auf den Weg gestreut; oder, Blühe liebes Veilchen"—beginnen und dabey ihres Unglücks vergessen. Sie singen aber z. B. die lezte Melodie—wenigstens in Einer Gegend so, wie sie am Ende der Beylage angegeben ist, —wobey die von ihnen erfundene zweyte Stimme so richtig nachgezeichnet ist, als möglich.

N. T. entweder *Langsame*, die man sehr artig Werbungstänze nennt; oder *Geschwinde*, die Zigeuner- oder Volkstänze heissen. Von beyden lege ich ein Paar bey.

Der Ungar beschreibt bey seinen Tänzen immer einen Zirkel. Bey dem Werbungstanz stellen sich blos die Mannspersonen in einem Kreis an, machen nach Massgabe der Töne verschiedene, aber meistens gut in die Augen fallende gemässigte Figuren mit den Fussen, und schlagen mit ihren klingenden Sporen, und mit den Händen, den Takt so ordentlich, dass dadurch selten der Wohlklang der Töne gestöhrt, wohl aber das Pathetische des Tanzes merklich erhoben wird. An den geschwinden Tänzen nimmt auch das schöne Geschlecht Theil. Hier beobachtet der Tänzer die nämliche Gewohnheit mit Händen und Füssen und macht fast eben die Figuren, wie bey dem erstern, nur verhältnissmässig geschwinder, und mit einigen Drehern verbunden. Das Frauenzimmer steht ihm mit dem Gesicht zugekehrt gegenüber, die eine oder wohl beyde Hände in die Seite gestemmt, und den Blick auf die Füsse des Tänzers gerichtet, der ihren Gang, ihre Stellungen und Wendungen, durch seine eigenen Figuren leitet. Zuweilen nähern sich beyde tanzende Personen einander, der Mann umfasst die Taille der Tänzerin, indess diese ihre Hände auf seine Achseln legt, und so drehen sie sich eine Weile in der Runde herum. Ein andermal aber dreht sich das Frauenzimmer, auf das Zeichen des Tänzers mit der Hand, allein, welche Stellung eine der schönsten im Tanze ist. Ich freue mich immer, wenn ich eine schlanke Blondine—mit ihrem kleinen Kopfputze, wo oft vier bis sechs niedliche Haarflechten um eine silberne Nadel gewunden sind, oder deren Locken natürlich über die Schultern fallen, deren enges, mit Gold reich geziertes Mieder die schöne Taille bezeichnet, und deren runde Röcke, die am untersten Rande meistens mit einer Borde besezt sind, und nicht bis zur Ferse reichen—und die schönen Füsse, welche sich beym Drehen eben nicht missgünstig zeigen, sehe."

Text C) Foreword to *22 Originelle Ungarische Nationaltänze für das Clavier* (Vienna: Chemische Druckerey, 1806/1807; H-KE 807), the first volume of an anonymous four-volume collection that was published in Vienna between 1806/1807 and 1812. Transcribed from Géza Papp, ed., *Hungarian Dances 1784–1810*, Musicalia Danubiana 7 (Budapest: Magyar Tudományos Akadémia, Zenetudományi Intézet, 1986), 356.

"Vorbericht.

Die einheimische Musick einer Nation zeiget von ihrem Geiste. Der national Ungar beobachtet das Metrum in seinen Melodien genau; aber dieser liebt besonders auffallende Uebergänge in andere Töne. Auch sein Vortrag ist von jenem anderer Nationen vollkommen unterschieden. Der stärkere Ausdruck fällt gemeiniglich auf den Niederschlag (:Thesis:) [und] seine Lieblingstriller sind in Terzen, Quarten, Quinten, manchmal auch in Sexten. Ich habe zu deren richtigen Vortrag ein eignes Zeichen angenommen; es ist folgendes * und die Noten über welche es sich befindet (:es seyen solche halbe, oder viertel Noten:) sind dreymal durchstrichen.

Der Sammler."

Text D) "Ungarische Tänze," *Allgemeine musikalische Zeitung* 9, no. 25 (18 March 1807): cols. 402–6.

"Vor zwanzig bis dreysig Jahren, ehe die Anglaise die meisten, figurirten Tänze in Deutschland verschlang, und dadurch, wie Pharao's dürre Kühe, selbst nur immer magerer ward, u. immer mehr vom wahren englischen Tanz abwich, bis sie jetzt fast nur zu einem, gewiss nichts weniger als schönen Hüpfen zusammengefallen ist—vor zwanzig bis dreysig Jahren, sag' ich, kannten, liebten und übten die feinern deutschen Gesellschaften, ausser dem deutschen, englischen und französischen Tanz, auch die wahre Polonaise, (nicht die dürftige, bequeme Promenade, die jetzt an vielen Orten so heisst—) und noch manchen Nationaltanz, vornämlich den kosakischen, den masurischen, den ungarischen; und wichen sie auch von dem eigentlich Nationalen derselben in gar manchem ab—machten sie sich dieselben, theils künstlicher, theils mehr fussgerecht: so blieb doch von jedem etwas, und es kam einiger Charakter, grosse Mannichfaltigkeit, und viel Schönes auf unsre Bälle, die jetzt dem Zuschauer, der nicht etwa ein ganz anderes Interesse, als am Tanz, nimmt, nur Langeweile machen können. Seit ganz kurzem scheint es jedoch, als ob man wenigstens in einigen von den deutschen Hauptstädten, wo den Leuten nicht vor dem Marschiren alles Tanzen vergeht, wieder an jene vernachlässigten Tänze dächte, und so wieder etwas mehr Abwechselung u. Geschmack in die Tanzgesellschaften bringen wollte.

Verdient nun aber irgend einer dieser fast vergessenen Tänze, und zwar vornämlich von Deutschen, wieder eingeführt zu werden: so ist es der ungarische, der so viel Anständiges, Schönes, und dem deutschen Charakter Angemessenes, dabey auch eine so originelle, charakteristische Musik hat! Dieser Tanz, wie ihn nämlich die Ungarn selbst behandeln, ist aber von zweyerley Art, und zwar die eine von der andern durchaus und ganzlich verschieden. Der ursprünglich-nationale, der vornehme ungarische Tanz ist pathetisch, heroisch, stolz, hat aber auch etwas Sanft-Schwärmerisches in seinen Wendungen—wie denn dies alles auch in dem Charakter des Ungarn selbst liegt. Seine Musik hat ebenfalls ganz diesen Ausdruck, und nimmt sich—in ihrem Wechsel von Moll und Dur, in ihren, oft kühnen, harmonischen Ausbeugungen, in ihren kräftigen Rhythmen, die der Tänzer bey den Haupteinschnitten mit Händeklatschen und Sporengeklirr noch mehr, aber gar nicht unangenehm, verstärkt—trefflich aus. Der zweyte ungarische, ist der rasche, gemeinere Volks- —eigentlich, der Zigeuner-Tanz, in welchen denn auch, wie jetzt in unsre Anglaisen und Quadrillen, der schnelle Dreher aufgenommen ist. Er hat ebenfalls ausserordentlich viel Interessantes und zugleich das Ausgezeichnete, dass hier beyde Geschlechter nothwendig ganz in ihrem Geschlechtscharakter auftreten müssen—der Mann, wie bey jenem ersten, nur lebhafter und behender, das Weib anmuthig, graziös, lieblich und gewandt. (Es ist z. B. jeder Tänzerin hier durch die Sache selbst nothwendig gemacht, überall nur nach ihrem Tänzer, aber auch diesem blos, ausgenommen beym Drehen, auf die Füsse zu blicken—folglich dem Zuschauer mit niedergeschlagenen Augen zu erscheinen, die sie dann, wenn der Dreher beginnt, mit den Armen zugleich, langsam erhebt—was alles, wie man leicht glauben wird, sich ganz allerliebst ausnimmt und gewiss auch den zartesten Reizen der Tänzerinnen einen weiten, aber anständigen Spielraum verschafft. Die Musik zu diesem Tanze drückt ebenfalls ganz das aus, was er selbst ausdrückt, ist folglich auch gewöhnlicher in Dur, und mehr melodisch, als harmonisch geschrieben; hat aber doch auch ihre Ausweichungen in Moll, wenigstens in die nächste Moll-Tonart.

Zu diesen Zeilen veranlasst mich eine kleine Sammlung ungarischer Tänze, die der fürstl. Esterhazysche Konzertmeister, Hr. Hummel in Wien, für's Pianoforte komponirt und so eben auf anderthalb Bogen herausgegeben hat—

Balli ongaresi per Pianoforte, comp. e ded. a—la Principessa de Liechtenstein—par Hummel—Op. 23. A Vienna, nel Contor delle Arti—(Pr. 50 Xr.)

ein Werkchen, das freylich für den Künstler, als solchen, nichts Ausgezeichnetes hat, aber gut genug gerathen ist, um, zur Verbreitung jener wiedererwachenden Liebhaberey am charakteris[tis]chen Tanze sein Scherflein beytragen zu können. Hr. H. hat den Charakter überall ziemlich, und einigemal, z. B. in No. 1.[,] in No. 7., sehr gut getroffen; nur hätte er dem Basse an mehrern Stellen, z. B. S. 3. oftmals, eine bequemere Lage geben sollen, da dergleichen Sächelchen doch zunächst für Dilettanten und Dilettantinnen kommen, die nur wenig vermögen, aber hier, wo sie für die Sache gewonnen werden sollen, besondere Rücksicht verdienen. Auch ist es nicht zu loben, dass Hr. H. von der ersten, edlern Art dieses Tanzes nur Ein Stück gegeben hat. Da vielleicht noch nicht viele Leser d. m. Z. diese Art kennen, setze ich die zwey ersten Klauseln der No. 1. hieher; die dritte und vierte haben öfters, (und haben auch hier) nur irgend eine schwirrende, muntere Figur in Dur, welche sich blos in der Haupttonart und Dominante bewegt, und von den nationalen Musikern extemporirt, oder doch nach eigener Phantasie immer neu variirt wird—was man denn auch hier thun mag, und was noch besser ist, als das Niederschreiben und Abspielen Einer solchen Figur. [The first sixteen measures of Hummel's *Balli ongaresi*, no. 1 appear here.]

Die besondere Art des Vortrags, die, wie die der eigentlichen Polonaise, etwas äusserst pikantes hat, lässt sich freylich nicht durch Zeichen anschaulich machen, kann aber doch, der Hauptsache nach, aus der Musik selbst, zusammengedacht mit den Bewegungen der Tanzenden, so ziemlich errathen werden. Nur Eins will ich darüber anmerken! Der Triller auf den zwey halben Takt-Noten soll kein eigentlicher Triller seyn, sondern der Spieler des Hackebrets, eines nie fehlenden Hauptinstruments der Ungarn, lässt die Schlägel hierbey auf diesen längern Noten fortzittern, was man denn auf dem Pianoforte nicht durch den eigentlichen Triller, sondern durch ein sehr schnelles, gleichsam schwirrendes Wechseln dieser Töne nachahmen kann—etwa, wie: [the musical figure given in chapter 3 as ex. 3.4 appears here] u. so fort. Wahrscheinlich hat es Hr. H. auch so gemeynt. Er hat übrigens auch einigemal, um jenen musikal. Naturkindern näher zukommen, unsre Grammatik verleugnet, wie auch schon obiges Beyspiel zeigt; ich kann ihm darüber keinen Vorwurf machen."

Bibliography

Archival Sources

A-Wgm

Bengraf, Joseph. *Trois Divertissemens pour le Clavecin Seul avec un Ballet Hongrois Composés par Mr Joseph Bengraf, Recueil Premier.* VII 3445.

A-Wn

6 Deutsche Tänze nach Türkischen geschmack für's Clavier. Mus.Hs.12919 MUS MAG.

Contredanses Hongraises pour le Clavecin presentées à Son Altesse Royal Mad^e L'Archiduchesse Elisabeth à l'occasion, qu'Elle parut avec S. A. R^{le} Msg^r l'ArchiDuc François en habit Hongrais à la Redoute. ce 31. Janv. 1788. par un Masque hongrais. Mus.Hs.13010 MUS MAG.

Hummel, Johann Nepomuk. *Balli ongaresi per Pianoforte composti e dedicati A. S. A. S. la Principessa Leopoldina di Liechtenstein nata Principessa d'Esterhazy; da G.^{ni} N. Hummel di Vienna Maestro di Concerto di S. A. il Sig^{re} P^{pe} reg^{te} d'Esterhazy, Op. 23.* Vienna: Contor delle arti e d'industria, [1806]. L18.Kaldeck MS40603-qu.4° MUS MAG.

Kauer, Ferdinand. *XII. Neue Ungarische Tänze für das Forte piano gewiedmet Ihro Königlichen Majestet Maria Theresia.* Mus.Hs.13003 MUS MAG.

Kauer, Ferdinand. *XII. Neue Ungarische Tänze für zwey Violin und Bass gewiedmet Ihro Königlichen Majestet Maria Theresia.* Mus.Hs.11351 MUS MAG.

Ossowski, Stanislaus. *6 Hongroisses Pour le Clavecin Composses Pour [!] Mr Stanislaus d'ossowsci.* Mus.Hs.13007 MUS MAG.

Ossowski, Stanislaus. *12 Deutsche Nach Ungarischen Geschmack für das Clavier Del Siegn: Sta: d'Ossowski.* Mus. Hs.12864 MUS MAG.

US-CAt

Gumpenhuber, Philipp. *Repertoire de Tous les Spectacles, qui ont été donné au Theatre de la Ville.* Kärntnertortheater, 1763 volume. MS Thr 248.3: 1763, seq. 409–410.

I-Tn

[Starzer, Joseph]. *Ballets de Nations. Tome premier. Contient Les Ballets Suivants. Les Ameriquains. L'Espagnol. L'Hongrois. Les Savoiards. Les Chinois. Les Maures. Tous ces Ballets sont de la composition de Monsieur Hilverding.* Rehearsal parts for two violins and *basso.* Fondo Foà 102, 103, 104.

CZ-K

[Starzer, Joseph]. *Ungareso. Ballo. Con 2 Violini, 2 Oboe o Traversi, 2 Corni, e Basso. Parti 7.* No. 25, K-II.

Significant Articles in Eighteenth- and Nineteenth-Century Journals and Newspapers

"Aus Siebenbürgen, vom 26 Febr." *Preßburger Zeitung,* 13 March 1784, 3–4.

"Bétsi víg múlatságok." *Magyar Hírmondó,* 1 December 1781, 736–41.

"Geschichte der Musik in Siebenbürgen." *Allgemeine musikalische Zeitung* 16, no. 46 (16 November 1814): cols. 765–76.
"Inländische Begebenheiten. Wien." *Wiener Zeitung,* 9 January 1788, 61–63.
M. † Z. "Uebersicht des Zustandes der Musik in Königsberg." *Allgemeine musikalische Zeitung* 11, no. 40 (5 July 1809): cols. 630–40.
"Mind itt van." *Magyar Kurír,* 13 June 1787, 378–79.
"Nachrichten: Kurze Uebersicht des Bedeutendsten aus dem gesammten jetzigen Musikwesen in Wien." *Allgemeine musikalische Zeitung* 3, no. 4 (22 October 1800): cols. 65–69.
"Nachrichten: Pest in Ungarn, d. 6ten Febr." *Allgemeine musikalische Zeitung* 12, no. 24 (14 March 1810): cols. 369–78.
"Ueber die Nationaltänze der Ungarn." *Allgemeine musikalische Zeitung* 2, no. 35 (28 May 1800): cols. 609–16.
"Uebersicht des gegenwärtigen Zustandes der Tonkunst in Wien." *Vaterländische Blätter für den österreichischen Kaiserstaat,* 27 May 1808, 39–44.
"Ungarische Tänze." *Allgemeine musikalische Zeitung* 9, no. 25 (18 March 1807): cols. 402–6.
"Vermählungs-Feyer des Erzherzogs Franz mit ihrer Durchl. der Prinzessin Elisabeth von Würtemberg. Wien, den 12. Jan. 1788." *Journal des Luxus und der Moden* 3 (February 1788): 50–59.
"Wien den 1. Christmonat." *Anhang zur Wiener Zeitung Nro. 97,* 5 December 1781, cols. 1–5.
"Wien den 28. Wintermon." *Anhang zur Wiener Zeitung Nro. 95,* 28 November 1781, cols. 1–5.

Primary Sources

Anderson, Emily, ed. *The Letters of Mozart and His Family.* 3rd ed. New York: W. W. Norton, 1985.
Angiolini, Gasparo. *Lettere di Gasparo Angiolini a Monsieur Noverre sopra i balli pantomimi.* Milan: G. B. Bianchi, 1773.
ANNO (AustriaN Newspapers Online). Historische Zeitungen und Zeitschriften. Österreichische Nationalbibliothek. https://anno.onb.ac.at.
Arnold [Johann Rautenstrauch]. *Schwachheiten der Wiener. Aus dem Manuskript eines Reisenden.* Vol. 3. Vienna and Leipzig: August Hartmann, 1786.
ARTFL Project. "Dictionnaires d'autrefois." https://artfl-project.uchicago.edu/content/dictionnaires-dautrefois.
Bright, Richard. *Travels from Vienna Through Lower Hungary; with Some Remarks on the State of Vienna During the Congress, in the Year 1814.* Edinburgh: Printed for Archibald Constable and Co., 1818.
Brown, Edward. *A Brief Account of some Travels in Hungaria, Servia, Bulgaria, Macedonia, Thessaly, Austria, Styria, Carinthia, Carniola, and Friuli. As also Some Observations on the Gold, Silver, Copper, Quick-silver Mines, Baths, and Mineral Waters in those parts: With the Figures of some Habits and Remarkable places.* London: Printed by T. R. for Benj. Tooke, 1673.
"Bundesgesetzblatt für die Republik Österreich. 230. Verordnung. 31 August 2018." https://www.ris.bka.gv.at/Dokumente/BgblAuth/BGBLA_2018_II_230/BGBLA_2018_II_230.pdfsig.
Burney, Charles. *Dr. Burney's Musical Tours.* Vol. 1, *An Eighteenth-Century Musical Tour in France and Italy Being Dr. Charles Burney's Account of his Musical Experiences As It Appears in His Published Volume with Which Are Incorporated His Travel Experiences According to His Original Intention.* Edited by Percy A. Scholes. London: Oxford University Press, 1959.
Burney, Charles. *Dr. Burney's Musical Tours.* Vol. 2, *An Eighteenth-Century Musical Tour in Central Europe and the Netherlands Being Dr. Charles Burney's Account of his Musical Experiences.* Edited by Percy A. Scholes. London: Oxford University Press, 1959.
Compan, Charles. *Dictionnaire de danse.* Paris: Cailleau, 1787.
Craven, Lady Elizabeth. *A Journey through the Crimea to Constantinople. In a Series of Letters from the Right Honourable Elizabeth Lady Craven to His Serene Highness the Margrave of*

Brandebourg, Anspach, and Bareith. Written in the Year MDCCLXXXVI. London: Printed for G. G. J. and J. Robinson, 1789.

de Luca, Ignaz. *Topographie von Wien*. Vol. 1. Vienna: In Kommission bey Thad. Edlen v. Schmidbauer und Komp. am Graben zur blauen Krone, 1794.

de Luca, Ignaz. *Wiens gegenwärtiger Zustand unter Josephs Regierung*. Vienna: Wucherer, 1787.

Feldtenstein, Carl Joseph von. *Erweiterung der Kunst nach der Chorographie zu tanzen, Tänze zu erfinden, und aufzusetzen; wie auch Anweisung zu verschiedenen National-Tänzen; Als zu Englischen, Deutschen, Schwäbischen, Pohlnischen, Hannak- Masur- Kosak- und Hungarischen; mit Kupfern; nebst einer Anzahl Englischer Tänze*. Braunschweig: n.p., 1772. Reprint edited by Kurt Petermann, Leipzig: Zentralantiquariat der deutschen demokratischen Republik, 1984.

Feldtenstein, Carl Joseph von. *Die Kunst nach der Choregraphie zu Tanzen und Tänze zu schreiben, nebst einer Abhandlung über die äusserliche Wohlanständigkeit im Tanzen*. Braunschweig: im Verlage der Schröderschen Buchhandlung, 1767.

Furetière, Antoine. *Dictionnaire universel, contenant generalement tous les mots françois, tant vieux que modernes, et les termes des sciences et des arts*. Vol. 2. The Hague: chez Pierre Husson, Thomas Johnson, Jean Swart, Jean van Duren, Charles le Vier, la Veuve van Dole, 1727.

Khevenhüller-Metsch, Johann Joseph. *Aus der Zeit Maria Theresias. Tagebuch des Fürsten Johann Joseph Khevenhüller-Metsch, kaiserlichen Obersthofmeisters 1742–1776*. Vol. 3 (1752–1755). Edited by Rudolf Graf Khevenhüller-Metsch and Dr. Hanns Schlitter. Vienna: Adolf Holzhausen and Leipzig: Wilhelm Engelmann, 1910.

Khevenhüller-Metsch, Johann Joseph. *Aus der Zeit Maria Theresias. Tagebuch des Fürsten Johann Joseph Khevenhüller-Metsch, kaiserlichen Obersthofmeisters 1742–1776*. Vol. 8 (1774–1780). Edited by Maria Breunlich-Pawlik and Hans Wagner. Vienna: Adolf Holzhausen, 1972.

Koch, Heinrich Christoph. *Musikalisches Lexikon*. Frankfurt am Main: August Hermann dem Jüngern, 1802. Reprint Hildesheim: Bärenreiter, 1964.

Koch, Heinrich Christoph. *Versuch einer Anleitung zur Composition*. Vol. 3. Leipzig: bey Adam Friedrich Böhme, 1793.

[Kringsteiner, Joseph Ferdinand]. *Der Tanzmeister: Eine Posse mit Gesang in drey Aufzügen vom Verfaßer des Zwirnhändlers*. Vienna: bey Matthias Andreas Schmidt, Universitäts-Buchdrucker, 1807.

Lannoy, Eduard von. "Nationalliteratur, Nationaldichter, Nationalmusik." In *Aesthetisches Lexikon: Ein alphabetisches Handbuch zur Theorie der Philosophie des Schönen und der schönen Künste. Nebst Erklärung der Kunstausdrücke aller ästhetischen Zweige, als: Poesie, Poetik, Rhetorik, Musik, Plastik, Graphik, Architektur, Malerei, Theater, &c.*, vol. 2, edited by Ignaz Jeitteles, 119–20. Vienna: Carl Gerold, 1837.

Ledyard, John. *John Ledyard's Journey through Russia and Siberia 1787–1788: The Journal and Selected Letters*. Edited by Stephen D. Watrous. Madison: University of Wisconsin Press, 2011.

Liszt, Franz. *Des Bohémiens et de leur musique en Hongrie*. Paris: Librairie Nouvelle, 1859.

Marx, Adolf Bernhard. *Die Lehre von der musikalischen Komposition*. Vol. 2. Leipzig: Breitkopf und Härtel, 1837–1838.

Mémoires historiques du Comte Betlem-Niklos, Contenant l'Histoire des derniers Troubles de Transilvanie. Amsterdam: Jean Swart, 1736.

[Montagu, Lady Mary Wortley]. *Letters of the Right Honourable Lady M- -y W- -y M- - - -e: Written, during her Travels in Europe, Asia and Africa, to Persons of Distinction, Men of Letters, &c. in different Parts of Europe. Which Contain, among other curious Relations, Accounts of the Policy and Manners of the Turks; Drawn from Sources that have been inaccessible to other Travellers*. Vol. 1. London: Printed for T. Becket and P. A. De Hondt, 1763.

[Montagu, Lady Mary Wortley]. *Turkish Embassy Letters*. Introduction by Anita Desai, text edited and annotated by Malcolm Jack. Athens: University of Georgia Press, 1993.

Neuestes Sittengemählde von Wien. Vol. 1. Vienna: bey Anton Pichler, 1801.

Nicolai, Friedrich. *Beschreibung einer Reise durch Deutschland und die Schweiz, im Jahre 1781. Nebst Bemerkungen über Gelehrsamkeit, Industrie, Religion und Sitten.* Vols. 1, 3–5. Berlin and Stettin: n.p., 1783–1785.

Pamela Censured. London: Printed for J. Roberts, 1741.

Perinet, Joachim. *Annehmlichkeiten in Wien.* Vienna: Lukas Hochenleitter, 1788.

Pezzl, Johann. *Neue Skizze von Wien.* Part 1. Vienna: J. V. Degen, 1805.

Pezzl, Johann. *Skizze von Wien.* 6 vols. Vienna and Leipzig: In der kraussischen Buchhandlung, 1786–1790.

Reichardt, Johann Friedrich. *Vertraute Briefe geschrieben auf einer Reise nach Wien und den Oesterreichischen Staaten zu Ende des Jahres 1808 und zu Anfang 1809.* Vol. 1. Amsterdam: Im Kunst- und Industrie-Comtoir, 1810.

Répertoire des théâtres de la ville de Vienne depuis l'année 1752 jusqu'à l'année 1757. Vienna: Johann Leopold van Ghelen, 1757.

[Richter, Joseph]. *Das alte und neue Wien, oder Es ist nicht mehr, wie eh. Ein satyrisches Gemählde entworfen von einem alten Laternputzer.* Vienna: Christoph Peter Rehm, 1800.

[Richter, Joseph]. *Taschenbuch für Grabennymphen auf das Jahr 1787.* Vienna: n.p., 1787.

Riesbeck, [Johann Kaspar]. *Travels through Germany, in a Series of Letters; Written in German by the Baron Riesbeck, and Translated by the Rev. Mr. Maty, Late Secretary to the Royal Society, and Under Librarian to the British Museum.* Vol. 2. London: Printed for T. Cadell, in the Strand, 1787. Translation of the original German edition of 1784.

Roth, Gottfried, ed. *Vom Baderlehrling zum Wundarzt: Carl Rabl, ein Mediziner im Biedermeier.* Linz: Oberösterreichischer Landesverlag, 1971.

Rousseau, Jean-Jacques. *Dictionnaire de musique.* Paris: Chez la Veuve Duchesne, 1768. Reprint Geneva: Editions Minkoff, 1998.

Schiller, Friedrich. *On the Aesthetic Education of Man in a Series of Letters.* Edited and translated with an introduction, commentary, and glossary of terms by Elizabeth M. Wilkinson and L. A. Willoughby. Oxford: Clarendon Press, 1982.

Schubart, Christian Friedrich Daniel. *Ideen zu einer Ästhetik der Tonkunst.* Edited by Ludwig Schubart. Vienna: J. V. Degen, 1806. Reprint with index and preface by Fritz Kaiser and Margrit Kaiser, Hildesheim: Georg Olms Verlagsbuchhandlung, 1969.

Schulz, J[ohann] A[braham] P[eter]. *Lieder im Volkston, bey dem Claviere zu singen.* Vol. 2. Berlin: George Jakob Decker, 1785.

Seume, I. G. [Johann Gottfried]. *Spaziergang nach Syrakus im Jahre 1802.* Braunschweig and Leipzig: n.p., 1803.

Smith, William. *Journal of a Voyage in the Missionary Ship Duff, to the Pacific Ocean in the Years 1796, 7, 8, 9, 1800, 1, 2, &c.: Comprehending Authentic and Circumstantial Narratives of the Disasters which Attended the First Effort of the "London Missionary Society." With an Appendix; Containing Interesting Circumstances in the Life of Captain James Wilson, the Commander of the Duff, when he was Engaged in the Wars in the East Indies, and taken Prisoner by Hyder Ally's troops,—his bold attempt to escape, and subsequent difficulties.* New York: Collins, 1813.

Sternberg, Kaspar. *Leben des Grafen Kaspar Sternberg von ihm selbst beschrieben.* Edited by Franz Palacký. Prague: Friedrich Tempsky, 1868.

Sulzer, Johann Georg. *Allgemeine Theorie der schönen Künste.* Vol. 2. Leipzig: Weidmann, 1792. Reprint Hildesheim: Georg Olms, 1967.

Townson, Robert. *Travels in Hungary, with a Short Account of Vienna in the Year 1793.* London: Printed for G. G. and J. Robinson, 1797.

Türk, Daniel Gottlob. *School of Clavier Playing, or Instructions in Playing the Clavier for Teachers and Students.* Translated with introduction and notes by Raymond H. Haggh. Lincoln: University of Nebraska Press, 1982. First published as *Klavierschule, oder Anweisung zum Klavierspielen für Lehrer und Lernende, mit kritischen Anmerkungen.* Leipzig: Schwickert and Halle: Hemmerde and Schwetschke, 1789.

Weiskern, Friedrich Wilhelm. *Beschreibung der k.k. Haupt und Residenzstadt Wien, als der dritte Theil zur österreichischen Topographie*. Vienna: Kurzböcken, 1770.
Wienerisches Kommerzialschema oder Auskunfts- und Geschäftsbuch für Inländer und Fremde. Vienna: Gerold, 1782–1798.
Wraxall, William. *Memoirs of the Courts of Berlin, Dresden, Warsaw and Vienna in the Years 1777, 1778, and 1779*. Vol. 2. 2nd ed. London: Printed by A. Strahan for T. Cadell and W. Davies, 1800.

Music Editions

Bónis, Ferenc, ed. *Ungarische Tänze für Klavier/Hungarian Dances for Piano*. Diletto Musicale 662. Vienna: Doblinger, 1993.
Papp, Géza, ed. *Hungarian Dances 1784–1810*. Musicalia Danubiana 7. Budapest: Magyar Tudományos Akadémia, Zenetudományi Intézet, 1986.

Secondary Sources

Agence France-Presse. "Austria's 'Ghetto' Language Classes Stir Segregation Fears." https://www.france24.com/en/20200118-austria-s-ghetto-language-classes-stir-segregation-fears.
Agnew, Vanessa. "Encounter Music in Oceania: Cross-Cultural Musical Exchange in Eighteenth- and Early Nineteenth-Century Voyage Accounts." In *The Cambridge History of World Music*, edited by Philip V. Bohlman, 183–201. Cambridge: Cambridge University Press, 2013.
Agnew, Vanessa. *Enlightenment Orpheus: The Power of Music in Other Worlds*. Oxford: Oxford University Press, 2008.
Allanbrook, Wye Jamison. *Rhythmic Gesture in Mozart:* Le Nozze di Figaro *and* Don Giovanni. Chicago: University of Chicago Press, 1983.
Anderson, Benedict. *Imagined Communities: Reflections on the Origin and Spread of Nationalism*. London: Verso, 1983.
Antolini, Bianca Maria. "Publishers and Buyers." In *Music Publishing in Europe 1600–1900: Concepts and Issues, Bibliography*, edited by Rudolf Rasch, 209–40. Berlin: Berliner Wissenschafts-Verlag, 2005.
Arkin, Lisa C., and Marian Smith. "National Dance in the Romantic Ballet." In *Rethinking the Sylph: New Perspectives on the Romantic Ballet*, edited by Lynn Garafola, 11–68. Hanover, NH: University Press of New England, 1997.
Balisch, Alex. "The *Wiener Zeitung* Reports on the French Revolution." In *Austria in the Age of the French Revolution, 1789–1815*, edited by Kinley Brauer and William E. Wright, 185–92. Minneapolis: Center for Austrian Studies, University of Minnesota, 1990.
Bartha, Dénes. "Mozart et le folklore musical de l'Europe centrale." In *Les Influences étrangères dans l'oeuvre de W. A. Mozart, Paris, 10–13 octobre 1956*, edited by André Verchaly, 157–81. Paris: Centre national de la recherche scientifique, 1958.
Bellman, Jonathan. "The Hungarian Gypsies and the Poetics of Exclusion." In *The Exotic in Western Music*, edited by Jonathan Bellman, 74–103. Boston: Northeastern University Press, 1998.
Bellman, Jonathan. *The* Style Hongrois *in the Music of Western Europe*. Boston: Northeastern University Press, 1993.
Bellman, Jonathan. "Toward a Lexicon for the *Style Hongrois*." *Journal of Musicology* 9, no. 2 (Spring 1991): 214–37.
Beneder, Beatrix. "Mädchenbedienung im Männerort: Geschlechter-Inszenierungen im Wirtshaus." In *Im Wirtshaus: Eine Geschichte der Wiener Geselligkeit*, edited by Ulrike Spring, Wolfgang Kos, and Wolfgang Freitag, 242–47. Vienna: Czernin Verlag, 2007.
Blanning, T. C. W. *The Culture of Power and the Power of Culture: Old Regime Europe 1660–1789*. Oxford: Oxford University Press, 2003.

Bloechl, Olivia, and Melanie Lowe. "Introduction: Rethinking Difference." In *Rethinking Difference in Music Scholarship*, edited by Olivia Bloechl, Melanie Lowe, and Jeffrey Kallberg, 1–52. Cambridge: Cambridge University Press, 2015.

Bohlman, Philip V. "On the Unremarkable in Music." *19th-Century Music* 16, no. 2 (Autumn 1992): 203–16.

Bohlman, Philip V. "Vernacular Music." *Grove Music Online*. www.oxfordmusiconline.com.

Bohlman, Philip V., and Federico Celestini. "Editorial: Musicians at the Borders." *Acta Musicologica* 88, no. 1 (2016): 1–4.

Bónis, Ferenc. "Beethoven und die ungarische Musik." In *Bericht über den internationalen musikwissenschaftlichen Kongress Bonn 1970*, edited by Carl Dahlhaus et al., 121–27. Kassel: Bärenreiter, 1970.

Bónis, Ferenc. "Heldentum und Sehnsucht nach Freiheit. Zur Frage: Beethoven und die ungarische Musik." In *Fidelio/Leonore: Annäherungen an ein zentrales Werk des Musiktheaters—Vorträge und Materialien des Salzburger Symposions 1996*, edited by Peter Csobádi et al., 347–57. Salzburg: Verlag Müller-Speiser, 1998.

Born, Georgina, and David Hesmondhalgh. "Introduction: On Difference, Representation, and Appropriation in Music." In *Western Music and Its Others: Difference, Representation, and Appropriation in Music*, edited by Georgina Born and David Hesmondhalgh, 1–58. Berkeley: University of California Press, 2000.

Botstein, Leon. Review of *Musical Life in Biedermeier Vienna*, by Alice M. Hanson. *Musical Quarterly* 72, no. 4 (1986): 529–35.

Bracewell, Wendy. "The Limits of Europe in East European Travel Writing." In *Under Eastern Eyes: A Comparative Introduction to East European Travel Writing on Europe*, edited by Wendy Bracewell and Alex Drace-Francis, 61–120. Budapest: Central European University Press, 2008.

Brown, Bruce Alan. "Appendix 3: Gumpenhuber's Descriptions of Ballets Performed in the Kärntnertortheater during 1759 (Excluding End of 1758–59 Season)." In *The Grotesque Dancer on the Eighteenth-Century Stage: Gennaro Magri and His World*, edited by Rebecca Harris-Warrick and Bruce Alan Brown, 312–19. Madison: University of Wisconsin Press, 2005.

Brown, Bruce Alan. *Gluck and the French Theatre in Vienna*. Oxford: Clarendon Press, 1991.

Brown, Bruce Alan. "'. . . les danses *confédérées*': Multinational Ballets on the Viennese Stages, 1740–1776." Paper presented at the 75th annual meeting of the American Musicological Society, Philadelphia, PA, November 2009.

Brown, Bruce Alan. "Magri in Vienna: The Apprenticeship of a Choreographer." In *The Grotesque Dancer on the Eighteenth-Century Stage: Gennaro Magri and His World*, edited by Rebecca Harris-Warrick and Bruce Alan Brown, 62–90. Madison: University of Wisconsin Press, 2005.

Brown, Bruce Alan. "Of Caricatures and Contexts: Some Representations of Jews (Real and Imagined) in the Habsburg Monarchy During the Eighteenth Century." PowerPoint presentation at the STIMU-Symposium: "Reinventing a Usable Past," Festival Oude Muziek, Utrecht, August 2016.

Brown, Julie Hedges. "Schumann and the *Style Hongrois*." In *Rethinking Schumann*, edited by Roe-Min Kok and Laura Tunbridge, 265–99. Oxford: Oxford University Press, 2011.

Brown, Marilyn R. *Gypsies and Other Bohemians: The Myth of the Artist in Nineteenth-Century France*. Ann Arbor, MI: UMI Research Press, 1985.

Burford, Freda, revised by Anne Daye. "Contredanse." *Grove Music Online*. www.oxfordmusiconline.com.

Burger, Hannelore. "Pässe für Fremde." In *Grenze und Staat: Paßwesen, Staatsbürgerschaft, Heimatrecht und Fremdengesetzgebung in der österreichischen Monarchie, 1750–1867*, edited by Waltraud Heindl, Edith Saurer, Hannelore Burger, and Harald Wendelin, 76–87. Vienna: Böhlau, 2000.

Buurman, Erica. "The Annual Balls of the Pensionsgesellschaft bildender Künstler, 1792–1832: Music in the Viennese Imperial Ballrooms from Haydn to Lanner." In *Beethoven und andere Hofmusiker seiner Generation: Bericht über den internationalen musikwissenschaftlichen Kongress Bonn, 3. bis 6. Dezember 2015*, edited by Birgit Lodes, Elisabeth Reisinger, and John D. Wilson, 221–35. Bonn: Beethoven-Haus, 2018.

Buurman, Erica. *The Viennese Ballroom in the Age of Beethoven*. Cambridge: Cambridge University Press, 2022.

Campianu, Eva. "Langaus, Quadrille, Zingarese: Joseph Haydn und der Tanz." *Morgen* 6, no. 23 (June 1982): 171–77.

Case, Holly. "Goulash Democracy. Hungary: A Nation in Fear of the Future." *Times Literary Supplement*, 20 June 2018, 14.

Chew, Geoffrey. "The Austrian Pastorella and the *Stylus Rusticanus*: Comic and Pastoral Elements in Austrian Music, 1750–1800." In *Music in Eighteenth-Century Austria*, edited by David Wyn Jones, 133–93. Cambridge: Cambridge University Press, 1996.

Chew, Geoffrey. "Pastorella." *Grove Music Online*. www.oxfordmusiconline.com.

Croll, Gerhard. "'Fremdländische' Redouten-Tänze zur Zeit Mozarts." In *Telemanniana et alia musicologica: Festschrift für Günter Fleischhauer zum 65. Geburtstag*, edited by Dieter Gutknecht, Hartmut Krones, and Frieder Zschoch, 189–92. Michaelsteiner Forschungsbeiträge 17. Oschersleben: Ziethen Verlag, 1995.

Crowe, David. "The Gypsies in Hungary." In *The Gypsies of Eastern Europe*, edited by David Crowe and John Kolsti, 117–31. Armonk, NY: M. E. Sharpe, 1991.

Crowe, David M. *A History of the Gypsies of Eastern Europe and Russia*. New York: St. Martin's Press, 1994.

Cusick, Suzanne G. "Gender and the Cultural Work of a Classical Music Performance." *repercussions* 3, no. 1 (Spring 1994): 77–110.

Cusick, Suzanne G. "Gender, Musicology, and Feminism." In *Rethinking Music*, edited by Nicholas Cook and Mark Everist, 471–98. Oxford: Oxford University Press, 1999.

Cypess, Rebecca. *Women and Musical Salons in the Enlightenment*. Chicago: University of Chicago Press, 2022.

Daverio, John. *Crossing Paths: Schubert, Schumann, and Brahms*. Oxford: Oxford University Press, 2002.

Dean-Smith, Margaret. "Hornpipe (ii)." *Grove Music Online*. www.oxfordmusiconline.com.

Dobszay, László. *A History of Hungarian Music*. Translated by Mária Steiner. Translation revised by Paul Merrick. Budapest: Corvina, 1993.

Domokos, Maria. "Kiegészítések a verbunkos zene es tánc bécsi adataihoz." *Zenetudományi Dolgozatok* (1985): 95–111.

Do Paço, David. *L'Orient à Vienne au dix-huitième siècle*. Oxford University Studies in the Enlightenment. Oxford: Voltaire Foundation, 2015.

Do Paço, David. "Viennese Delights: Remarks on the History of Food and Sociability in Eighteenth-Century Central Europe." EUI Working Paper MWP 2014/23. https://cadmus.eui.eu/bitstream/handle/1814/33473/MWP_2014_23.pdf?sequence=1&isAllowed=y.

Dózsa, Katalin. "Court and City Costume, 18th to 20th Centuries." In *Historic Hungarian Costume from Budapest*, with a foreword by Francis W. Hawcroft, 16–46. Manchester: Whitworth Art Gallery, 1979.

During, Simon. "Rousseau's Patrimony: Primitivism, Romance and Becoming Other." In *Colonial Discourse/Postcolonial Theory*, edited by Francis Baker, Peter Hulme, and Margaret Iversen, 47–71. Manchester: Manchester University Press, 1994.

Ehmer, Josef. "Worlds of Mobility: Migration Patterns of Viennese Artisans in the Eighteenth Century." In *The Artisan and the European Town, 1500–1900*, edited by Geoffrey Crossick, 172–99. Aldershot: Scolar Press, 1997.

Evans, R. J. W. *Austria, Hungary, and the Habsburgs: Central Europe c. 1683–1867*. Oxford: Oxford University Press, 2006.

"Factsheet: Sebastian Kurz." Compiled by the Bridge Initiative Team. https://bridge.georgetown.edu/research/factsheet-sebastian-kurz/.

Fink, Monika. *Der Ball: Eine Kulturgeschichte des Gesellschaftstanzes im 18. und 19. Jahrhundert*. Lucca: Libreria musicale italiana, 1996.

Földi-Dózsa, Katalin. "Die ungarische Nationaltracht als Hofkleidung." In *Kaiser und König, 1526–1918*, edited by István Fazekas and Gábor Ujváry, 23–28. Vienna: Collegium Hungaricum, 2001.

Fort, Joseph Giovanni. "Incorporating Haydn's Minuets: Towards a Somatic Theory of Music." PhD diss., Harvard University, 2015.

Frazer, Michael L. *The Enlightenment of Sympathy: Justice and the Moral Sentiments in the Eighteenth Century and Today*. Oxford: Oxford University Press, 2010.

Gelbart, Matthew. *The Invention of "Folk Music" and "Art Music": Emerging Categories from Ossian to Wagner*. Cambridge: Cambridge University Press, 2007.

Geselle, Andrea. "Reisende Frauen." In *Grenze und Staat: Paßwesen, Staatsbürgerschaft, Heimatrecht und Fremdengesetzgebung in der österreichischen Monarchie, 1750–1867*, edited by Waltraud Heindl, Edith Saurer, Hannelore Burger, and Harald Wendelin, 410–14. Vienna: Böhlau, 2000.

Goodman, Dena. "Suzanne Necker's *Mélanges*: Gender, Writing, and Publicity." In *Going Public: Women and Publishing in Early Modern France*, edited by Elizabeth C. Goldsmith and Dena Goodman, 210–23. Ithaca, NY: Cornell University Press, 1995.

Gramit, David. *Cultivating Music: The Aspirations, Interests, and Limits of German Musical Culture, 1770–1848*. Berkeley: University of California Press, 2002.

Hanks, Sarah E. "Pantaleon's Pantalon: An 18th-Century Musical Fashion." *Musical Quarterly* 55, no. 2 (April 1969): 215–27.

Hanson, Alice M. *Musical Life in Biedermeier Vienna*. Cambridge: Cambridge University Press, 1985.

Harris-Warrick, Rebecca, and Bruce Alan Brown, eds. *The Grotesque Dancer on the Eighteenth-Century Stage: Gennaro Magri and His World*. Madison: University of Wisconsin Press, 2005.

Head, Matthew. "Haydn's Exoticisms: 'Difference' and the Enlightenment." In *The Cambridge Companion to Haydn*, edited by Caryl Clark, 77–92. Cambridge: Cambridge University Press, 2005.

Head, Matthew. "'If the Pretty Little Hand Won't Stretch': Music for the Fair Sex in Eighteenth-Century Germany." *Journal of the American Musicological Society* 52, no. 2 (Summer 1999): 203–54.

Head, Matthew. *Orientalism, Masquerade and Mozart's Turkish Music*. London: Royal Musical Association, 2000.

Head, Matthew. *Sovereign Feminine: Music and Gender in Eighteenth-Century Germany*. Berkeley: University of California Press, 2013.

Heartz, Daniel. *Haydn, Mozart and the Viennese School, 1740–1780*. New York: W. W. Norton, 1995.

Heartz, Daniel, and Patricia Rader. "Branle." *Grove Music Online*. www.oxfordmusiconline.com.

Heise, Ulla. *Kaffee und Kaffeehaus: Eine Kulturgeschichte*. Hildesheim: Olms, 1987.

Helyard, Erin. *Clementi and the Woman at the Piano: Virtuosity and the Marketing of Music in Eighteenth-Century London*. Oxford University Studies in the Enlightenment. Liverpool: Liverpool University Press, 2022.

Hirschkop, Ken. "The Classical and the Popular: Musical Form and Social Context." In *Music and the Politics of Culture*, edited by Christopher Norris, 283–304. London: Lawrence & Wishart, 1989.

Historic Hungarian Costume from Budapest. Foreword by Francis W. Hawcroft. Manchester: Whitworth Art Gallery, 1979.

Hitchcock, H. Wiley. *Music in the United States: A Historical Introduction*. 3rd ed. Englewood Cliffs, NJ: Prentice Hall, 1988.

Hoare, M. E. "'Cook the Discoverer': An Essay by Georg Forster, 1787." *Records of the Australian Academy of Science* 1, no. 4 (November 1969): 7–16.
Hooker, Lynn M. *Redefining Hungarian Music from Liszt to Bartók.* Oxford: Oxford University Press, 2014.
Hunter, Mary. "The *Alla Turca* Style in the Late Eighteenth Century: Race and Gender in the Symphony and the Seraglio." In *The Exotic in Western Music*, edited by Jonathan Bellman, 43–73. Boston: Northeastern University Press, 1998.
Islamov, Tofik M. "From *Natio Hungarica* to Hungarian Nation." In *Nationalism and Empire: The Habsburg Empire and the Soviet Union*, edited by Richard L. Rudolph and David F. Good, 159–83. New York: St. Martin's Press, 1992.
Istvánffy, Tibor. "All'Ongarese: Studien zur Rezeption ungarischer Musik bei Haydn, Mozart und Beethoven." PhD diss., Ruprecht-Karls-Universität Heidelberg, 1982.
Jones, David Wyn. *Music in Vienna 1700, 1800, 1900.* Woodbridge: Boydell Press, 2016.
Jordanova, Ludmilla. *Sexual Visions: Images of Gender in Science and Medicine between the Eighteenth and Twentieth Centuries.* Milwaukee: University of Wisconsin Press, 1989.
Joubert, Estelle. "Analytical Encounters: Global Music Criticism and Enlightenment Ethnomusicology." In *Studies on a Global History of Music: A Balzan Musicology Project*, edited by Reinhard Strohm, 42–60. London: Routledge, 2018.
"Journeys to Authority: Reassessing Women's Travel Writing, 1763–1863." Special issue of *Women's Writing* 24, no. 2 (2017).
Judson, Pieter M. *The Habsburg Empire: A New History.* Cambridge, MA: Belknap Press of Harvard University Press, 2016.
Kallberg, Jeffrey. *Chopin at the Boundaries: Sex, History, and Musical Genre.* Cambridge, MA: Harvard University Press, 1996.
Karnes, Kevin C. "Inventing Eastern Europe in the Ear of the Enlightenment." *Journal of the American Musicological Society* 71, no. 1 (Spring 2018): 75–108.
Katz, Ruth, and Carl Dahlhaus, eds. *Contemplating Music: Source Readings in the Aesthetics of Music.* Vol. 2, *Import.* Stuyvesant, NY: Pendragon Press, 1989.
Kauffmann, Kai. *"Es ist nur ein Wien!" Stadtbeschreibungen von Wien 1700 bis 1873.* Vienna: Böhlau, 1994.
Komlós, Katalin. *Fortepianos and Their Music: Germany, Austria, and England, 1760–1800.* Oxford: Clarendon Press, 1995.
Komlós, Katalin. "'Ich Praeludirte und Spielte Variazionen': Mozart the Fortepianist." In *Perspectives on Mozart Performance*, edited by R. Larry Todd and Peter Williams, 27–54. Cambridge: Cambridge University Press, 1991.
Korhonen, Joonas. *Social Choreography of the Viennese Waltz: The Transfer and Reception of the Dance in Vienna and Europe, 1780–1825.* Helsinki: Academia Scientiarum Fennica, 2014.
Kosáry, Domokos. *Culture and Society in Eighteenth-Century Hungary.* Budapest: Corvina, 1987.
Kürti, László. "Hungary." In *International Encyclopedia of Dance*, vol. 3, edited by Selma Jeanne Cohen, 407–24. Oxford: Oxford University Press, 1998.
Lager, Herbert, and Hilde Seidl. *Kontratanz in Wien: Geschichtliches und Nachvollziehbares aus der theresianisch-josephinischen Zeit.* Vienna: Österreichischer Bundesverlag, 1983.
Landes, Joan B. "The Public and the Private Sphere: A Feminist Reconsideration." In *Feminists Read Habermas: Gendering the Subject of Discourse*, edited with an introduction by Johanna Meehan, 91–116. New York: Routledge, 1995.
Landes, Joan B. *Women and the Public Sphere in the Age of the French Revolution.* Ithaca, NY: Cornell University Press, 1988.
Landon, H. C. Robbins. *Mozart and Vienna.* New York: Schirmer, 1991.
Laqueur, Thomas. *Making Sex: Body and Gender from the Greeks to Freud.* Cambridge, MA: Harvard University Press, 1990.
Le Guin, Elisabeth. *Boccherini's Body: An Essay in Carnal Musicology.* Berkeley: University of California Press, 2006.

Leppert, Richard. "Music, Domestic Life, and Cultural Chauvinism: Images of British Subjects at Home in India." In *Music and Society: The Politics of Composition, Performance, and Reception*, edited by Richard Leppert and Susan McClary, 63–104. Cambridge: Cambridge University Press, 1987.

Leppert, Richard. *Music and Image: Domesticity, Ideology and Socio-Cultural Formation in Eighteenth-Century England*. Cambridge: Cambridge University Press, 1988.

Litschauer, Walburga, and Walter Deutsch. *Schubert und das Tanzvergnügen*. Vienna: Verlag Holzhausen, 1997.

Locke, Ralph P. *Music and the Exotic from the Renaissance to Mozart*. Cambridge: Cambridge University Press, 2015.

Locke, Ralph P. *Musical Exoticism: Images and Reflections*. Cambridge: Cambridge University Press, 2009.

Loesser, Arthur. *Men, Women & Pianos: A Social History*. New York: Simon & Schuster, 1954.

Loya, Shay. *Liszt's Transcultural Modernism and the Hungarian-Gypsy Tradition*. Eastman Studies in Music 87. Rochester, NY: University of Rochester Press, 2011.

Major, Ervin. "Miszellen: Ungarische Tanzmelodien in Haydns Bearbeitung." *Zeitschrift für Musikwissenschaft* 11 (1928–1929): 601–4.

Makkai, László. "Habsburg Absolutism and Hungary (1711–1790)." In *A History of Hungary*, edited by Ervin Pamlényi, 179–205. Budapest: Corvina, 1973.

Mathew, Nicholas. "Heroic Haydn, the Occasional Work and 'Modern' Political Music." *Eighteenth-Century Music* 4, no. 1 (March 2007): 7–25.

Mathew, Nicholas. *Political Beethoven*. Cambridge: Cambridge University Press, 2013.

Mayerhofer, Claudia. *Dorfzigeuner: Kultur und Geschichte der Burgenland-Roma von der Ersten Republik bis zur Gegenwart*. Vienna: Picus, 1987.

Mayes, Catherine. "Eastern European National Music as Concept and Commodity at the Turn of the Nineteenth Century." *Music & Letters* 95, no. 1 (February 2014): 70–91.

Mayes, Catherine. "In Vienna 'Only Waltzes Get Printed': The Decline and Transformation of the *Contredanse Hongroise* in the Early Nineteenth Century." In *Consuming Music: Individuals, Institutions, Communities, 1730–1830*, edited by Emily H. Green and Catherine Mayes, 154–75. Eastman Studies in Music 138. Rochester, NY: University of Rochester Press, 2017.

Mayes, Catherine. "Reconsidering an Early Exoticism: Viennese Adaptations of Hungarian-Gypsy Music around 1800." *Eighteenth-Century Music* 6, no. 2 (September 2009): 161–81.

Mayes, Catherine. "Turkish and Hungarian-Gypsy Styles." In *The Oxford Handbook of Topic Theory*, edited by Danuta Mirka, 214–37. Oxford: Oxford University Press, 2014.

Maynes, Mary Jo. *Schooling in Western Europe: A Social History*. Albany: State University of New York Press, 1985.

McKee, Eric. "Ballroom Dances of the Late Eighteenth Century." In *The Oxford Handbook of Topic Theory*, edited by Danuta Mirka, 164–93. Oxford: Oxford University Press, 2014.

Melton, James Van Horn. *Absolutism and the Eighteenth-Century Origins of Compulsory Schooling in Prussia and Austria*. Cambridge: Cambridge University Press, 1988.

Melton, James Van Horn. "From Image to Word: Cultural Reform and the Rise of Literate Culture in Eighteenth-Century Austria." *Journal of Modern History* 58, no. 1 (March 1986): 95–124.

Melton, James Van Horn. *The Rise of the Public in Enlightenment Europe*. Cambridge: Cambridge University Press, 2001.

Melton, James Van Horn. "School, Stage, Salon: Musical Cultures in Haydn's Vienna." In *Haydn and the Performance of Rhetoric*, edited by Tom Beghin and Sander M. Goldberg, 80–108. Chicago: University of Chicago Press, 2007.

Mitchell, A. Wess. *The Grand Strategy of the Habsburg Empire*. Princeton, NJ: Princeton University Press, 2018.

Oberzill, Gerhard H. *Ins Kaffeehaus! Geschichte einer Wiener Institution*. Vienna: Jugend und Volk, 1983.

Outram, Dorinda. *The Enlightenment*. 4th ed. Cambridge: Cambridge University Press, 2019.
Papp, Géza. "Die Quellen der 'Verbunkos-Musik': Ein bibliographischer Versuch. A) Gedruckte Werke I. 1784–1823." *Studia Musicologica* 21, nos. 2–4 (1979): 151–217.
Pethő, Csilla. "*Style Hongrois*: Hungarian Elements in the Works of Haydn, Beethoven, Weber and Schubert." *Studia Musicologica* 41, nos. 1–3 (2000): 199–284.
Philp, Mark. *Radical Conduct: Politics, Sociability and Equality in London 1795–1815*. Cambridge: Cambridge University Press, 2020.
Pressler, Gertraud. "Brigittakirtag." In *Oesterreichisches Musiklexicon Online*, edited by Rudolf Flotzinger and Barbara Boisits. https://www.musiklexikon.ac.at/ml/musik_B/Brigittakirtag.xml.
Reichart, Sarah. "The Influence of Eighteenth-Century Social Dance on the Viennese Classical Style." PhD diss., City University of New York, 1984.
Reichart, Sarah. "The Thuillier Contredanses." *Proceedings of the Society of Dance History Scholars* 8 (1985): 98–110.
Resch, Katharina, Marie Gitschthaler, and Susanne Schwab. "Teacher's [sic] Perceptions of Separate Language Learning Models for Students with Immigrant Background in Austrian Schools." *Intercultural Education* 34, no. 3 (2023): 288–304.
Ribeiro, Aileen. *Dress in Eighteenth-Century Europe, 1715–1789*. New Haven, CT: Yale University Press, 2002.
Rice, John A. *Empress Marie Therese and Music at the Viennese Court, 1792–1807*. Cambridge: Cambridge University Press, 2003.
Roider, Karl A., Jr. *Austria's Eastern Question, 1700–1790*. Princeton, NJ: Princeton University Press, 1982.
Rosen, Charles. *The Classical Style: Haydn, Mozart, Beethoven*. New York: W. W. Norton, 1997.
Rousseau, G. S., and Roy Porter. "Introduction: Approaching Enlightenment Exoticism." In *Exoticism in the Enlightenment*, edited by G. S. Rousseau and Roy Porter, 1–22. Manchester: Manchester University Press, 1990.
Sachs, Curt. *World History of the Dance*. Translated by Bessie Schönberg. New York: W. W. Norton, 1963.
Salmen, Walter, ed. *Mozart in der Tanzkultur seiner Zeit*. Innsbruck: Helbling, 1990.
Salmen, Walter. "Spielleute und Ballmusiker." In *Mozart in der Tanzkultur seiner Zeit*, edited by Walter Salmen, 51–56. Innsbruck: Helbling, 1990.
Salmen, Walter. "Tanzinstrumente und -ensembles." In *Mozart in der Tanzkultur seiner Zeit*, edited by Walter Salmen, 57–58. Innsbruck: Helbling, 1990.
Sárosi, Bálint. *Gypsy Music*. Translated by Fred Macnicol. Budapest: Corvina, 1978.
Sárosi, Bálint. "Parallelen aus der ungarischen Volksmusik zum 'Rondo all'Ongarese'-Satz in Haydns D-dur Klavierkonzert Hob. XVIII:11." In *Bericht über den internationalen Joseph Haydn Kongress Wien 1982*, edited by Eva Badura-Skoda, 222–26. Munich: G. Henle, 1986.
Sárosi, Bálint. *Sackpfeifer, Zigeunermusikanten ... Die instrumentale ungarische Volksmusik*. Translated by Ruth Futaky. Budapest: Corvina, 1999.
Schaller-Pressler, Gertraud. "Volksmusik und Volkslied in Wien." In *Wien Musikgeschichte*, vol. 1, *Volksmusik und Wienerlied*, edited by Elisabeth Theresia Fritz and Helmut Kretschmer, 3–147. Vienna: Lit, 2006.
Schenk, Erich. "Der Langaus." *Studia Musicologica* 3, nos. 1–4 (1962): 301–16.
Scheutz, Martin. "Von den 'höchst-verbottenen Zusammenkünften': Das Wirtshaus der frühen Neuzeit." In *Im Wirtshaus: Eine Geschichte der Wiener Geselligkeit*, edited by Ulrike Spring, Wolfgang Kos, and Wolfgang Freitag, 76–83. Vienna: Czernin Verlag, 2007.
Schindler, Otto G. "Das Publikum des Burgtheaters in der josephinischen Ära." In *Das Burgtheater und sein Publikum: Festgabe zur 200-Jahr-Feier der Erhebung des Burgtheaters zum Nationaltheater*, edited by Margret Dietrich, 11–95. Vienna: Veröffentlichungen des Instituts für Publikumsforschung, 1976.
Schneider, David E. *Bartók, Hungary, and the Renewal of Tradition: Case Studies in the Intersection of Modernity and Nationality*. Berkeley: University of California Press, 2006.

Semmens, Richard. "Branles, Gavottes and Contredanses in the Later Seventeenth and Early Eighteenth Centuries." *Dance Research: The Journal of the Society for Dance Research* 15, no. 2 (Winter 1997): 35–62.

Solie, Ruth. "Whose Life? The Gendered Self in Schumann's *Frauenliebe* Songs." In *Music and Text: Critical Inquiries*, edited by Steven P. Scher, 219–40. Cambridge: Cambridge University Press, 1992.

Steidl, Annemarie. "Between Home and Workshop: Regional and Social Mobility of Apprentices in 18th and 19th Centuries [sic] Vienna." *Mélanges de l'École française de Rome—Italie et Méditerranée modernes et contemporaines* (2016). https://journals.openedition.org/mefrim/2491.

Stoklásková, Zdenka. "Der Reisepass als Voraussetzung für den Eintritt von Fremden nach Österreich." In *Grenze und Staat: Paßwesen, Staatsbürgerschaft, Heimatrecht und Fremdengesetzgebung in der österreichischen Monarchie, 1750–1867*, edited by Waltraud Heindl, Edith Saurer, Hannelore Burger, and Harald Wendelin, 632–47. Vienna: Böhlau, 2000.

Suchoff, Benjamin. "Editor's Preface." In Béla Bartók, *The Hungarian Folk Song*, edited by Benjamin Suchoff. Translated by M. D. Calvocoressi, with annotations by Zoltán Kodály. Albany: State University of New York Press, 1981.

Szabolcsi, Bence. *A Concise History of Hungarian Music*. Translated by Sára Karig. Translation revised by Florence Knepler. London: Barrie and Rockliff in cooperation with Corvina Press Budapest, 1964.

Szabolcsi, Bence. "Joseph Haydn und die ungarische Musik." *Beiträge zur Musikwissenschaft* 2 (1959): 62–73.

Tanzer, Gerhard. *Spectacle müssen seyn: Die Freizeit der Wiener im 18. Jahrhundert*. Vienna: Böhlau, 1992.

Taruskin, Richard. "Nationalism." *Grove Music Online*. www.oxfordmusiconline.com.

Taruskin, Richard. *The Oxford History of Western Music*. Vol. 2, *Music in the Seventeenth and Eighteenth Centuries*. Oxford: Oxford University Press, 2010.

Teibenbacher, Peter, Diether Kramer, and Wolfgang Göderle. "An Inventory of Austrian Census Materials, 1857–1910. Final Report." Mosaic Working Paper WP2012-007 (December 2012). Max Planck Institute for Demographic Research. https://www.researchgate.net/publication/355145590_An_Inventory_of_Austrian_Census_Materials_1857-1910_Final_Report (accessed 16 January 2025).

Thompson, Carl. "Journeys to Authority: Reassessing Women's Early Travel Writing, 1763–1862." *Women's Writing* 24, no. 2 (2017): 131–50.

Tompkins, Jane. *Sensational Designs: The Cultural Work of American Fiction, 1790–1860*. Oxford: Oxford University Press, 1985.

Tóth, István György. *Literacy and Written Culture in Early Modern Central Europe*. Budapest: Central European University Press, 2000.

Trouillot, Michel-Rolph. *Global Transformations: Anthropology and the Modern World*. New York: Palgrave Macmillan, 2003.

van der Merwe, Peter. *Roots of the Classical: The Popular Origins of Western Music*. Oxford: Oxford University Press, 2004.

Vermes, Gábor. *Hungarian Culture and Politics in the Habsburg Monarchy, 1711–1848*. Budapest: Central European University Press, 2014.

Vial, Stephanie D. *The Art of Musical Phrasing in the Eighteenth Century: Punctuating the Classical "Period."* Eastman Studies in Music 55. Rochester, NY: University of Rochester Press, 2008.

Vocelka, Karl. *Glanz und Untergang der höfischen Welt: Repräsentation, Reform und Reaktion im habsburgischen Vielvölkerstaat*. Vienna: Carl Ueberreuter, 2001.

Weber, William. *Music and the Middle Class: The Social Structure of Concert Life in London, Paris and Vienna*. New York: Holmes & Meier, 1975.

Weinmann, Alexander. "Vollständiges Verlagsverzeichnis der Musikalien des Kunst- und Industrie Comptoirs in Wien 1801–1819. Ein bibliographischer Beitrag." *Studien zur Musikwissenschaft* 22 (1955): 217–52.
Wheatcroft, Andrew. *The Habsburgs: Embodying Empire*. London: Viking, 1995.
Winkler, Gerhard J. "Der 'Style Hongrois' in der europäischen Kunstmusik des 18. und 19. Jahrhunderts: Ein geschichtlicher Abriss." In *Musik der Roma in Burgenland: Referate des internationalen Workshop-Symposions Eisenstadt, 5.–6. Oktober 2001*, edited by Gerhard J. Winkler, 63–81. Eisenstadt: Burgenländisches Landesmuseum, 2003.
Withers, Charles W. J. *Placing the Enlightenment: Thinking Geographically about the Age of Reason*. Chicago: University of Chicago Press, 2007.
Witzmann, Reingard. *Der Ländler in Wien: Ein Beitrag zur Entwicklungsgeschichte des Wiener Walzers bis in die Zeit des Wiener Kongresses*. Vienna: Arbeitsstelle für den Volkskundeatlas in Österreich, 1976.
Wolff, Larry. "The Global Perspective of Enlightened Travelers: Philosophic Geography from Siberia to the Pacific Ocean." *European Review of History—Revue européenne d'histoire* 13, no. 3 (September 2006): 437–53.
Wolff, Larry. *Inventing Eastern Europe: The Map of Civilization on the Mind of the Enlightenment*. Stanford, CA: Stanford University Press, 1994.
Wolff, Larry. *The Singing Turk: Ottoman Power and Operatic Emotions on the European Stage from the Siege of Vienna to the Age of Napoleon*. Stanford, CA: Stanford University Press, 2016.
Wolff, Larry. "Travel Literature." In *Encyclopedia of the Enlightenment*, vol. 4, edited by Alan Charles Kors, 188–94. Oxford: Oxford University Press, 2003.
Wolff, Larry, and Marco Cipolloni, eds. *The Anthropology of the Enlightenment*. Stanford, CA: Stanford University Press, 2007.
Women's Travel Writing, 1780–1840: A Bio-Bibliographical Database. https://btw.wlv.ac.uk.
Woodfield, Ian. "Collecting Indian Songs in Late 18th-Century Lucknow: Problems of Transcription." *British Journal of Ethnomusicology* 3 (1994): 73–88.
Woodfield, Ian. *Music of the Raj: A Social and Economic History of Music in Late Eighteenth-Century Anglo-Indian Society*. Oxford: Oxford University Press, 2000.
Yonan, Michael. *Empress Maria Theresa and the Politics of Habsburg Imperial Art*. University Park: Pennsylvania State University Press, 2011.
Yonan, Michael E. "Veneers of Authority: Chinese Lacquers in Maria Theresa's Vienna." *Eighteenth-Century Studies* 37, no. 4 (Summer 2004): 652–72.
Zohn, Steven. *Music for a Mixed Taste: Style, Genre, and Meaning in Telemann's Instrumental Works*. Oxford: Oxford University Press, 2008.
Zotti, Herbert, and Susanne Schedtler. "'Vom Trübsalblasen gar ka Spur': Musik im Wirtshaus." In *Im Wirtshaus: Eine Geschichte der Wiener Geselligkeit*, edited by Ulrike Spring, Wolfgang Kos, and Wolfgang Freitag, 216–21. Vienna: Czernin Verlag, 2007.
Zvara, Edina. *Egy tudós hazafi Bécsben: Görög Demeter és könyvtára*. Budapest: Országos Széchényi Könyvtár—Gondolat Kiadó, 2016.

Index

For the benefit of digital users, indexed terms that span two pages (e.g., 52–53) may, on occasion, appear on only one of those pages.

Figures and tables are indicated by *f* and *t* following the page number.

advertisements, 19, 103–4, 106–7, 117–18, 136, 137–40, 141–45
Agnew, Vanessa, 6–7, 14, 120
Allgemeine musikalische Zeitung (periodical)
   amateur music-making described in, 116–18
   Hungarian national dances described in, 122, 158–59
   Hungarian Romani music described in, 22–23, 95–96, 108–9
   sheet music reviewed and advertised in, 104–5, 126–28, 127*f*
amateur musicians, 18–19, 104–6, 116–20, 125–29, 130–31
Anderson, Benedict, 105n12, 124–25
Angiolini, Gasparo, 49–50, 51–52, 55–59, 61–62, 63–64, 156–58
anthropology, 6–7, 67, 94, 102–3, 120
aristocracy. *See* Habsburg court; *natio Hungarica*
artisans, 31–32
assimilation, 20–24, 85n56, 122–23, 161–62
audiences, 61–63, 65–67, 156
Augarten, 68–69
authenticity, 93–94, 104–5, 115–16

ballets de nations, 30, 49–64
Balli ongaresi (Hummel), 104–5, 126–28, 126*f*–27*f*, 158–59
Bánffy, Dénes, 85, 87–88
beerhouses, 72–73, 79–82, 87–88
Beethoven, Ludwig van, 3–4, 8–9, 10–11, 15–16, 68–69, 123
Bellman, Jonathan, 8–9, 10–11
Bengraf, Joseph, 103–4, 106–7, 108–9, 111–16, 112*f*
Bernardi, Charles, 49, 53*t*
Bibiena (theater), 65
Bodin, Louise Joffroy, 55–59
Bohlman, Philip V., 13–14, 65–66
Born, Georgina, 12–13, 17–18

Boscovich, Ruggiero Giuseppe, 27
Botstein, Leon, 11–12
Bracewell, Wendy, 26
Bright, Richard, 20–22, 27
Bronevskii, V. B., 26
Brown, Bruce Alan, 31n18, 49n54, 51–52, 53*t*, 59, 61–62
Brown, Edward, 25
bureaucracy, 21, 34–37
Burgtheater (Vienna), 49, 52–55, 53*t*, 59–63, 65, 68n6. *See also* court theaters
Burney, Charles, 6–7, 14, 27–29, 67–68, 74, 93–96
Buurman, Erica, 15–16, 139–40, 141–42, 147–48, 154–56

casinos, 71, 79, 141–42
Catherine the Great, 40–42, 46
Catholic Church, 20–21, 47–48, 88–90
character dance, 62–64. See also *divertissements*; pantomime ballets
Charles VI, Emperor (1685–1740), 38, 40, 65
Charles VII, Emperor (1697–1745), 38
Chew, Geoffrey, 120–21
choreography, 49–51, 141–44, 146–59, 151*f*
class (socioeconomic)
   and access to music, 65–67, 82–83
   and education, 88–90
   and gender, 18, 66–67, 78–83, 88–90, 99–101
   and historiography, 13–14
   and music literacy, 87–88
   in pantomime ballet, 50–51, 59–63
   in perceptions of Eastern Europe, 28–30
   and social dance, 7–8, 19, 70–73, 74–78, 132–37, 140–41, 148–49, 153–60
   in Vienna, 19, 68–72, 74–83, 136–37, 153–54, 155–60
Clementi, Muzio, 40–42
clothing, 31–32, 33–34, 35*f*–36*f*, 40, 41*f*, 42–43, 48–49

coffeehouses, 72–74, 75f, 79
collections of dances. *See* dances, sets of
Condillac, Abbé Étienne Bonnot de, 105–6
contredanse, 7–8, 19, 136–37, 138–42, 144–48, 150–52, 153–60. *See also* social dance
Contredanses Hongraises pour le Clavecin, 132–36, 133f, 134f, 144–45, 147, 159–60
Cook, James, 91–92, 100–1
Cossack dances, 78, 138–40, 141–42, 145–46, 158–59
costumes, 42–43, 46–47
court theaters, 29–30, 49–64, 65, 67–68
Craven, Lady Elizabeth, 96–97
cultural appropriation, 63–64, 122–24
cultural work, 104–6, 131
Cusick, Suzanne G., 13–14, 105n11

dance
 and embodiment, 6, 15–16
 and the Enlightenment, 6, 27–30
 See also choreography; contredanse; *divertissements*; national dances; pantomime ballets; social dance
dance halls, 71–72, 74, 153–54, 155–56
dance instruction, 140–44, 149–53
dances, sets of, 19, 109–10, 116, 132–36, 137–40, 143–46
de Luca, Ignaz, 1n3, 5, 68n6, 69–70, 73–74, 79–80, 140–41, 153–54
dialogism, 18–19
diversity, 1–3, 4–5, 100–1, 163–64
divertissements, 42–49, 62–64, 156–58
domestic settings, music and dance in, 18–19, 104–6, 116–19, 130–31, 136–37, 139–40, 159–60. *See also* amateur musicians
Durazzo, Count Giacomo, 52–55
During, Simon, 125, 130

Eastern Europe, Western European constructions of, 17–18, 25–30, 40, 63–64, 120–21
education, 88–90, 161–62
Ehmer, Josef, 32
Elisabeth of Württemberg, Archduchess, 19, 132–36, 159
embodiment, 6, 15–16, 105–6, 125–29
Enlightenment
 anthropology in, 6–7, 67, 94, 102–3, 120
 conceptualization of Eastern Europe in, 17–18, 25–30, 40, 63–64, 120–21
 elevation of music in, 6, 27–29, 102–3
 and embodiment, 105–6
 and emotion, 120, 123–24

 and the exotic, 130
 feminine ideal in, 82–83, 97–100
 and publication, 99–100
 role of dance in, 6, 27–30
Ephemerides Vindobonenses (newspaper), 43, 45
exoticism, 2, 12–13, 130

fashion. *See* clothing
Feldtenstein, Carl Joseph von, 149–53
Fichte, Johann Gottlieb, 28–29
La Foire de Zamoysck, ou Le Cosaque jaloux (Starzer/Hilverding), 53t, 61–62
food and drink establishments, 72–78, 75f–76f, 77f, 79–82
form (music), 109, 110–15, 146–47
Forster, Georg, 100–1
Fortis, Alberto, 27
Franz I, Emperor (Francis Stephen of Lorraine, 1708–1765), 38, 156–58
Franz II, Emperor (Franz I of Austria, 1768–1835), 19, 132, 136, 159
Frazer, Michael L., 123–25
French language, 3, 22, 30–31, 37–38, 89–90

gardens, 68–69, 70–71
gender
 eighteenth-century discourses on, 97–100, 116, 148–49
 and musical simplicity, 119–20
 and professional vs. amateur musicians, 127–29
 and social dance, 148–52
 and socioeconomic class, 18, 66–67, 78–83, 88–90, 99–101
 and travel, 7–8, 96–98
 See also women
General School Ordinance of 1774, 88–89
German language, 3, 21, 22, 37–38
global music, 102–3, 122–23. *See also* national music
Gluck, Christoph Willibald, 40–42, 53t, 63–64
Goldmark, Carl, 122–23
Görög, Demeter, 132–36, 159–60
Gramit, David, 28–29, 65–66, 120–21
Gumpenhuber, Philipp, 51–52

Habermas, Jürgen, 98–100
Habsburg court, 14–15, 17–18, 40–49, 62–64, 132–36, 156–58, 159–60
Habsburg Monarchy, 5, 20–23, 29–30, 38, 46–48, 85–86, 88–89, 161–62
Hadi és Más Nevezetes Történetek (periodical), 132–36

INDEX 187

Hanslick, Eduard, 15–16
Hanson, Alice, 11–12
Harmoniemusik (wind band music), 70–71, 74, 138–39
harmony and key, 95–96, 106–8, 109–10, 111–15, 146–47
Haussard, Jean-Baptiste, 35*f*–36*f*
Hawkesworth, John, 92
Haydenreich, Joseph, 137–40
Haydn, Joseph, 3–4, 8–9, 15–16, 40–42, 123
Head, Matthew, 116, 119–20
Helyard, Erin, 127–29
Herder, Johann Gottfried, 123–25
Hesmondhalgh, David, 12–13, 17–18
Hilverding, Franz, 49–52, 53*t*, 55, 63–64. See also *L'Hongrois* (Starzer/Hilverding)
Hirschkop, Ken, 18–19
Hoffmeister, Franz Anton, 137–39, 143–44
L'Hongrois (Starzer/Hilverding), 49, 52–64, 57*t*, 58*f*, 60*f*–61*f*
Hummel, Johann Nepomuk, 104–5, 126*f*–27*f*, 126–28, 158–59
Hungarian dance music
　absence from scholarship on Vienna, 6, 15–16
　development of, 23
　documentation of, 13–14, 15–17, 19, 63–64, 109–10
　popularity of, 5, 103
　terminology for, 23–24
　See also keyboard music; Romani music; *Ungarische*
Hungarian identity, 17–18, 21–22, 23, 29–30, 46–49. *See also* nationalism
Hungarian language, 21–22, 37–38
Hungarian nobility. See *natio Hungarica*
Hungarians
　clothing and appearance of, 31–32, 33–34, 35*f*–36*f*, 40, 41*f*, 42–43, 48–49
　elite presence in Vienna, 30–32, 33–40, 43, 46–49
　in Vienna's population, 5, 30–37
Hungary
　described in travel writing, 25–29, 48–49, 145–46
　Magyar dominance within, 22, 37–38, 48–49
　privileged position within the Habsburg Monarchy, 5, 38–40, 46–49

illiberalism, 161–63
imagined community (Anderson), 7–8, 18–19, 105–6, 124–25, 158–60
improvisation, 87–88, 106–8, 126–29, 152–53

inns, 66–67, 72–73, 74, 78, 85
Islamophobia, 161–62

Jahn, Ignaz, 68–69
Joseph II, Emperor (1741–1790)
　at court, 45–48, 62–63
　decrees by, 21–23, 37–38, 68–69, 161–62
　geopolitical vulnerability of, 29–30, 45–48
　in Hungarian dress as a child, 40, 41*f*
Journal des Luxus und der Moden (periodical), 119

Kaisersammlung, 19, 132, 136, 143–44
Kärntnertortheater (Vienna), 49, 52–55, 53*t*, 67–68. *See also* court theaters
Kauer, Ferdinand, 103, 136
keyboard music
　accessibility of, 7–8, 115–20, 125–27
　advertisements for, 103–4, 106–7, 136, 139–40
　Romani musicians evoked in comments on, 7–8, 18, 104–9, 125–27
　for social dance, 19, 132–40, 143–45
　stylistic features of, 109–16, 120–21, 125–27
　women and, 7–8, 18–19, 116–19, 120, 127–29, 130–31
keyboard playing, 7–8, 18, 103–6, 116–19, 120, 125–29, 130–31
Khevenhüller-Metsch, Prince Johann Joseph, 156–58
Koch, Heinrich Christoph, 150–52
Komlós, Katalin, 119
Kosakische. *See* Cossack dances
Koželuch, Leopold, 119
Kringsteiner, Joseph Ferdinand, 141–42
Kurz, Sebastian, 161, 162–63

Ländler, 138–40, 141–42
language, 3, 21–22, 30–31, 37–38, 89–90, 161–62
Lannoy, Eduard von, 122
Lázar, János, 162–63
Leopold I, Emperor (1640–1705), 38
Lindner, Andreas, 143–44
Liszt, Franz, 8–11, 146n35
literacy, 88–91. *See also* music literacy; reading
literature, 90, 91–98, 128–31. *See also* travel writing
Locke, Ralph P., 12–13, 156
Lothringer Bierhaus, 79–80

Magyar Hírmondó (newspaper), 43–44, 46–47, 48–49

Magyar Kurír (newspaper), 20–21, 66–67, 83–85, 86–88
Le Marché aux poissons (Gluck/Bernardi), 53t
Maria Feodorovna, Grand Duchess (Sophia Dorothea of Württemberg), 40–42, 46, 62–63, 156
Maria Theresa, Empress (1717–1780)
 at court, 156–58
 and forced assimilation of Roma, 20–21, 22–23, 24, 85
 and the Hungarian nobility, 38–40
 other policies and decisions by, 33, 65, 80–82, 88–89
Marie Therese, Empress (Maria Theresa of Naples and Sicily, 1772–1807), 19, 136
Mathew, Nicholas, 16, 160
Mattheson, Johann, 119–20
medical science, 97–99
melody, 57, 106–7, 110–15, 120–21, 146–47
Melton, James Van Horn, 99–100
meter and rhythm, 106–7, 110–15, 146–47
Meytens, Martin van, 41f
migration, 30–32, 161–63
military dance, 44, 45, 46–47, 48–49
minuets, 55, 57, 58f, 138–42, 153–55
Montagu, Lady Mary Wortley, 1–2, 26, 92, 96–97
morality, 82–83, 99, 123–24, 128–30
Mozart, Wolfgang Amadeus
 in the Augarten, 68–69
 overemphasized in scholarship, 3–4, 15–16
 published music by, 119, 138–39
 at the Viennese court, 40–42, 62–64, 156, 159
music instruction, 117–19
music literacy, 87–88
musicology, limits of, 3–4, 8–9, 13–14, 15–16, 163
Musikalische Korrespondenz der teutschen Filarmonischen Gesellschaft (periodical), 104, 114–15
Musikalisches Magazin, 137–39, 143–45

natio Hungarica, 37–40, 43, 46–49
nation, concepts of, 30, 37–38, 48–49, 62–63
national dances, 42, 45–47, 122, 141–44, 152–53, 156–59. *See also* Hungarian dance music; *Ungarische*
national music, 22–23, 106–7, 108, 122–23
nationalism, 14–15, 22–23, 37–38, 161–63. *See also* Hungarian identity
Neuestes Sittengemählde von Wien (book), 153–54

newspapers, 13–14, 19, 42–46, 104, 136, 137–42. *See also* periodicals; *Wiener Zeitung*
Nicolai, Friedrich
 on elite Hungarians, 31–32, 37–38
 on observation of people, 1–2, 6, 100–1
 on Vienna's population, 1–2, 3, 5, 31–32, 161
 on Vienna's sites of sociability, 71–73, 74, 79–80
notation, 102–3, 108–9, 115–16. *See also* sheet music
Noverre, Jean-Georges, 156–58

opera, 12–13, 49, 59
Opitz, Georg Emanuel, 77f
Orbán, Viktor, 162–63
Originelle Ungarische Nationaltänze für das Clavier, 95–96, 109, 113f–26f, 114–15, 125, 144–45
ornamentation, 110–11, 114–15, 125–28, 146–47
Ossowski, Stanislaus, 137–39, 143–45
Otherness, 5, 17–19, 129, 161–63. *See also* self-othering

Pamela (Richardson), 129–30
Pamer, Michael, 141–42
pantomime ballets, 14–15, 17, 29–30, 49–64
Papp, Géza, 103, 109–10, 112f, 113f, 115–16, 131, 134f
parks, 68–69, 70–71
pastoralism, 120–21, 130
pastorella, 120–21
Paul, Grand Duke (1754–1801), 40–42, 46, 156
Pecháček, Franz Martin, 141–42
performance practice, 18–19, 104–9, 125–28
Perinet, Joachim, 79–80
periodicals, 102–5, 132, 160. *See also Allgemeine musikalische Zeitung*; newspapers
Pezzl, Johann
 on gender and socioeconomic class, 78–80, 89–90, 100–1
 on the Royal Hungarian Bodyguard, 33
 on Vienna's population, 1–3, 67–71, 161, 163–64
 on Vienna's sites of sociability, 68–69, 70–71, 72–78
Philp, Mark, 6
polka, 122–23
Les Polonois à la foire hongroise (Starzer/Salomone), 52–55, 62–63
Un Port de mer dans la Provençe (?/Salomone), 51–52, 53t, 59
postcolonialism, 12–13

Pragmatic Sanction, 38
Prater (park), 68–69, 76f, 78–79
presentational dance, 156–60. See also *divertissements*; pantomime ballets
Preßburger Zeitung (newspaper), 87–88
prostitution, 77f, 80–83, 81f, 84f
public sphere, 18, 67–83, 98–100

Rabl, Carl, 74–78
reading, 67, 88–91, 97–98, 100–1, 124–25, 128–30, 159–60
Reichardt, Johann Friedrich, 82–83
Révérend, Abbé, 145–46
Rice, John A., 136, 156–58
Richardson, Samuel, 129–30
Richter, Joseph, 80–83, 84f, 140–41
Riesbeck, Johann Kaspar, 28–29, 30–31, 39
Rigler, Franz Paul, 106–7, 145–46
Rochlitz, Friedrich, 122
Roma
  fascination with, 8–11
  forced assimilation of, 20–24, 85
  stigmatization of, 5, 85–86, 163
Romani music
  descriptions of, 22–23, 91, 95–96, 106–9
  evoked by non-Romani composers, 8–11, 106–16, 122–24, 125–28
  performed in Vienna, 66–67, 83–88
Romani musicians
  amateur keyboard players' identification with, 7–8, 18–19, 104–6, 125, 127–29, 130–31
  descriptions of, 66–67, 83–85, 86–88, 91, 95–96, 106–9, 115–16, 128–29
  evoked in comments on keyboard music, 7–8, 18, 104–9, 125–27
  performance practices of, 18–19, 106–9, 125–27
  working conditions of, 20–24, 83–88
Rosen, Charles, 3–4
Rousseau, Jean-Jacques, 150–52
Royal Hungarian Bodyguard, 33, 44, 45, 46–47
Russia, 26, 46, 48–49
Russian royal family, 17, 29–30, 40–42, 44, 45–46, 62–64

St. Brigitta fair, 68–69, 74–78
Salomone, Giuseppe, 49, 53t
Schiller, Friedrich, 155–56
Schindler, Otto G., 65, 68n6, 69–70
Schmidtbauer (music dealer), 141–42
Schönfeld, Johann Ferdinand Ritter von, 15–16
Schubert, Franz, 8–9, 10–11, 123

Schulz, J. A. P., 120–21
self-othering, 125, 128–29, 130
sets of dances. See dances, sets of
Seume, Johann Gottfried, 78
sheet music, 5, 102–5, 106–10, 115–16, 120–23, 137–40, 159–60. See also keyboard music; keyboard playing
simplicity, 109, 116–17, 119–21, 123–24, 131
Smith, William, 93
social dance
  choreography for, 141–44, 146–59, 151f
  instruction in, 140–44, 149–53
  music marketed for, 19, 136, 137–40, 141–46
  published descriptions of, 19, 136–37, 147–54, 158–59
  and socioeconomic class, 7–8, 19, 70–73, 74–78, 132–37, 140–41, 148–49, 153–60
  See also contredanse
socioeconomic class. See class
soft power, 39–40
Sophia Dorothea of Württemberg (Grand Duchess Maria Feodorovna), 40–42, 46, 62–63, 156
speculation, 13–14
Speer, Daniel, 145–46
Speidel, Ludwig, 122–24
Starzer, Joseph, 53t, 55, 56f, 57t, 58f, 60f–61f. See also *L'Hongrois* (Starzer/Hilverding)
Sternberg, Kaspar, 48–49
style hongrois, 8–11
style polonais (Zohn), 120–21
stylus rusticanus (Chew), 120–21
Sulzer, Johann Georg, 150–52
sympathy, 18, 123–25, 130–31

Tartars, 42, 46, 49
Taruskin, Richard, 15–16, 61–62
taverns, 72–73, 74, 80–83, 86–88
Telemann, Georg Philipp, 120–21
theatrical dance, 50, 63–64. See also pantomime ballets
Tompkins, Jane, 104–5
Townson, Robert, 25, 27, 28–29, 80–82, 145–46
Traeg, Johann, 103, 137–39, 144–45
traiteurs, 72–73, 74
Transylvania, 22–23
travel, 6–8, 25–29, 85–86, 94–98
travel writing, 1–3, 6–7, 14, 25–29, 91–98, 124–25. See also Burney, Charles; Nicolai, Friedrich; Pezzl, Johann; Wraxall, William
Le Turc généreux (Starzer/Hilverding), 59–62

Türk, Daniel Gottlob, 150–52

Ungarische, 132–40, 144–54, 151f, 158–60

Vanmour, Jean-Baptiste, 35f–36f
Varese, Giuseppe Maria, 52–55
Vaterländische Blätter für den österreichischen Kaiserstaat (newspaper), 3–4, 116–17
verbunk, 23
vernacular music
  defined, 65–66
  relatively privileged women's limited access to, 66–67, 82–83, 87–88
  venues for, 66–67, 74–78, 86–88, 100–1
Vienna
  diversity of, 1–3, 4–5, 100–1, 163–64
  education in, 89–90
  Hungarian population of, 5, 30–37
  Hungary viewed negatively from, 25–26
  limits of music scholarship on, 3–4, 8–9, 15–16, 163
  recreational spaces in, 68–69, 70–83
  restricted entry into, 85–86
  socioeconomic class divisions in, 19, 68–72, 74–83, 136–37, 153–54, 155–60
  theater audiences in, 65, 67–68
virtuosity, 87–88, 108–9, 115–16, 120
Volkston, 120–21

wages, 67–68, 69–70
Weninger (dancing master), 141–42
Wiener Zeitung (newspaper)
  music lessons advertised in, 117–18
  sheet music advertised in, 103, 106–7, 136, 137–40, 141–45
  Viennese court events described in, 40–42, 44, 156–58
Wienerisches Diarium (newspaper), 156–58
wine cellars, 72–73, 79–82, 87–88
Wolff, Larry, 17, 26, 63–64, 91, 120–21
women
  disenfranchisement of, 7, 18, 67, 99–100
  education of, 88–90
  eighteenth-century beliefs about, 97–100, 116, 148–49
  exclusion from public spaces, 18, 66–67, 78–83, 97–101
  identification with Romani musicians, 7–8, 18–19, 104–6, 125, 127–29, 130–31
  and keyboard music, 7–8, 18–19, 116–19, 120, 127–29, 130–31
  marginalized in musicological research, 13–14
  as readers, 67, 90–91, 97–98, 100–1, 128–30
  and travel, 92, 96–97
  as writers, 92, 96–97, 99
  See also gender
Wraxall, William, 30–31, 32, 67–68, 70–71, 78–79, 96–97
Württemberg family, 40–42, 44, 46–47. *See also* Elisabeth of Württemberg, Archduchess; Sophia Dorothea of Württemberg (Grand Duchess Maria Feodorovna)

xenophobia, 161–64

Zohn, Steven, 120–21